TERRORISM
AND THE NEWS MEDIA

Terrorism and the News Media

*A Selected,
Annotated Bibliography*

by A. ODASUO ALALI
and GARY W. BYRD

McFarland & Company, Inc., Publishers
Jefferson, North Carolina, and London

British Library Cataloguing-in-Publication data are available

Library of Congress Cataloguing-in-Publication Data

Alali, A. Odasuo, 1957–
    Terrorism and the news media : a selected, annotated bibliography
/ by A. Odasuo Alali and Gary W. Byrd.
      p. cm.
    Includes indexes.
    ISBN 0-89950-904-5 (lib. bdg. : 50# alk. paper) ∞
    1. Terrorism in mass media. 2. Terrorism and mass media.
I. Byrd, Gary W., 1943– . II. Title.
P96.T472A43 1994
016.3036′25 – dc20   94-2923
                                                    CIP

Manufactured in the United States of America

McFarland & Company, Inc., Publishers
  Box 611, Jefferson, North Carolina 28640

Table of Contents

Preface

The research literature on terrorism and the news media has increased in the past few decades with the rapid increase in terrorist activities. The bulk of this research focuses on content analysis of media reporting of terrorism. In addition to the research endeavors undertaken by academics, there have been political leaders, law enforcement agents and paid analysts who have voiced their opinions about the way the news media handle terrorist events. The analyses of the relationship between terrorism and the news media have produced divergent viewpoints that suggest that media coverage both does and does not encourage terrorism. While some of these views may have led to the development of theoretical explanations of the relationship, others seem to continue to fuel the debate about media handling of terrorism. In essence, we are still unable to fully understand the consequences of media coverage of terrorism.

We intend, through this book, to document the relevant studies and articles that pertain to media coverage of terrorism. In the process, we expect that this book will serve as a resource for those who wish to understand or further their knowledge of how terrorism is reported in the news media.

We believe that in addition to researchers and educators, this book will serve as a reference guide also for policy makers, law enforcement professionals, psychologists, and students at the undergraduate and graduate levels. We also believe that media practitioners will find this collection useful in their research and news gathering endeavors.

This book should not be regarded as inclusive of all studies and articles about terrorism in the media. Some might have eluded us. This is not to say that the present work is not comprehensive in nature; we are merely suggesting that no work of this nature ever captures all studies in its field. We feel strongly that the studies in this volume are the illuminators of the belief system that permeates analysis of media coverage of terrorism. We expect that this book will serve as a springboard for further research in the field, including the development of theoretical explanations of this complex phenomena.

One of the most exciting aspects of compiling this annotated bibliography was the help and cooperation we received from our colleagues, friends, and family. We are indebted to many people for their assistance in completing this project. Our special thanks go to Reza Azarmsa and Donna Elsdon, both at California State University, Bakersfield, for their technical support.

We wish to express our appreciation for the support we received from Sherri Cummins, Kenoye and Joy Eke, Fidelis Ejianreh, Charles Ibrahim, Clinton and Claudia Orugbani; and Bev and Dylan Byrd for their patience and understanding. We are grateful, and acknowledge our debt, for their sustained encouragement of our academic expeditions, particularly while we were preparing this book.

Finally, we are indebted to the victims of terrorism and their friends and relatives. We wish there were a less dramatic means of resolving the conflicts that took their lives and inflicted pain on others.

Chapter 1

Introduction

This book provides the reader with a comprehensive, annotated listing of research and articles that show how media operatives report terrorism in news programs. The research and articles we have assembled here show that terrorism, like any other phenomenon, attracts attention. The media, in turn, are fascinated and excited about covering terrorists and acts of terrorism. Central to this perspective are current research findings which show that the explosive nature of terrorist incidents makes attractive lead-in stories to the evening news; often, they receive a prominent play in the front pages of newspapers and on the covers of newsmagazines. As long as the media are attracted to events of terrorism, it is reasonable to expect that terrorists will continue to be interested in the media; it is possible that they will manipulate news reporters by timing their attacks for significance to the media.

Even though terrorism is an old problem, the 1980s will always be seen as the decade when the news media became more vulnerable to terrorists, who made effective use of the media to advance their agenda. Terrorists are no different from any other group that uses the media to its advantage. Perhaps the most illustrative example of this perspective is offered by Rada (1985), who argues that modern terrorism and public relations share a symbiotic relationship because both have the objectives of commanding attention, delivering a message, and influencing opinion.

It is under this backdrop that the most dramatic and "newsworthy" terrorist events have found themselves in the media. Examples include the hijacking of Trans World Airline (TWA) Flight 847 (June 1985), the Italian cruise liner *Achille Lauro* (October 1985), Egypt Air Flight 648 (November 1985), Pan Am Flight 73 (September 1986), and the bombings of U.S. Marine headquarters in Beirut (October 1983), TWA Flight

840 (April 1986), the Pan Am Flight 103 over Lockerbie, Scotland (December 1988), the World Trade Center (February 1993) and London's financial district (April 1993).

In each case, there have been critical opinions voiced on how the media handled the terrorists and the reports about the victims. Clearly, these opinions suggest the direction most discussions have taken about terrorism in the media. The one issue that continues to pervade all discussions is whether this seeming media gravitation towards terrorism creates a contagion effect on would-be terrorists who are determined to escape a political cul-de-sac. Reactions to this proposition vary, depending on who responds to it. But researchers like Robert Picard (1991) have indicated that the arguments in support of the contagion thinking represent government perspectives that are designed to influence public policy and mobilize national consensus for government actions against alleged terrorist organizations and countries that are suspected of supporting terrorism. Picard's argument casts doubt on the government's perspectives on terrorism and the media in the sense that their interpretations are based on dubious scientific data that are intended to advance the government's interest.

But despite the government's dubious intentions, there are reasonable inferences that news coverage of terrorism may have some effect on the perpetrators of terrorist acts. One might ask: Is it not probable that news coverage of terrorism would influence the terrorists and their likely targets, and victims, since terrorists tend to thrive on publicity?

While it is reasonable to expect that the perpetrators of terrorism would seem to benefit from media coverage, another concern or question pertains to the media audience. Does reportage on terrorism influence one's fear of the world, particularly of being a victim of terrorism or violence? Can the consumers of media products where terrorists and terrorism are featured divorce themselves from the tension, terror, and tragedy that are associated with terrorism?

One of the most telling indications of the media's impact on audiences is that media operatives have converted their perceptions of terrorism, terrorist groups, and their sponsors into household names to the extent that most Americans believe terrorism emanates from the Middle East. For example, when international terrorism is reported in the media, the typical consumer of media products is likely to suspect the origins of that terrorism, the perpetrators, and their victims and targets. Quite often, the perpetrators are associated with individuals such as Abul Abbas, Nabih Berri, Abu Nidal, Ahmed Jibril, Moammar Gadhafi, and most recently Sheik Omar Abdul Rahman. The mention of Shiite Muslims rings a bell, and organizations such as the Palestinian Liberation Front and Palestine Liberation Organization (PLO) remind us of Americans and Israelis who have been victims of terrorism. The mention of countries such as Iran, Iraq, Lebanon, Libya, and Syria in the news reminds us of those who allegedly sponsor or are associated with terrorism. And when we hear of the Middle East in the news, it tends to remind us that it is one of the most volatile regions of the world, where terrorism is a way of life. Clearly, we may not be passive observers of terrorism news.

Media conceptions of "terrorism" and the labels assigned to perpetrators of political violence seem to reflect the anti–Muslim, anti–Islamic feelings that permeate American newsrooms. Walker (1993, p. B3) suggests that media unfamiliarity with Islam has translated into biased reporting: "North American newsrooms have no lifelong, built-in familiarity with Islam, even though it has about 950 million adherents around the world." The consequence is reporting that creates specific impressions which contribute to the increase in negative reactions and attitudes toward Muslims around the world. It is not surprising that Serbian terrorist acts go unnoticed. Rather, reporters see such acts in terms defined by "the Serbian irregulars in Bosnia [who] keep telling Western journalists that they are fighting to prevent the establishment of a 'fundamentalist Islamic state.' They know our mythologies only too well. Muslim means fundamentalist. Fundamentalist means fanatic."

Perhaps, in the frenzy to identify an "Islamic Connection" to terrorism, the media have not sufficiently acknowledged that the labels "terrorism" and "terrorist" are relative to ideological definitions. When an act of political violence is terrorism and when the perpetrator of such an act is a terrorist are questions that are answered differently by persons of unlike cultures and varying perspectives. For example, prior to the establishment of Israel, many acts of what could easily be called terrorism were perpetrated against the Palestinians without such acts being assigned the pejorative label of "terrorism." In fact, this pattern of reporting continues today. Illustrative of this tendency is the tone that was used in reporting the massacre of 30 Palestinians during the Holy month of Ramadan in March 1994, at the mosque in Hebron. The bloodbath was described merely as an act of violence committed by a Jewish extremist and settler; it was *not* characterized as a terrorist act.

11

Indeed, examples of slanted media interpretation of political violence are abundant. A persistent obsession with the Irish Republican Army (IRA) has legitimized British policy in Northern Ireland as inherently reasonable. The United States' support of death squads in Central America and its support in overthrowing democratic governments, such as those in Guatemala (1954), Brazil (1964), and Chile (1973), appear to be irrelevant to the media. Similarly the U.S. media have been reluctant to characterize bombings and arson fires at U.S. abortion clinics as terrorist acts. Such acts have been followed by actual shootings and the murder of at least one physician who provides abortion. The rise in the incidence of terrorist bombings of clinics receives no press, yet political terrorism — the rate of which is declining — receives close attention from the press. *The Dallas Morning News* reports that data from the U.S. Bureau of Alcohol, Tobacco and Firearms indicate that there were 144 bombings or arsons at abortion clinics in the United States from 1982 to December 1993 (O'Connor, 1994, p. 1A). On the other hand, FBI statistics show only 51 incidents of terrorist activity in 1982 and 54 incidents between 1986 and 1990. One can only conclude that the acts of violence that are focal points of media coverage are not perceived in the same geopolitical and sociopolitical terms as those that receive little or no press.

Occasionally, media consumers have learned about the motivation behind a terrorist incident, that is if the media can reach the perpetrators to determine their motivations. In the past, several reasons for terrorist acts have been advanced. Some news reportage suggest that terrorism is an instrument of struggle for those who are desperate and see no other means for advancing their cause. Others suggest that terrorism may be motivated by the need for money to buy arms and finance their organization; or to undermine the authority of a state. As much as terrorists and terrorism are part of daily news programs, a question that remains unanswered is: Are audiences fully aware of the motivations behind each terrorist act, their origins, and the characters or perpetrators?

Amidst this complex web of reportage and concerns is the danger posed to the quality of journalism. Basically, this pertains to media behavior during terrorist activities. Are the media reluctant or enthusiastic participants in the coverage of terrorism? Do media operatives give too much airtime or space to terrorism? Does coverage of terrorism lead to escalation of terrorist acts? Is coverage of terrorism one-sided? Is violence needed for coverage of terrorists to take place? Is the coverage we get softer than reality? Is the quality of coverage immaterial as Bell (1978) contends? Should anchorpersons act as go-betweens in terrorist incidents as was demonstrated by CBS anchorman Dan Rather when TWA Flight 847 was hijacked? Does media coverage of terrorists elevate their status? Does it tend to legitimize their actions? Typical is the circus-like atmosphere that the press corp created at Beirut airport during the TWA Flight 847 hijacking. Should the media mention likely targets when terrorist incidents are anticipated?

Equally important are questions surrounding the media's inability to uncover terrorist activity. An example is the alleged involvement of the Iraqis in terrorist activities prior to the invasion of Kuwait on August 2, 1990. The media watched, without reporting, when Iraq was removed from the State Department's list of nations sponsoring terrorism. Iraq was quietly added to the list in September 1990 after the invasion of Kuwait, while Syria's alleged role as a supporter of terrorism was downplayed by the State Department (Friedman, 1990, p. A16).

Along these lines is how the media omit terrorist incidents in other parts of the world, particularly in South America, Latin America, and Africa. While it can be argued that the situation in the Middle East is not comparable to situations elsewhere, the lack of equity in terrorism news coverage serves as an indictment of the media. Why do the media spend more time covering one region than the other?

Lastly, it is not clear who determines the label used to describe acts of political violence. What factors precipitate the descriptive labeling of terrorists? Who is a "terrorist" and who is a "freedom fighter"? When does a "freedom fighter" become a "terrorist"? What are governments' roles in terrorism? Are all acts of political violence, including those which are government sponsored, terrorist acts? For example, does the United States' invasion of Grenada and Panama constitute terrorism? What about the U.S. mining of Nicaraguan harbors? Does the labeling change simply because the victims are not Americans? Brian Simmons (1991) found that when U.S. citizens were victims of political violence, "newsmagazines chose to use the label *terrorist* to describe the perpetrators on nearly 80% of the occasions. However, when U.S. citizens were not involved, they used the term only 51% of the time" (p. 30). Are we being judgmental, as suggested by Rubenstein (1987)? "To call an act of political violence terrorist is not merely to describe it but to judge it. Descriptively, terrorism suggests violent acts by individuals or small groups. Judgmentally, it implies illegitimacy" (p. 17). Eke and Alali (1991) suggest that "defining terrorism is like a chimera." Following are various definitions of terrorism they found:

"...the act of terrorizing, use of force or threats to demoralize, intimidate, and subjugate, esp. such use as a political weapon or policy; the demoralization and intimidation produced in this way."

— *Webster's New World Dictionary*

"...the unlawful use or threatened use of force or violence by a revolutionary organization against individuals or property with the intention of coercing or intimidating governments or societies, often for political or ideological purposes."

—U.S. Department of Defense, 1983

"...the unlawful use of force or violence against persons or violence against persons or property to intimidate or coerce a government, the civilian population, or any segment thereof, in furtherance of political or social objectives."

—Federal Bureau of Investigations, 1983

"...premeditated, politically motivated violence perpetrated against noncombatant targets by subnational groups or clandestine state agents."

—U.S. State Department, 1984

"...violent criminal conduct apparently intended: (a) to intimidate or coerce a civilian population; (b) to influence the conduct of a government by intimidation or coercion, or (c) to affect the conduct of a government by assassination or kidnapping."

—U.S. Department of Justice, 1984

"...the unlawful use or threat of violence against persons or property to further political or social objectives. It is usually intended to intimidate or coerce a government, individuals or groups or to modify their behavior or policies."

—The Vice President's Task Force
on Combatting Terrorism, 1986

"Clearly, the complexity of the term not only has created definitional problems for society, but also has confused and indeed polluted the debate on how to characterize acts of political violence" (Eke and Alali, 1991, p. 6).

New Areas of Concern

There is no doubt that American interests overseas were the focus of terrorist acts in the 1980s. While it has been difficult for terrorists to penetrate the United States mainland (the World Trade Center bombing in February 1993 may have altered that belief), the media occasionally alluded to their presence in the United States. In the early 1980s, for example, an alleged Libyan "Hit Squad" was widely reported in the media; the military action against Iraq, "Operation Desert Storm," created fear among the United States populace regarding possible terrorism because the media reported about the possibility of Iraqi sponsoring terrorism in the United States. This fear was heightened in small communities in the United States when it was reported that agents of the Federal Bureau of Investigation (FBI) paid occasional visits to Arab nationals who might have been sympathetic to Iraq; some were allegedly monitored by agents of the Bureau. It might suffice to say that none of these speculations materialized. Yet they created fear and indignation among the populace.

The shifting global arrangement, characterized by the end of the Cold War and the prospect of peace in the Middle East, seems to create new concerns regarding terrorism. Asia and Africa might now be the focus of acts of political violence because of the political upheavals in these regions. The African situation lends itself to terrorism because of increasing unemployment, inflation, famine, political instability, and civil war. Also, inadequate security measures at the airports of most African countries would most likely attract terrorists. Already, two incidents of terrorist hijacks occurred within one week in Ethiopia. On August 29, 1992, an Ethiopian Airlines Boeing 737 was hijacked by a group who claimed to be victims of political prosecution in Ethiopia. Two weeks later, on September 4, 1992, another Ethiopian jetliner was hijacked to Djibouti. These two incidents and the political unrest and instability in South Africa, Algeria, Nigeria, and other nations that are embracing democracy would shift the threat of terrorism to new regions that were thought to be safe.

Recommendations for Further Research

Most analyses of how the media covered terrorism in the past have revolved around the contagion argument. While the contagion perspective has been advanced by government officials and scholars alike, it has done little to answer critical questions that may provide relief to how the media influence terrorism.

Researchers must try to develop criteria to determine whether the news media give too much air time to terrorists. Additionally, attention needs to be focused on ethical issues of media coverage of terrorism. For example, is it ethical for anchor persons and reporters to act as go-betweens for governments and terrorists? Should reporters deliver terrorists' messages to governments, regardless of their policy towards terrorists? To what extent are reporters perceived as neutral observers when they serve as conduits for terrorists?

Thirdly, even though the terrorist overtake of the U.S. Embassy in Teheran gave birth to respected news programs such as "Nightline," is the quality of terrorism coverage sufficient? In other words, do viewers understand the historical context of the terrorism incident? Is the quantity of coverage satisfactory? Should news programs cover a broader spectrum of terrorism news? (Should they accord *less* coverage to terrorism?) Is actual violence necessary for coverage to take place?

Research efforts may try to resolve the conflict that now exists between local news coverage and network coverage of terrorism. Should local news organizations enter the terrorism arena by dispatching their reporters to volatile areas even when the violence has no local impact or significance?

What role do the so-called "experts" play in the analysis of terrorism, especially when they are thousands of miles away from the locale? Additionally, how credible is terrorism coverage when primary sources (the terrorists themselves) are rarely quoted in the stories?

What are the possible solutions to problems in the media coverage of terrorism? Is censorship a useful tool? What about network imposed guidelines for covering terrorism? In short, what ways can the quality of coverage be improved?

Lastly, most articles on the topic of terrorism are either content studies or are written from the perspective of political leaders and policy analysts. Researchers must begin to develop methodologies and theoretical explanations on how terrorism is reported in the media.

Organization of the Book

This book is organized into four chapters. The present chapter has addressed some of the concerns often voiced about the media and how terrorism is reported in the news; points out new areas of concerns; and gives recommendations for further research.

The annotated entries begin in Chapter 2, "Understanding Terrorism." Here, the reader is provided with a collection of books, book chapters, and journal articles about terrorism. These studies should help the novice to understand the terrorism phenomena.

In Chapter 3, a number of studies and conference papers that reflect research on and analysis of how the electronic media cover terrorism are listed; and Chapter 4 presents works on the relationship of the print media and terrorism.

Sources of Entry

The summary annotations in this book are a combination of our interpretations of studies, summaries, and the abstracts that were provided by the authors or reviewers of each study. We obtained most of the entries from numerous sources, including scholarly journals, periodicals, indexes, and abstracts. Additional entries were obtained through a computer and manual search of databases such as *Dissertation Abstracts International (DAI)*, the *Educational Resources Information Center Clearinghouse (ERIC)*, the *National Technical Information Service (NTIS)*, *Psychological Abstracts*, *Readers Guide*, *Social Science Index*, *Social SciSearch*, *Sociological Abstracts*, *Magazine Index*, and *PsycLIT*. We also obtained some opinion pieces and articles from the indexes of major newspapers.

REFERENCES

Bell, J.B. (1978, May-June). Terrorist scripts and live-action spectaculars. *Columbia Journalism Review,* pp. 47–50.

Eke, K.K., and Alali, A.O. (1991). Introduction: Critical issues in media coverage of terrorism. In A.O. Alali, & K.K. Eke (eds.) (1991). *Media coverage of terrorism: Methods of diffusion* (pp. 3–11). Newbury Park, CA: Sage Publications, Inc.

Friedman, T.L. (1990, September 11). Baker will go to Syria for help against Iraqis. *New York Times,* p. A16.

O'Connor, Colleen (1994, January 10). Abortion clinics face increase in violence: Militants say scripture backs them. *The Dallas Morning News,* p. 1A+.

Picard, R.G. (1991). News coverage as the contagion of terrorism: Dangerous charges backed by dubious science. In A.O. Alali & K.K. Eke (eds.) *Media coverage of terrorism: Methods of diffusion* pp. 49–62). Newbury Park, CA: Sage Publications, Inc.

Rada, S.E. (1985, Fall). Trans-national terrorism as public relations. *Public Relations Review,* 11, 3:26–33.

Terrorism and the News Media

Rubenstein, R. (1987). *Alchemist of revolution: Terrorism in the modern world.* New York: Basic Books.

Simmons, B.K. (1991). U.S. newsmagazines' labeling of terrorists. In A.O. Alali & K.K. Eke (eds.) *Media coverage of terrorism: Methods of diffusion* (pp. 23–39). Newbury Park, CA: Sage Publications, Inc.

Walker, Robert (1993, April 5). Most Muslims aren't terrorists but do we make that clear? *The Gazette* (Montreal), p. B3.

Chapter 2

Understanding Terrorism

1. Adams, J. (1987). The financing of terror. In Paul Wilkinson & Alasdaire M. Stewart (eds.), *Contemporary research on terrorism* (pp. 393–405). Aberdeen, MA: Aberdeen University Press.

   Both the British government and the terrorists appear to have unwittingly joined forces to perpetuate the myth of NORAID's significance in the IRA scheme of things. The British government, anxious to undercut any potential political interference from the United States, and in particular from the U.S. Congress, has played on the guilt of the American people by constantly trading off the influence of NORAID — portrayed as the main supplier of guns and money to the IRA — and that of the terrorist bombing in the province. This has successfully defused any coherent and effective U.S. political support for the campaign to get Britain out of Northern Ireland.

2. Ahmad, Eqbal (1986). Terrorists struggle against oppressive governments. In Bonnie Szumski (ed.), *Terrorism: Opposing viewpoints* (pp. 58–61). St. Paul, MN: Greenhaven Press.

   The author argues that the causes of terrorism are multiple, but that these causes are all related to government indifference and violence. Author asserts that young people turn to terrorism to release the feelings of anger and the hopelessness their living conditions generate.

3. Alesevich, Eugene (1978). Police terrorism. In Marius H. Livingston with Lee Bruce Kress & Marie G. Wanek (eds.), *International terrorism in the contemporary world* (pp. 269–275). Westport, CT: Greenwood Press.

   Author suggests that targets of terror and violence perpetrated by members of the American police system at the federal, state, and municipal level can be labeled criminals (organized and individual), extremists, radicals, and the like, who under pressure curtail or cease criminal activity within the jurisdiction of the agency perpetrating acts of terror. (Includes three notes.)

4. Alexander, Yonah (ed.) (1976). *International terrorism: National, regional, and global perspectives.* New York: Praeger Publishers, 390p.

This is a general overview of international terrorism, including discussions of what constitutes terrorism. Additional analysis suggests how society should deal with terrorism. The essays in this book present terrorism from national, regional and international perspectives. (Includes a selected bibliography and index.)

5. _____ (ed.) (1987). *The 1986 Annual on terrorism.* Higham, MA: Kluwer Academic Publishers.

This annual series, of which only the 1986 edition is devoted to terrorism, captures recent works in many fields, including terrorism in the news media.

6. _____, Carlton, David, and Wilkinson, Paul (eds.) (1979). *Terrorism: Theory and practice.* Boulder, CO: Westview Press, 280p.

This book offers an interesting as well as long-term appraisal of terrorist phenomena. It relates the theory and practice of terrorism to wider changes in social behavior, attitudes, and conditions and to advances in scientific knowledge and technology. A valuable feature of many of the contributions is the effort to assess the development and implications of modern terrorism and the broader canvas of trends in international relations and conflict. (Includes a selected bibliography and index.)

7. _____, and Finger, Seymour M. (eds.) (1977). *Terrorism: Interdisciplinary perspectives.* London: McGraw-Hill Book Company (UK) Limited, 377p.

The editors assembled numerous experts whose perspectives on terrorism are reflected in some of the definitional and historical questions that occupy discussions about terrorism. Authors provide reader with the political and strategic issues that pertain to terrorism; interposed with questions on how the media react to and report terrorism in the news. The discussions on current challenges and future implications are added dimensions to this book. (Includes a selected bibliography and index.)

8. _____, and Kilmarx, R.A. (eds.) (1979). *Political terrorism and business: The threat and response.* New York: Praeger Publishers, 345p.

This book is a comprehensive analysis of the threat of political terrorism to business. Led by Alexander and Kilmarx, various experts articulate their perspectives on terrorism and its impact on corporate activities. Discussions include responses to such threat. (Includes five tables, five figures, a selected bibliography, two appendices, and index.)

9. _____, and Pluchinsky, Dennis (1992). *Europe's Red terrorist: The fighting Communist organizations.* London: Frank Cass and Company Ltd., 258p.

This book is an overview of the challenges of contemporary terrorism. The focus is on a particular strain of terrorist groups in Western Europe. Examines terrorist actors, the terrorist network, methods of operation and targets.

10. Anderson, Bill (1986). Economics — not oppression motivates terrorists. In Bonnie Szumski (ed.), *Terrorism: Opposing viewpoints* (pp. 62-68). St. Paul, MN: Greenhaven Press.

In the discussion of terrorism, there is often debate over the religious and or political motivations for such acts of violence. The author suggests that this type of discussion is irrelevant; terrorists care little about ideology or about the oppression of their fellow men. Terrorists should be seen as groups attempting to gain political economic power in the least expensive way available. (Includes one graphic.)

11. Anderson, Thomas P. (1978). Political violence and cultural patterns in Central America. In Marius H. Livingston with Lee Bruce Kress & Marie G. Wanek (eds.), *International terrorism in the contemporary world* (pp. 153-159). Westport, CT: Greenwood Press.

This analysis focuses attention on the three neighboring countries of Guatemala, El Salvador, and Honduras; excluding the countries Nicaragua and Costa Rica. The former is excluded because violence there has largely become institutionalized in its governmental processes and the latter because an entirely different set of economic and cultural circumstances have left the Costa Ricans immune to the malady of violence. The author also focuses on that type of violence associated with political life in the twentieth century: ideological violence. (Includes eight notes.)

12. Arnold, Terrell E. (1988). *The violence formula: Why people lend sympathy and support to terrorism.* Lexington, MA: Lexington Books, 203p.

    The spread of terrorism and insurgency in the early 1980s speaks to the dismal nature of decisions made by society. The impact of these actions point to how difficult it has been for the United States to make national policy decisions; the greatest and most continuous democratic experiment in the world was in trouble because it could not make lasting decisions. The author observes that the useful life of major decisions, especially on controversial issues, was becoming shorter. The reason is clear: protest strategies were emerging as an alternative to institutional decision making. (Includes 12 chapters, notes, and index.)

13. Aston, C.C. (1982). *A contemporary crisis: Political hostage-taking and the experience of Western Europe.* Westport, CT: Greenwood Press, 213p.

    This study focuses on how political hostage incidents represent a new form of crisis for governments. It is not concerned with the underlying causes of political terrorism nor with the actual or potential reaction to such acts by the international community. Rather, the author is solely concerned with the question of response at the national level; not the capabilities but the constraints on host government's response. The basic premise of the work is that if political hostage incidents represent a new form of crisis, they should share certain common characteristics with the more conventional forms of international crisis. (Includes four parts, nine chapters, ten tables, two appendices, bibliography, and an index.)

14. Austin, W. Timothy (1989, September). Living on the edge: The impact of terrorism upon Philippine villagers. *International Journal of Offender Therapy and Comparative Criminology, 33,* 2:103–119.
    See entry 567.

15. Ball, George (1986). Retaliatory attacks will not eliminate terrorism. In B. Szumski (ed.), *Terrorism: Opposing viewpoints* (pp. 204–208). St. Paul, MN: Greenhaven Press.

    The author argues that retaliatory attacks can only escalate the violence and result in the deaths of hundreds of innocent people. (Includes one drawing.)

16. Bandura, Albert (1990). Mechanisms of moral disengagement. In W. Reich (ed.), *Origins of terrorism: Psychologies, ideologies,*

22

theologies, states of mind (pp. 161-191). Woodrow Wilson Center Series. New York: Cambridge University Press.

Author explores the psychological mechanisms that enable terrorists to do what they do, in particular, to kill persons who are, by most criteria, not responsible for whatever wrong terrorists may be trying to right.

17. Barcus, F. Earl (1983). Newspaper coverage of violence in Boston public schools, August 1981–April 1983. Boston, MA: Report for the Safe Schools Commission.

This report analyzes the coverage of violence in Boston public schools by two daily newspapers. The study found that 13 percent of the 1,000 newspaper stories pertaining to Boston schools dealt with violence.

18. Bartalotta, Giuseppe (1981, October). Psicologia analitica e terrorismo politico [Analytical psychology and political terrorism]. *Rivista di Psicologia Analitica,* 12, 24:21-30.

This article examines the psychological roots of modern terrorism. Draws a profile of a typical modern-day terrorist, who is young, well-educated, and skillfully manipulated by ruthless and power-crazed international leaders.

19. Beeman, William O. (1986). Stricter penalties will not eliminate terrorism. In Bonnie Szumski (ed.), *Terrorism: Opposing viewpoints* (pp. 215-217). St. Paul, MN: Greenhaven Press.

The author suggests that terrorism is a response by beleaguered communities to political and social injustice. Using more severe punishments for individual terrorists will not reduce terrorism. Rather, the author argues that attempts must be made to correct the conditions under which these people live.

20. Bell, B. (1978). *A time of terror: How democratic societies respond to revolutionary violence.* New York: Basic Books, Inc., 286p.

There is no common wisdom, no consensus on an appropriate democratic response, often not even agreement on a national policy. Yet the fact remains that something must be done — to stop the hijacking, or rescue the hostages, or end sanctuary. And during the last few years a lot has been done, not all desirable, it is true, but not all futile either. Nowhere in the growing literature on terrorism, however, does there exist a rigorous, cross-national analysis of how to respond to this threat. (Includes four parts, 12 chapters, bibliography and an index.)

21. Bell, J. Bowyer (1978). Terror: An Overview. In Marius H. Livingston with Lee Bruce Kress & Marie G. Wanek (eds.), *International terrorism in the contemporary world* (pp. 36–43). Westport, CT: Greenwood Press.

    This overview argues that there appears to be a continuing phenomenon with inadequate analytical tools. There is no consensus and no common language; in fact, it may be that the very word terror is a hindrance in the investigation of violence.

22. Bender, David L., Leone, Brunno, and Szumski, Bonnie (eds.) (1986). *Terrorism: Opposing viewpoints.* St. Paul, MN: Greenhaven Press, 240p.

    The purpose of this "Opposing Viewpoints Series" is to present balanced, and often difficult to find, opposing points of view on complex and sensitive issues. This volume comprises views by 34 authors; they express their views about terrorism, its causes, and determine whether it is justified. Additional discussions try to determine whether superpowers sponsor terrorism and if terrorism can be eliminated. (Includes an extensive bibliography and index.)

23. Beres, Louis Rene (1986, Fall). How to reduce the threat of terrorism. *Social Science Record,* 24, 1:17–19.

    Argues that the answer to reducing the threat of terrorism lies in improved understanding of the linkage between United States foreign policy and anti–American terrorism. Author reviews geopolitical developments to suggest that U.S. safety from terrorism will depend upon our ability to disengage from the present course of all-consuming anti–Sovietism.

24. Bill, James A. (1988, June). The Shah, the Ayatollah, and the United States. *Headline Series* (Foreign Policy Association, New York), vol. 285, 76p. Excerpted from James A. Bill, *The Eagle and the Lion: The tragedy of American-Iranian relations.* New Haven, CT: Yale University Press.

    Author outlines the political turmoil in Iran in the 1970s and 1980s and Iranian–U.S. relations during this period. The book concludes that the Iranian hostage crisis will continue to shape future U.S. policy towards Iran. Includes questions for classroom discussion and a 13-item reading list.

25. Bishop, Clifford M. (1991). *International terrorism: A guide to United States Government Documents,* 83p. (ED 332667).

Guide is intended as an introduction to published government information on the issue of terrorism. Indicates the range of the abundance of materials and the variety of government agencies concerned about terrorism.

26. Bremmer, L. Paul, III (1988, February 4). Terrorism: myths and reality. U.S. Department of State, Bureau of Public Affairs, *Current Policy* No. 1047, pp. 1–3.
     Argues against placating terrorists because there is no evidence that such a policy works and no justification for acts of violence and destruction. Also, argues that firmness can be a virtue.

27. Brock, Bernard L., and Howell, Sharon (1989, Fall-Winter). The evolution of the PLO: A rhetoric of terrorism. *Central States Speech Journal,* 39, 3–4: 281–292.
     Examines the Palestine Liberation Organization (PLO) and its effectiveness in use of rhetoric of terrorism as a strategy. Concepts from protest rhetoric of the 1960s are applied in this analysis. Argues that current terrorist rhetoric is similar to the New Left's confrontational strategies.

28. Burgess, Parke G. (1973). Crisis rhetoric: Coercion vs. force. *Quarterly Journal of Speech,* 59: 61–73.
     This article discusses the ability to make decisions about what to say, or not to say, in response to different situations. Author argues that people are not random sentence generators. Even the most unsophisticated person has the ability to choose what to say and how to say it. How does one respond to a certain question? Are the responses of different people to the same question similar and does this similarity show that there are rules to these responses? These are some of the questions involved in the study of crisis rhetoric. The author suggests that not much is known about how humans have learned this process. Some unresolved questions are when and how people learn to use speech, whether cultural differences play a part in how different cultures use speech, and whether peoples of different cultures have similar communication patterns. The author seeks to determine how the media cover terrorism, and how the mass audience responds to such coverage.

29. Cairns, Ed, and Wilson, Ronnie (1989). Coping with political violence in Northern Ireland. *Social Science and Medicine,* 28, 6:621–624.

Examines coping with political violence in Northern Ireland within the following dimensions: "the relationship between the appraisal of violence, coping with violence, and trait neuroticism." Suggests that people in Northern Ireland use "distancing" to cope with political violence.

30. Calero, Adolfo, Cruz, Arturo J., and Callejas, Alfonso R. (1980). U.S. sponsored Contras are freedom fighters. In Bonnie Szumski (ed.), *Terrorism: Opposing viewpoints* (pp. 142–145). St. Paul, MN: Greenhaven Press.

    The authors describe the Contras as the "genuine voice" of the Nicaraguan people. They believe the Contras fight for pluralism, freedom, and human rights.

31. Casey, William J. (1986, November). Conquering the cancer of terrorism. *USA Today* (Magazine), 115, 2498: 10–12.

    Reflects views of then-director of the Central Intelligence Agency on developing a worldwide counterterrorism network. Discussion includes tackling international terrorism, plugging media leaks, and the need for responsible caution.

32. Chamorro, Edgar (1986). U.S. sponsored Contras are terrorists. In Bonnie Szumski (ed.), *Terrorism: Opposing viewpoints* (pp. 137–141). St. Paul, MN: Greenhaven Press.

    The author, who served as a director of the Nicaraguan Democratic Force from 1982 to 1984, has emerged as an outspoken opponent of the Contras. He describes how the violent, terrorist methods used by the Contras ultimately disillusioned him from their cause. (Includes one cartoon.)

33. Chomsky, Noam (1988, July/August). Scenes from the uprising. *Zeta Magazine,* pp. 9–20.

    Argues that the conflict in the West Bank is more complicated than is illustrated in most discourse. Suggests that the origins and agendas of the parties in conflict should be examined before blame is assigned to one source.

34. Clark, Dennis (1978). Terrorism in Ireland: Renewal of a tradition. In Marius H. Livingston with Lee Bruce Kress & Marie G. Wanek (eds.), *International terrorism in the contemporary world* (pp. 77–83). Westport, CT: Greenwood Press.

Since 1969 Northern Ireland has been in the grip of violent events that have resulted in military rule for that unhappy province in all but a formal legal sense. Americans are confronted by various obstacles in comprehending what has transpired in Northern Ireland over the last six years. The mass media have acted as a distorting filter through which news of varying quality has been channeled to the United States. For these reasons, in addition to the importance of the subject itself, it is appropriate to review the implications of recent events in Northern Ireland. (Includes 16 notes.)

35. Clifford-Vaughan, F. McA. (1987). Terrorism and insurgency in South Africa. In Paul Wilkinson & Alasdaire M. Stewart (eds.), *Contemporary research on terrorism* (pp. 270–289). Aberdeen, MA: Aberdeen University Press.

Studies of terrorism commence with difficulties of nomenclature. This is especially true of the activities of those groups in Southern Africa whose proclaimed aims are "national liberation," "freedom" and "justice" — and whose opponents are thus presumed to resist these desirable states. Such terms as "freedom fighters," "guerrillas," "liberation forces" and "democratic, progressive, peace-loving movements" would seem to preclude any discussion of their aims. But the outrages perpetrated by these groups in South Africa force the conclusion that such groups' methods rather than their stated aims are the criterion for understanding them. (Includes 69 notes.)

36. Clutterbuck, Richard (1978). *Kidnap and ransom: The response.* London/Boston: Faber and Faber, 186p.

The author describes briefly the operation of kidnapping and hostage-taking in many countries and details the differing methods, operations and motives of those responsible and the difficulties in countering them. The book proposes the tentative conclusion that, given definite resources of manpower, organization, equipment and weapons, a government's success or failure in countering kidnapping will almost certainly be determined primarily by the reaction of the government or security forces to each particular incident, their preparedness, experience and perhaps most important their relationship with the society they serve. (Includes four topics, 18 chapters, bibliography, and index.)

37. _____. (1987). *Kidnap, hijack and extortion: The response.* London: Macmillan Press, 220p.

Since 1977 the author has been a non-executive director of Control Risks Ltd. (CR), and this book is his own interpretation of the organization's experience in advising many hundreds of clients all over the world on threat assessment and prevention, and in advising on the handling of 200 such crimes. Of the case studies which make up a major part of this book, CR was involved in some but not others and, though the book is based on their collective practical experience, CR's abiding principle of protecting client privacy has been adhered to. The author has only recorded names, places and events where these have been published in the press or elsewhere. The research department of CR, headed by Sheila Latham, maintains records of most known cases worldwide, whether CR was involved or not. (Includes four parts, 20 chapters, bibliography, and index.)

38. Comay, Michael (1976). Political terrorism. *Mental Health and Society,* 3, 5–6: 249–261.

Suggests that differences exist among political, state, criminal, and psychopathic modes of terrorism as well as that of urban guerrillas.

39. Commager, Henry S. (1986). Both superpowers encourage terrorism. In Bonnie Szumski (ed.), *Terrorism: Opposing viewpoints* (pp. 175–177). St. Paul, MN: Greenhaven Press.

The author argues that while terrorism may not be morally justified, it is certainly understandable. Throughout history, major countries have resorted to terror tactics. Today's terrorists are merely participating in a longstanding tradition.

40. Cordes, B. (1987). Euroterrorists talk about themselves: A look at the literature. In Paul Wilkinson & Alasdaire M. Stewart (eds.), *Contemporary research on terrorism* (pp. 318–336). Aberdeen, MA: Aberdeen University Press.

Much research has been devoted to examining what terrorists have done in the past and identifying trends for predicting what they might do in the future. Less attention, however, has been focused on terrorist motivations or indeed, on terrorists' self-perception. The author suggests that using the primary materials provided by the terrorists themselves—i.e., memoirs, statements, interviews and communiques—much information about the terrorist mindset and decision making can be gleaned. (Includes an extensive bibliography and 59 notes.)

41. _____ (1986, Fall). Major contemporary terrorist organizations. *Social Science Record,* 24, 1: 51–53.

The author compiled a list of 100 guerrilla and terrorist organizations around the world from RAND Corporation's database and the 1983 book by Peter Janke, *Guerrilla and terrorist organizations: A world directory and bibliography.*

42. Corrado, Raymond R., and Evans, R. (1988). Ethnic and ideological terrorism in Western Europe. In Michael Stohl (ed.), *The politics of terrorism* (pp. 373–444). New York: Marcel Dekker, Inc.

In this chapter, political terrorism is viewed as an explicitly political tactic employed by self-appointed individuals who are members of small clandestine groups; they want to destabilize a political regime by provoking the government to retaliate, thereby encouraging a repressive response and eventually sowing dissension in the ranks of those upholding the existing system. (Includes 172 notes.)

43. Corsi, Jerome R. (1981, March). Terrorism as a desperate game: Fear, bargaining, and communication in the terrorist event. *Journal of Conflict Research,* 25, 1: 47–85.

Presents a typology and characteristics of terrorist events using 539 events of international terrorism occuring between January 1970 and July 1974. Also examined are the negotiations involved in hostage situations, government/terrorist response options, and event outcomes. Assumptions of theoretical model are tested. (Includes 50 references.)

44. Council of Europe (1983). *A cultural and educational approach to the problem of violence. Report of the Committee on Culture and Education.* Strasbourg, France, 235p.

This Council of Europe report on the problem of violence opens with two recommendations: 1) on cultural and educational means of reducing violence; and 2) on a European Award for Non-Violence. An explanatory memorandum provides a general introduction and explains the report's focus on terrorism, violence in the media, violence and sports, and positive approaches through education.

45. Cox, Robert (1983). Total terrorism: Argentina, 1969 to 1979. In Martha Crenshaw (ed.), *Terrorism, legitimacy, and power: The Consequences of political violence* (pp. 121–142). Middletown, CT: Wesleyan University Press.

The author attempts to describe why Argentina was a laboratory for terrorism in the 1970s. In the first half of the decade terrorism became an integral part of everyday life and seemed likely to become endemic, like gangsterism in Chicago in the 1920s. But by the end of 1979 official barbarism had surpassed that of the terrorists in savagery. Argentina, rich in anomalies and long held up to the world as an extravagantly bad example of almost everything, from its telephone system to its catastrophic rate of inflation, became a terrorist state without terrorists. (Includes 14 footnotes.)

46. Crelinsten, Ronald D. (1987). Power and meaning. Terrorism as a struggle over access to the communication structure. In Paul Wilkinson & Alasdaire M. Stewart (eds.), *Contemporary research on terrorism* (pp. 419–450). Aberdeen, MA: Aberdeen University Press.

Author examines how the mass media fit into the communication structure of terrorism. In an age in which we have come to speak of our world as an electronic global village, the power of the mass media to affect political discourse on an ever-widening scale has become the object of increasing scientific attention. One special focus has been the reporting of "news" and the processes of selection, interpretation and presentation which mediate between events as they happen and events as they are reported to readers, listeners and viewers. Two common findings have been that: a) the media tend to be attracted to violent incidents and, in reporting them, tend to ignore their historical antecedents and their social or political contexts; and b) the primary sources of information for reporting on political life tend to be those who represent authority or who belong to the existing power structure. Accordingly, the author distinguishes between these "primary definers," such as politicians, police spokespersons or government officials, and what they call "secondary definers," such as political or social activists or reformers who remain outside the existing power structure. Such secondary definers are used much less frequently by the media than are primary definers. (Includes one figure and 56 notes.)

47. _____ (1987). Terrorism as political communication: The relationship between the controller and the controlled. In Paul Wilkinson & Alasdaire M. Stewart (eds.), *Contemporary research on terrorism* (pp. 3–23). Aberdeen: Aberdeen University Press.

The author intended to demonstrate what he considers to be a fruitful approach to the study of terrorism which avoids some of the major pitfalls which plague contemporary research of this complex phenomenon. First, the author outlines the nature of these pitfalls and why he thinks they are so prevalent. The author points to various conceptual and methodological approaches which offer more promise for developing an adequate research framework for analyzing terrorism.

Finally, the author develops this framework by means of a schematic model. (Includes three figures and 31 notes.)

48. _____, Laberge-Altmejd, D., and Szabo, D. (1979). *Terrorism and criminal justice.* Lexington, MA: Lexington Books, 131p.
This book is a collection of articles presented at a conference entitled "The Impact of Terrorism and Skyjacking on the Operations of the Criminal Justice System," held in February 1976 in Rochester, Michigan. The proceedings are presented in three parts. (Includes one figure, four tables, notes, and index.)

49. Crenshaw, Martha (1992, January–March). Current research on terrorism: The academic perspective. *Studies in Conflict and Terrorism,* 15, 1: 1–11.
Extensive review of theories regarding the nature of terrorism and suggestion of specific research agendas for the future. Argues that the study of terrorism must draw on research from diverse fields. This interdisciplinary approach does not imply that other factors relating to strategic rationales for terrorism should be ignored.

50. _____ (1981, April). The causes of terrorism. *Comparative Politics,* 13, 3: 379–399.
Author outlines an approach to the analysis of the causes of terrorism. Analysis centers on three key questions: Why terrorism occurs; how the process of terrorism works; and what its social and political effects are. Specific cases are used to determine the causal factors in terrorism. (Includes 52 notes.)

51. _____ (1990). Questions to be answered, research to be done, knowledge to be applied. In Walter Reich (ed.), *Origins of terrorism: Psychologies, theologies, state of mind* (pp. 247–260). New York: Cambridge University Press.
Argues that understanding terrorism requires application of psychological theory in analysis of the phenomenon. Suggests that the intent of the terrorist actor and the emotional reactions of the audiences must be analyzed in attempts to explain terrorism. Author proposes research questions for students of terrorism.

52. _____ (ed.) (1983). *Terrorism, legitimacy, and power: The consequences of political violence.* Middletown, CT: Wesleyan University Press, 162p.

The essays contained in this volume are the products of a symposium, "Terrorism: The Challenge to the State," held in January 1982 to commemorate the sesquicentennial anniversary of the founding of Wesleyan University. The conference, one in a series of symposia on important public issues, focused on the impact of terrorism on state, society, and individual, particularly the dilemma it poses for liberal democracy. The essays are linked by their attention to the social and political effects of terrorism, particularly its impact on democratic institutions and values. (Includes a selected bibliography, and index.)

53. Dale, Stephen F. (1988, March). Religious suicide in Islamic Asia: Anticolonial terrorism in India, Indonesia, and the Philippines. *Journal of Conflict Resolution,* 32, 1: 37–59.

Demonstrates a relationship between the suicidal attacks used for centuries in three Asian Muslim communities and those of Middle Eastern Muslims. "Provides insights into the dynamics of terrorist attacks, and illustrates the necessity of political solutions to the problems of terrorism."

54. de Boer, Connie (1979, Fall). The polls: Terrorism and hijacking. *Public Opinion Quarterly,* 43, 3: 410–418.

Analysis of public opinion about terrorism and hijacking suggests that 85 percent of those polled in the United Kingdom in June 1978 viewed terrorism as a very serious problem.

55. de Dunayevich, Julia B., and Puget, Janice (1989, Summer). State terrorism and psychoanalysis. *International Journal of Mental Health.* 18, 2: 98–112.

Examines state terrorism and the psychological effects on Argentines during the period of dictatorship (1976–1983). Also examines the post-dictatorship period.

56. Deeb, Marius (1988, April). Shia movements in Lebanon: Their formation, ideology, social basis, and links with Iran and Syria. *Third World Quarterly,* 10, 2: 683, 692–698.

The article focuses on Hezbullah in Lebanon, an offshoot of Iran's Islamic revolution. Suggests that the revolution in Iran encouraged the development of revolutionary groups in the Middle East. (Includes 19 footnotes.)

57. Denemark, R.A., and Welfling, M.B. (1988). Terrorism in Sub-Saharan Africa. In Michael Stohl (ed.), *The politics of terrorism* (pp. 445–495). New York: Marcel Dekker, Inc.

In this chapter the authors work with a definition similar to Gurr's (see annotation in entry 108). However, in examining the African context the authors do not exclude terrorist activity that is a part of other, more generalized violent activity, as Gurr chooses to do in his data collection. The authors compare certain more general indices of violence and the incidence of terrorism, especially in the very difficult area of state terrorism. (Includes eight tables, 25 notes, and 51 references.)

58. Dobson, Christopher, and Payne, Ronald (1977). *The Carlos complex: A pattern of violence.* New York: Putnam, 245p.

This book expresses the author's belief that Ilich Ramirez Sanchez's (Carlos the Killer) importance goes much beyond his notoriety. They argue that as the symbol of international terrorism, Carlos has made ordinary people aware that there is a worldwide network of revolutionaries determined for a variety of reasons to destroy the fabric of modern society. Carlos is also important because most of the strands of this network come together in him; the authors have sought to use him as a guide through the network. The authors found that the network is so comprehensive, with its "hit-men," its support groups, and its intellectual sympathizers, that every turning had its surprises. Wherever the authors trod they came across the footprints of the heavy-booted men of the KGB—for the Kremlin, even when it is not involved, wants to know what is going on. (Includes 15 chapters and index.)

59. _____, and _____ (1979). *The terrorists: Their weapons, leaders, and tactics.* New York, N.Y.: Facts On File, 228p.

Ten chapters examine the phenomenon of terrorism with attempts to understand reasons and motivations behind terrorism; terrorists' training, weapon of choice, and sponsors; and the tactics used to execute acts of violence. Authors also examine the strategies used by democratic societies to fight terrorism.

60. Dowling, Ralph E. (1988, March). The contributions of speech communication scholarship to the study of terrorism: Review and preview. Paper presented at the Conference on Communication in Terrorist Events: Functions, Themes, and Consequences (Boston, MA, March 3–5, 1988), 41p. (ED 315818).

Existing research about terrorism examines the terrorist phenomenon from different perspectives. The author notes that few studies have been done within the discipline of speech communication. Consequently, this paper sets the stage for such analysis; "it defines the discipline of speech communication and rhetorical studies, reviews the few existing rhetorical studies of terrorism, and goes on to show the ways in which a rhetorical perspective would alter and improve research carried out from other perspectives." The author argues that the rhetorical perspective can add to the interdisciplinary study of terrorist phenomena. (Includes a 119-item bibliography on rhetoric and the rhetorical dimensions of terrorism.)

61. _____, and Nitcavic, Richard G. (1989, November 20). Visions of terror: A Q-methodological analysis of American perceptions of international terrorism. Paper presented at the Annual Meeting of the Speech Communication Association (75th, San Francisco, CA, November 18–21, 1989), 33p. (ED 312698).

Public perceptions of events, particularly international terrorism, are influenced by specific variables. To explain these variables, the authors examine the efficacy of Q-methodology as a tool to explain these perceptions. "To develop their instrument, the researchers interviewed 16 individuals and based the structure of the Q-sort on the themes presented, resulting in an instrument with 49 statements." The authors found that the Q-methodology is a useful tool for examining public perceptions of international terrorism and about the effects of media coverage on terrorism. "Viewing terrorists as driven by human needs and possibly noble motives distinguished the 'Humanist/Cold-War Patriots' and the 'Pacifist-Isolationist' from the 'Frightened Philosopher' and the 'Aggressive Patriot.'" The authors say the results of this preliminary study should provide researchers with useful information for revision of the terrorism Q-sort — a process already under way. (Includes two tables of data, one figure, 26 references, and an appendix that contains research instrument and data.)

62. Drake, R. (1987). Contemporary terrorism and the intellectuals: The case of Italy. In Paul Wilkinson & Alasdaire M. Stewart (eds.), *Contemporary research on terrorism* (pp. 130–140). Aberdeen, MA: Aberdeen University Press.

For the last several years both left-wing extremists and some other groups have contributed to Italy's toll of political violence. After 1982 there was a sharp statistical decline in terrorist acts as a whole, but Italy has not yet entered the post-terrorist era of her history. (Includes 38 notes.)

63. Dror, Y. (1983). Terrorism as a challenge to the democratic capacity to govern. In Martha Crenshaw (ed.), *Terrorism, legitimacy, and* *power: The consequences of political violence* (pp. 65–90). Middletown, CT: Wesleyan University Press.

Politically, terrorism poses one more challenge to governments and rulers already overloaded quantitatively and qualitatively; it constitutes both a danger of failure with immediate and long-term consequences and an opportunity to reassert the requisites of a viable democratic capacity to govern. Terrorism demonstrates some main features of modern policy predicaments, posing an additional challenge to policymaking capacities and serving as an indicator of the present quality of policy-making. Little wonder that the literature on terrorism is booming with a mixture of serious studies and fictional treatments, sometimes with hard-to-discern borders between them. (Includes 46 footnotes.)

64. Dutter, Lee E. (1987). Ethno-political activity and the psychology of terrorism. *Terrorism,* 10, 3: 145–163.

Uses the example of South Moluccans in the Netherlands to illustrate the political behavior of ethnic groups, the theoretical connections between a society's ethnic cleavages, the development of ethno-political terrorism, and the implications of functioning of institutions of a country.

65. Duvall, R.D., and Stohl, Michael (1988). Governance by terror. In Michael Stohl (ed.), *The politics of terrorism* (pp. 231–271). New York: Marcel Dekker, Inc.

There are few efforts to identify systematically situations which fall outside the scope of the conventional use of the word terrorism but which, nevertheless, do satisfy the denotative criteria of that analytical concept. In this chapter, the authors attempt a partial correction of this situation by focusing on terrorism that generally receives far less attention: the terrorism practiced by "legally" constituted governments of nation-states. In doing so, the authors recognize that they must confront a couple of potential problems if they are to be at all persuasive in their argument. One is a conceptual issue; the other is an emotional issue. (Includes two tables, 37 notes, and 53 references.)

66. Editors for the Federal Bureau of Investigation, Terrorist Research and Analytical Center, Terrorism Section, Criminal Investigative Division (1988). *Terrorism at home and abroad: The U.S. government view.* In Michael Stohl (ed.), *The politics of terrorism* (pp. 295–372). New York: Marcel Dekker, Inc.

To give a clearer picture of the trends and dimensions of the terrorism in the United States, this report examines terrorist-related activities, defined as criminal acts which are committed either in support of or as a result of terrorism, but which are not intended to intimidate or coerce, in furtherance of political or social objectives. Author suggests that a bank robbery committed for the purpose of financing a terrorist group is an example of terrorist-related activity that falls short of meeting the incident criteria. This chapter also includes a section on incidents of terrorism, and revised statistical data from previous publications. (Includes seven tables, 16 figures, two appendixes, and four notes.)

67. Editors of *The Progressive* (1986). U.S. support of terrorists is immoral. In Bonnie Szumski (ed.), *Terrorism: Opposing viewpoints* (pp. 128–132). St. Paul, MN: Greenhaven Press.

One of the most debated aspects of terrorism is whether the U.S., by supporting dictatorial leaders throughout the world, is sponsoring terrorism. The author argues that the people living under these corrupt, U.S.–sponsored dictatorships begin to despise and resent the United States. Because their rights to legitimate forms of protest are denied, they turn to terrorism in a final attempt to achieve justice for themselves and their countries. (Includes one drawing.)

68. Editors of The Vice President's Task Force on Combatting Terrorism (1986). All political violence is terrorism. In Bonnie Szumski (ed.), *Terrorism: Opposing viewpoints* (pp. 16–21). St. Paul, MN: Greenhaven Press.

The Vice President's Task Force on Combatting Terrorism comprised 14 government officials appointed by Vice President George Bush in July 1985. In February 1986 the group issued its final report recommending policies and approaches to counteract terrorism. In this excerpt, the task force defines terrorism as a serious political threat to the United States and emphasizes that all legal political violence must be actively opposed.

69. Ehrenfeld, R., and Kahan, M. (1987). The "doping" of America: The ambivalence of the narco-terrorist connection and a search for solutions. In Paul Wilkinson & Alasdaire M. Stewart (eds.), *Contemporary research on terrorism* (pp. 241–255). Aberdeen, MA: Aberdeen University Press.

The authors argue that narco-terrorism is a particularly sinister manifestation of the international terrorist phenomenon; its unique effects are insidious, persistent and more difficult to identify than are the sporadic, violent outbursts of the armed assailant. (Includes 16 notes.)

70. Ellenberg, Edward S. (1978). The PLO and its place in violence and terror. In Marius H. Livingston with Lee Bruce Kress & Marie G. Wanek (eds.), *International terrorism in the contemporary world* (pp. 165-176). Westport, CT: Greenwood Press.

During the last few years, it has become more and more evident that the Palestine Liberation Organization (PLO) is playing a central role in the steadily developing international terrorist community. Although its so-called *raison d'être* is within the Middle Eastern political and historical context, the PLO has lately achieved the role of the main center of international terrorist linkup.

71. El-Sherbini, Magda (1990). Terrorism: Current readings. *Reference Services Review,* 18, 4: 49-63, 48.

Author presents selected readings on terrorism, 1985-1990. References cover books, periodicals, encyclopedias and dictionaries, directories, bibliographies, and online databases. These materials offer definitions of terrorism, psychological and religious aspects of terrorism, and preventive measures. (Includes 92 references.)

72. Emerson, Steven and Duffy, Brian (1990). *The fall of Pan Am 103: Inside the Lockerbie investigation.* New York: G.P. Putnam's Sons, 297p.

The book examines the bombing of Pan Am Flight 103 over Lockerbie, Scotland, and the investigation that followed. The authors provide an excellent account of the joint government investigation of a terrorist act of international proportion.

73. Enders, Walter, and Sandler, Todd (1991, January-March). Causality between transnational terrorism and tourism: The case of Spain. *Terrorism,* 14, 1: 49-58.

Analysis suggests that terrorism significantly reduced Spanish terrorism between 1970 and 1988.

74. Evans, Ernest H. (1979). *Calling a truce to terror: The American response to international terrorism.* Westport, CT: Greenwood Press, 180p.

This book examines the causes of terrorism and the strategies employed by terrorists. These issues are analyzed within the context of international politics and the United States' efforts to attain multilateral deterrence. Author also examines the "repoliticalization" of American policy response to international terrorism. (Includes three figures, four appendices, eight tables of data and a bibliography and index.)

75. Faucher, Leo J. (1983, August). FBI statistics on U.S. terrorism. *Security Management,* 27: 95–98.

This article is a chronology of domestic terrorist groups operating in the United States, and their targets. List includes Armenian groups, Croatian groups, Cuban groups, Jewish groups, and Libyan groups.

76. Fearey, Robert A. (1978). Introduction to international terrorism. In Marius H. Livingston with Lee Bruce Kress & Marie G. Wanek (eds.), *International terrorism in the contemporary world* (pp. 25–35). Westport, CT: Greenwood Press.

Author suggests that international terrorism is distinguished by three characteristics. First, as with other forms of terrorism, it embodies an act which is essentially criminal; second, international terrorism is politically motivated; and finally, international terrorism transcends national boundaries, through the choice of a foreign victim or target, the commission of the terrorist act in a foreign country, or an effort to influence the policies of a foreign government.

77. Feehan, John M. (1986). IRA terrorism is justified. In Bonnie Szumski (ed.), *Terrorism: Opposing viewpoints* (pp. 96–104). St. Paul, MN: Greenhaven Press.

The author argues that the Irish Republican Army (IRA) has no choice but to use violence to attain its goals. A native of Ireland, Feehan has authored many books on the Irish political situation as well as biographies of Irish rebels, including "Bobby Sands and the Tragedy of Northern Ireland," from which this article is excerpted.

78. Finger, Seymour M. (1988, March). The United Nations and international terrorism. *The Jerusalem Journal of International Relations,* 10, 1: 14–24.

Argues that because terrorism is an international problem, the United Nations has an obligation to assist in alleviating the problem. Author suggests that U.N. efforts may be thwarted because of the various definitions that blocs of nations attach to the concept terrorism.

79. Fisk, Robert (1978). The effect of social and political crime on the police and British Army in Northern Ireland. In Marius H. Livingston with Lee Bruce Kress & Marie G. Wanek (eds.), *International terrorism in the contemporary world* (pp. 84–93). Westport, CT: Greenwood Press.

Author argues that there is ambiguity about the British army's functions in Northern Ireland and about the nature of those considered the enemy. The IRA, when they clearly emerged in the shape of the Provisionals in 1970, were described in fashionable if slightly easy terms as "thugs and murderers"; they were considered common criminals with no genuine political aspirations. (Includes 20 notes.)

80. Fleming, Dan B. (1986, Fall). The treatment of terrorism in social studies texts. *Social Science Record,* 24, 1: 20–22.

Author suggests ways teachers can help students define and understand terrorism.

81. Fleming, P.A., Schmid, Alex P., and Stohl, Michael (1988). The theoretical utility of typologies of terrorism: Lessons and opportunities. In Michael Stohl (ed.), *The politics of terrorism* (pp. 153–195). New York: Marcel Dekker, Inc.

The primary utility of typologies can be found in the ability to make use of underlying variables in discovering relationships. Researchers create typologies by combining variables that are thought to be theoretically interesting. These resultant typologies provide the researcher with an opportunity to make general statements about classes of social phenomena. One of the most important classes in the understanding and managing of terrorism concerns terrorist organizations and types of groups. This chapter examines inter alia efforts to categorize and indicates the weaknesses in typology development that exist at present. (Includes one table, four models, one figure, design charts, nine notes, and 62 references.)

82. Flynn, E.E. (1987). Victims of terrorism: Dimensions of the victim experience. In Paul Wilkinson & Alasdaire M. Stewart (eds.), *Contemporary research in terrorism* (pp. 337–356). Aberdeen, MA: Aberdeen University Press.

The purpose of this article is to synthesize and critically assess the dimensions of knowledge of the victim experience in terrorism. Drawing on sociology, general principles are identified to further the understanding of the phenomenon, to aid in preparing persons at risk for the experience of victimization, and to assist in the development of an improved system response to victims. (Includes 56 notes.)

83. Flynn, Kevin, and Gerhardt, Gary (1989). *The "Silent Brother-hood": Inside America's racist underground.* London: Collier Mac-millan Publishers, 410p.

Both authors were among several reporters for the *Rocky Mountain News* in Denver assigned to cover the story. Gerhardt had the task of covering Denver police and federal agents as the story developed. Flynn was the only reporter to locate and attend the secret graveside services for Berg in Chicago. The story, however, didn't accelerate in the public eye until after the FBI had already dealt the fatal blow to the "Silent Brotherhood." In the months that followed, as bits and pieces of the story leaked out, Flynn, Gerhardt, and a news colleague, John Accola, criss-crossed the continent tracking down new developments. They stayed with the story through arrests and trials.

84. Fontaine, Roger W. (1988). *Terrorism: The Cuban connection.* New York: Crane Russak & Company, 199p.

Cuba's sponsorship of terrorism is still poorly understood, and that is no accident. It is one mark of Fidel Castro's remarkable career that he has successfully cloaked his support of terrorists with the romantic garb of the heroic guerrilla. Thus, in contrast to other states sponsoring terrorism (Iran, Libya, Syria, even the Soviet Union), Cuba's involvement in terrorism has never made headlines and more importantly has avoided nearly all serious inquiry. (Includes two appendices and a selected bibliography.)

85. Foreign Policy Association (1986). International terrorism: In search of a response. *Great Decisions '86* (pp. 35–44). New York: Foreign Policy Association.

Examines international terrorism and how the United States should respond to terrorists and terrorism. Analyzes the "causes" or issues terrorists claim to represent. Topics of analysis include definition of terrorism; regional terrorism; state-sponsored terrorism; examination of the Soviet connection; and terrorism and the media. (Includes an activity book, photographs, and illustrations.)

86. Fowler, William W. (1980, July). An agenda for quantitative research on terrorism. *The RAND Paper Series* P-6591. Santa Monica, CA: The RAND Corporation, 11p.

Suggests how databases containing numeric data on terrorism should be analyzed by researchers: the first part should be devoted to a definitional issues; the second section to design and context of data as they relate to quantitative methods; the third section discusses the level and importance of analysis; the fourth part presents a general strategy and specifies how data are to be analyzed; and the last section presents an agenda for research.

87. Francis, Samuel T. (1986). The Soviet Union sponsors terrorism. In Bonnie Szumski (ed.), *Terrorism: Opposing viewpoints* (pp. 145–151). St. Paul, MN: Greenhaven Press.

   In this excerpt from the author's book *The Soviet Strategy of Terror,* Soviet involvement in various revolutionary movements throughout the world is documented. Author concludes that the Soviets support international terror in order to help achieve their ultimate goal, the takeover of the United States. (Includes one cartoon.)

88. Frey, Raymond G., and Morris, Christopher W. (eds.) (1991). *Violence, terrorism, and justice.* New York: Cambridge University Press, 319p.

   Editors assembled a group of distinguished scholars to address the problem of terrorism. The essays try to determine, among other issues, the purposes of terrorism; the political significance of terrorism; and state terrorism. (Includes 12 chapters.)

89. _____, and _____ (1991). Violence, terrorism, and justice. In Raymond G. Frey & Christopher W. Morris (eds.), *Violence, terrorism, and justice* (pp. 1–17). New York: Cambridge University Press.

   This introductory chapter tackles the issue of terrorism, asking what exactly is terrorism; why is it wrong; and what is the justification for terrorism. Summarizes chapters in the book.

90. Friedland, Nehemia, and Merari, Ariel. (1985, December). The psychological impact of terrorism: A double-edged sword. *Political Psychology,* 6, 4: 591–604.

   Authors surveyed 1,500 respondents to determine the degree of fear and concern for personal safety caused by terrorist activities in Israel; attitudes toward political solutions to the Palestinian problem; and attitudes toward various counterterrorist measures. Shows impact of terrorism as a tool for political influence. (Includes 12 references.)

91. Friedlander, Robert A. (1979). *Terrorism: Documents of international and local control.* Vols. 1–5. Dobbs Ferry, NY: Oceana Publications, Inc.

   A comprehensive documentation of terrorism in five volumes. An excellent resource for researchers, which includes discussions on legislative issues.

92. _____ (1990). *Terrorism: Documents of international and local control,* vol. V. New York: Oceana Publications, Inc., 425p.

The resumption of this documentary series is due to the hard fact and cold reality that global terrorism has steadily expanded during the Dangerous Decade of the 1980s. This volume is primarily concerned with the United States' role in confronting the terrorist dilemma. No country has provided more detailed statistics about terrorism and its bloody consequences. One reason is that United States citizens, property, and diplomatic personnel continue to present major targets for the perpetrators of terror-violence. The studies contained in the first section of the present volume well delineate the tragic record of terrorism's seemingly inexorable challenge.

93. Galvin, Deborah M. (1983). The female terrorist: A socio-psychological perspective. *Behavioral Sciences and the Law,* 1, 2: 19–32.

Suggests that there is no archetypal female terrorist because women tend to get involved in terrorism on their own initiative or through a secondary other. Argues that the power of the female terrorist is less than that of her male counterpart. (Includes 52 references.)

94. Gerbner, George (1991). Symbolic functions of violence and terror. In Yonah Alexander & Robert G. Picard (eds.), *In the camera's eye: News coverage of terrorist events* (pp. 3–9). New York: Brassey's (U.S.) Inc.

See entry 95.

95. _____ (1988, July). Symbolic functions of violence and terror. Terrorism and the news media research project. Association of Education in Journalism and Mass Communication, 8p. (ED 312725).

The highly selective and politically shaped portrayals of violence and terror conceal rather than reveal the actual incidence and distribution of real violence and terror. These portrayals, including the choice of labels, serve as projective devices that isolate acts and people from meaningful contexts and set them up to be stigmatized and victimized. Symbolic uses benefit those who control them. They are usually states and media establishments, not small-scale or isolated actors or insurgents. The mass ritual of television presents a world which is power oriented. Though perpetrators of small-scale acts of violence and terror may occasionally force media attention and, in that sense, seem to advance their cause, in the last analysis such a challenge serves to enhance media credibility ("just reporting the facts") and is used to mobilize support for repression, often in the form of wholescale state violence and terror or military action, presented as justified by the provocation. Concludes that prolonged exposure to stories and scenes of violence and terror can mobilize aggressive tendencies; desensitize some and isolate others; trigger violence in a few; and intimidate the many. (Includes ten notes and ten references.)

96. _____, and Gross, Linda (1976). Living with television: The violence profile. *Journal of Communication,* 26, 2: 172–199.

Does TV entertainment incite or pacify violence, or both? New approach to research uses "Cultural Indicators" as a framework for a progress report on a long-range study of trends in television content and effects. Its findings have relevance to terrorism in the media. (Includes eight graphs, five tables, and 16 references.)

97. _____, _____, Jackson-Beeck, Marilyn, Jeffries-Fox, Suzanne, and Signorielli, Nancy (1978, Summer). Violence on the screen. *Journal of Communication,* 28, 3: 176–207.

This report discusses the expansion, diversification, and application of the Cultural Indicators research design that was popularized by Gerbner and his associates at the Annenberg School of Communication, University of Pennsylvania. The authors stress methodology, current findings on the distribution of power in the world of television drama, and some behavioral correlates of viewing. A full Technical Report is also available. The research consists of two interrelated parts, Message System Analysis (monitoring of the world of television drama) and Cultivation Analysis — all of which determines the conceptions of social reality that television tends to cultivate in different groups of (child and adult) viewers. The analyses provide information about the geographer, demography, character profiles, and action structure of the world of television, and focus these images and lessons upon specific issues, policies, and topics. The analyses have relevance to media coverage of terrorism. (Includes three graphs, 13 tables, and 31 references.)

98. Gerrits, Robert P.J.M. (1992). Terrorists' perspectives: Memoirs. In David L. Paletz & Alex P. Schmid (eds.), *Terrorism and the media* (pp. 29–61). Newbury Park, CA: Sage.

This chapter analyzes the uses of publicity by insurgent terrorists in Europe since 1968 based on memoirs by the terrorists themselves. An important analytical distinction is drawn between the psychological aims the terrorists pursue and the concrete ways in which these aims are brought about through publicity. Psychological aims include the demoralization of the opponent, exploiting the repression of the authorities, demonstrating the movement's strength, gaining sympathy, causing unrest and polarization, and demonstrating the necessity of violence to change the situation. Among the tactics of publicity are raising the news value of operations, organizing special sections for publicity, publicity-conscious selection of the times and places for actions and statements, and picking symbolically resonant targets. (Includes one figure and 24 references.)

99. Gladis, Stephen D. (1979, September). The hostage/terrorist situation and the media. *The FBI Law Enforcement Bulletin,* 48, 9: 10–15.
This is an examination of the relationship between the hostage/terrorist and the media. The author suggests that the conduct of the news media at hostage scenes has become a problem as they can, at times, instigate the violence and affect the way terrorists act. Because journalists are competing for the first and best story, they tend to get in the way of the police and aggravate the incident. Advancements in technology, such as the mini-cam, are also discussed as they enable newscasters to air live footage as the event is taking place. This poses a problem as journalists may not use good judgment as to what the audience should be shown, even when other stations decide not to cover the event live. Both CBS and NBC have established a set of guidelines to follow in the event of a hostage situation. The relationship of the media and law enforcement officials is also discussed here. Communication between the two seems to be the safest and most effective way to handle a crisis such as terrorism. A public information officer usually serves as a liaison between a law enforcement agency and the media. This arrangement facilitates the dissemination of information to the media, thereby, eliminating freelancers who may obstruct police work.

100. Glover, Jonathan (1991). State terrorism. In Raymond G. Frey & Christopher W. Morris (eds.), *Cambridge studies in philosophy and public policy* (pp. 256–275). New York: Cambridge University Press.
Author discusses some of the important characteristics of state terrorism and compares them with some prevalent features of individual terrorism. Suggests that state terrorism is morally worse than individual terrorism because of its frequency. It also tackles the reasons why state officials rely upon terrorism.

101. Golan, Galia (1990). *Gorbachev's "New Thinking" on terrorism.* New York: Praeger, 117p.

Traces and reevaluates Soviet attitude and policy toward terrorism from the 1960s and 1970s to 1983-1984. Suggests that during the 1960s and 1970s, the Soviet attitude toward terrorism was negative; the 1980s saw a dramatic, hardening Soviet attitude toward terrorism. Author suggests that the apparent behavioral change was motivated by an ideological shift.

102. Goldberg, Joseph E. (1991, Spring). Understanding the dimensions of terrorism. *Perspectives on Political Science,* 20, 2: 78–88.

A critical analysis of articles which suggests the definition of terrorism is based on the onlooker's politics. The author insists that one's ideological orientation influences how one defines terrorism. Suggests that identifying terrorism should not be conditioned by politics; states must balance the security interest of many over individual protection.

103. Grabosky, P.N. (1988). The urban context of political terrorism. In Michael Stohl (ed.), *The politics of terrorism* (pp. 59–84). New York: Marcel Dekker, Inc.

The chapter draws from examples widely dispersed over time and space but does not present a systematic survey of urban terrorist activity. Rather, it is intended specifically to show how the structure of cities conditions various aspects of terrorist organization and practice, both repressive and insurrectionary. (Includes 68 references.)

104. Greer, S.C. (1987). The supergrass system in Northern Ireland. In Paul Wilkinson & Alasdaire M. Stewart (eds.), *Contemporary research in terrorism* (pp. 510–535). Aberdeen, MA: Aberdeen University Press.

Apart from the number of defendants involved in supergrass cases, three main features distinguish the supergrass as a type of witness from run-of-the-mill accomplices who decide to give evidence for the prosecution. First, almost without exception, supergrasses in the U.K. have been the products of deliberate law-enforcement initiatives directed specifically at organized acquisitive crime mostly in the south of England or paramilitary activity in Northern Ireland. Second, they have been deeply involved in these serious, violent crimes rather than any other type of offense. Third, in almost every case they have been motivated by a highly developed sense of self-interest. Other accomplices turning Queen's evidence, on the other hand, may emerge anywhere in the U.K., may have committed any offense involving more than one participant and may take this step at the impetus of any one or more of a variety of motives including genuine contrition, the desire for revenge or the hope of obtaining some personal advantage, e.g., leniency in punishment, immunity from prosecution or a financial or other material reward. (Includes one table and 95 notes.)

105. Groebel, Jo (1989). The problems and challenges of research on terrorism. In Jo Groebel & Jeffrey H. Goldstein (eds.), *Terrorism: Psychological perspectives.* Series in psychobiology (pp. 15–38). Seville, Spain: Publicaciones de la Universidad de Sevilla.

Author presents some of the results that emerged from empirical analyses of terrorism in West Germany and discusses the theory, methods, and problems related to scientific research in this area. Makes several suggestions for future empirical analyses that probably can be applied in other nations or cultures where terrorism is of any significance.

106. _____, and Goldstein, Jeffrey H. (eds.) (1989). *Terrorism: Psychological perspectives.* Seville, Spain: Publicaciones de la Universidad de Sevilla.

Editors assembled a number of authors to present some of the research findings and perspectives that inform their views of the development, the phenomenology, and the consequences of terrorism. Special attention is drawn to the psychological factors involved in the occurrence and consequences of terrorism.

107. Gurr, Ted R. (1988). Political terrorism in the United States: Historical antecedents and contemporary trends. In Michael Stohl (ed.), *The politics of terrorism* (pp. 549–578). New York: Marcel Dekker, Inc.

Author identifies four distinctive species of political and social terrorism, based on the political status and situation of the perpetrators. 1) *Vigilante terrorism* is initiated by private groups but is aimed at other private groups in resistance to threatening social change. It is by far the most common kind of terrorism in U.S. history, as we show below. 2) *Insurgent terrorism,* which is the subject of most popular concern and journalistic treatment, is directed by private groups against public authorities and aims at bringing about radical political change. 3) *Transnational terrorism* is the third general category. It is distinct not in its purposes but in its international implications: its objectives, targets, or the terrorists themselves originate in another country than the one in which the terrorist incident occurs. 4) *State terrorism* is used by authorities to intimidate private citizens or groups and is generally very different in its causes, objectives, and consequences from terrorism initiated by private groups. (Includes two tables, ten notes, and 44 references.)

108. _____ (1988). Some characteristics of political terrorism in the 1960s. In M. Stohl (ed.), *The politics of terrorism* (pp. 31–58). New York: Marcel Dekker, Inc.

This chapter surveys the use of "terrorist" tactics by private groups for political purposes. The interpretative problems are sidestepped by using an empirical definition of this kind of "political terrorism" that makes no *a priori* assumptions about what effects the users hope to accomplish by their actions or about how their would-be victims react. The definition has three objective elements. The first is that destructive violence is used by stealth rather than in open combat. Explosives and incendiary devices are the archetypal weapons of political terrorism, but there are others, including sniping, kidnapping, hijacking, biological agents, and atomic devices, the latter two thus far feared rather than used. The second element in the definition is that some, at least, of the principal targets are political ones. The third definitional element is that these actions be carried out by groups operating clandestinely and sporadically. (Includes ten tables of data, two figures, appendix, and 16 notes.)

109. Gutteridge, W. (ed.) (1986). *The new terrorism.* London: Mansell Publishing Limited, 225p.

The authors examine the new forms of terrorism and the diplomatic immunities extended to state-sponsored terrorism. Case studies and incidents of terrorism in Western Europe: France, Spain (ITA) threat to Basque democracy), Italy (Red Brigades), and West Germany (Red Army), are discussed in the book.

110. Hacker, Frederick J. (1976). *Crusaders, criminals, crazies: Terror and terrorism in our time.* New York: Bantam Books.

This book explores two distinct kinds of fear arousal — terror and terrorism; what they are, what they do, what they do to us, what they do for us, and what can be done about them.

111. Hanle, Donald J. (1989). *Terrorism: The newest face of warfare.* New York: Pergamon–Brassey's Terrorism Library, International Defense Publishers, Inc., 255p.

The book seeks to answer the question, Is terrorism a form of war? In determining this answer, the author examines the ramifications of strategies for neutralizing this threat. Author argues that these issues demand the importance of understanding of terminologies such as war and terrorism. It is here that the complexity of the question at hand comes to light. With a quick glimpse at the table of contents the reader will note that it requires four of ten chapters simply to isolate, define, and come to an understanding of the phenomenon of war. It takes an additional chapter to define terrorism.

112. Harris, Louis, and Associates (1977, December 5). Terrorism. *The Harris Survey,* press release, 3p.

A public opinion poll in December 1977 shows that 90 percent of Americans who responded to the poll say terrorism is a "very serious" world problem: only 60 percent considered it a very serious domestic problem.

113. Hatcher, C. (1987). A conceptual framework in victimology: The adult and child hostage experience. In Paul Wilkinson & Alasdaire M. Stewart (eds.), *Contemporary research in terrorism* (pp. 357–375). Aberdeen, MA: Aberdeen University Press.

The study of "within-incident" behavior produced information which has contributed significantly to the successful resolution of many subsequent hostage-takings. The study of "after-incident" behavior began to show that even relatively brief hostage periods produced a range of short- and long-term reactions in a large percentage of the victims and their families. Only recently, however, have psychologists and other professionals begun to assist in the re-adjustment process of the ex-hostage. In order to do this effectively, the author suggests that one should ask the following questions: a) Is there a typical hostage behavior pattern, and what is the range of that hostage behavior? b) Is hostage behavior the same as other victim reactions or does it have some unique aspects? c) Do individuals of different backgrounds react differently? (Includes 20 notes.)

114. Heath, Linda, Gordon, Margaret T., and LaBailly, Robert (1981). What newspapers tell us (and don't tell us) about rape. *Newspaper Research Journal,* 2, 4: 48–55.

The authors hypothesized that the public's understanding of rape can be hindered by the frightening and erroneous view of rape that is presented in newspaper stories. However, a content analysis of 8,015 crime stories, in newspapers published in three cities (Philadelphia, Chicago, and San Francisco) did not confirm their hypothesis; it revealed that newspapers give a fairly accurate picture of rape when they present the details. Authors contend that newspapers need to run stories that will more adequately inform the public about rape.

115. Held, Virginia (1991). Terrorism, rights, and political goals. In Raymond G. Frey & Christopher W. Morris (eds.), *Cambridge studies in philosophy and public policy* (pp. 59–85). New York: Cambridge University Press.

After considering various characteristics of terrorism, the author defines terrorism as "a form of violence, which aims to achieve political goals, often through the creation of fear." Also examined is the question of the moral distinction between combatant and noncombatant and possible rights violations.

116. Hendel, Samuel (1978). The price of terror in the USSR. In Marius H. Livingston with Lee Bruce Kress & Marie G. Wanek (eds.), *International terrorism in the contemporary world* (pp. 122–130). Westport, CT: Greenwood Press.

This essay is a thorough analysis of the scope and price of terror in the Soviet Union.

117. Herman, Edward S. (1986). Soviet-backed terrorism is U.S. propaganda. In Bonnie Szumski (ed.), *Terrorism: Opposing viewpoints* (pp. 152–158). St. Paul, MN: Greenhaven Press.

The article is an excerpt from the author's book, *The Real Terrorist Network*. The author argues that the Soviet Union "terror network" is a United States concoction to rally support for a new wave of Communist scares. (Includes a cartoon.)

118. _____, and Mickolus, Edward F. (1980, June). Observations on "Why violence spreads." *International Studies Quarterly, 24,* 299–305.

The study of terrorism has undergone a number of developments in recent years. One of the most important is the adoption of the quantitative method of analysis. Long mired in unproductive arguments over the *a priori* disadvantages of statistical techniques in studying violence, the field has discovered that terrorist activity is amenable to systematic analysis. As in all new fields, however, the quantitative study of terrorism is fraught with obstacles of data reliability, the selection of a level of analysis and universe of discourse, and difficulties in making the transition from quantitative analysis to substantive argument and explanation. (Includes one table, 11 references, and five footnotes.)

119. _____, and O'Sullivan, Gerry (1984). *The terrorism industry: The experts and institutions that shape our view of terror.* New York: Pantheon Books, 303p.

This book is about cultural processes that make certain victims important, their trials and tribulations heartrending, and that mobilize public opinion on their behalf, but that cause other victims to remain unnoticed or even to be transmuted into victimizers. (Includes four appendices, 12 tables, notes, and index.)

120. Hewitt, Christopher (1992). Public's perspectives. In David L. Paletz & Alex P. Schmid (eds.), *Terrorism and the media* (pp. 170–207). Newbury Park, CA: Sage.

This chapter classifies the public into three main audiences: the terrorists' constituency, the terrorists' enemy, and the uninvolved. Nationalist terrorists define these categories in ethnic terms; revolutionary terrorists define them using class-ideological criteria. An analysis of public opinion polls from several countries indicates that terrorism arouses a high degree of public concern, but rarely succeeds in getting the terrorist cause on to the political agenda. Nationalist terrorists receive more support from their constituency than revolutionaries do from theirs. As a means of intimidating the enemy, revolutionary terrorism is an unsuccessful strategy, but nationalist terrorism is sometimes effective. (Includes three figures, 13 tables, 17 notes, and 69 references.)

121. Hitchens, Christopher (1989, Summer). Terrorism: A cliche in search of a meaning. *ETC,* 46, 2: 147–152.

Central to this paper is the question, "Does an 'act of terrorism' always refer to the kind of action taken or does it sometimes depend on who takes the action?" Author posed the definitional question of terrorism to Terrell E. Arnold so as to determine whether there is a universally accepted definition of the term. Responses suggest that there is no universally acceptable definition of terrorism.

122. Hoffman, Bruce (1986, Fall). Defining terrorism. *Social Science Record,* 24, 1: 6–7.

Author recognizes the lack of a concise meaning for the word terrorism. Develops a working definition which states that terrorism is the deliberate creation and attainment of fear through violence or the threat of violence in the attainment of political objectives.

123. _____ (1987). Terrorism in the United States during 1985. In Paul Wilkinson & Alasdaire M. Stewart (eds.), *Contemporary research on terrorism* (pp. 230–240). Aberdeen, MA: Aberdeen University Press.

> The author argues that the United States is, and has long been, the number one target of a variety of foreign terrorist organizations. Indeed, of the approximately 450 acts of terrorism recorded in 1985 by the RAND Corporation's terrorism chronology, 111 were directed at American targets. (Includes 16 notes.)

124. _____ (1986, Fall). Why persons become terrorists. *Social Science Record,* 24, 1: 8–9.

> States that alienation from society is a characteristic found in people who become terrorists. Certain events and life stages of individuals are typically associated with the development of terrorists.

125. Holden, Constance (1979, January). Study of terrorism emerging as an international endeavor. *Science,* 203, 4375: 33–35.

> Suggests the need for further study of the dynamics of terrorist groups, even though increased attention is being given to study of the political, social, and psychological aspects of terrorism.

126. Hollander, Nancy C. (1992, September). Psychoanalysis and state terrorism in Argentina. *American Journal of Psychoanalysis,* 52, 3: 273–289.

> Examines political repression in Argentina during the period characterized as the "Dirty War" (1976–1983). State terrorism, the author argues, was designed to repress those who opposed the government.

127. Homer, F.D. (1988). Terror in the United States: Three perspectives. In Michael Stohl (ed.), *The politics of terrorism* (pp. 197–229). New York: Marcel Dekker, Inc.

> This chapter is limited to the presentation of three perspectives that help organize the reader's knowledge of terror so as to integrate future events into their experience. These perspectives highlight several viewpoints concerning the role of terror in America, each embodying propositions about the relationship of terror to social change and exploring ideas about the appropriateness of terror to bring about change. Each addresses definitional issues about terror. (Includes ten notes and 65 references.)

128. Horchem, H.J. (1987). Terrorism in Germany: 1985. In Paul Wilkinson & Alasdaire M. Stewart (eds.), *Contemporary research on terrorism* (pp. 141-163). Aberdeen, MA: Aberdeen University Press.

> During the past twenty years, the majority of the Western European countries have been subject to attempts and actions committed by politically motivated terrorists. The international terrorism of Middle East organizations constituted a specific problem in this context. The author examines terrorism in Germany and suggests that terrorists involved in these activities are still operating with the assumption that they will be offered a refuge where they will not be pursued in connection with their activities.

129. Horowitz, Irving Louis (1983). The routinization of terrorism and its unanticipated consequences. In Martha Crenshaw (ed.), *Terrorism, legitimacy, and power: The consequences of political violence* (pp. 38-51). Middletown, CT: Wesleyan University Press.

> The author argues that most analyses have emphasized the causes and forms rather than the consequences of terrorism. Studies of government policies toward terrorism have also proliferated, but the outcomes of campaigns of terrorism have been largely ignored. Such a neglect of results, the author suggests, characterizes studies of political violence in general. (Includes 16 footnotes.)

130. _____ (1989). The texture of terrorism: Socialization, routinization, and integration. In Roberta S. Sigal (ed.), *Political learning in adulthood: A sourcebook of theory and research* (pp. 386-414). Chicago, IL: University of Chicago Press.

> Author examines and defines different types of political terrorism. Discusses political socialization of political terrorists. Concludes with specific observations and speculations about terrorism and its impact on daily affairs of many societies.

131. Hubbard, David G. (1986). Terrorism is criminal activity. In Bonnie Szumski (ed.), *Terrorism: Opposing viewpoints* (pp. 26-32). St. Paul, MN: Greenhaven Press.

> The author claims terrorism is no more than ordinary crime with a political motive. By defining terrorism as a serious threat, the United States and the world give terrorism far too much importance.

132. Inciardi, James A. (1991). Narcoterrorism: A Perspective and commentary. In J. Kelly, E. Donal, & J. MacNamara (eds.), *Perspectives*

on deviance: Dominance, degradation and denigration (pp. 89–103). Cincinnati, OH: Anderson Publishing Co.
  See entry 431.

133. Jaehnig, Walter B., Weaver, David H., and Fico, Frederick (1981, Winter). Reporting crime and fearing crime in three communities. *Journal of Communication,* 31, 1: 88–96.
  Newspaper emphasis on relatively infrequent violent crimes may contribute to a heightened public concern—and fear—among readers about their own safety. While conceding that the news media can assume useful information roles, critics argue that "objective" and comprehensive portrayals are unavailable to the public because press treatment of social problems is insufficient and superficial, and because newsroom values color the selection and presentation of information. The authors wanted to account for several factors in assessing how the press is used as a source of public information, so they adopted the following strategy: 1) look at communities of different sizes to see if public perceptions differed in increasingly concentrated urban environments; 2) see how press reports of crimes in those areas reflected the amount and nature of crimes actually committed according to police statistics, to see how "objective" or accurate a picture of area crime was presented by the press; 3) determine if personal experience or personal knowledge of crime would affect the definitions that would have been formed had media been the only source of information and 4) ascertain how public knowledge of crime and fear of being a victim of crime were related. Results have relevance to terrorism. (Includes three tables and 16 references.)

134. Jenkins, Brian M. (1981, August). Combating terrorism: Some policy implications. *The RAND Paper Series,* P-6666. Santa Monica, CA: The RAND Corporation, 11p.
  Author outlines a strategy for combating terrorism. Hints at the possibility of single terrorist incidents of greater magnitude within the U.S. mainland. Paper was prepared for a State Department conference on "Terrorism in the 1980s," May 21–22, 1981.

135. _____ (1981, February). Fighting terrorism: An enduring task. *The RAND Paper Series,* P-6585. Santa Monica, CA: The RAND Corporation, 8p.
  See entry 625.

136. _____ (1987). The future course of international terrorism. In Paul Wilkinson & Alasdaire M. Stewart (eds.), *Contemporary re-*

search on terrorism (pp. 581–589). Aberdeen, MA: Aberdeen University Press.

International terrorism emerged as a problem in the late 1960s, and despite increased governmental efforts to combat it, terrorism remains a serious problem in the 1980s. According to the author, terrorism will continue to pose a problem to society.

137. _____ (1981, March). International terrorism: Choosing the right target. *The RAND Paper Series,* P-6597. Santa Monica, CA: The RAND Corporation, 8p.

Answers the question: Is the Soviet Union supporting and fostering international terrorism? Argues that inasmuch as Moscow might be a culprit in terrorism, "we should be careful not to diminish opportunities to do something effective to combat international terrorism." Concludes that the best approach is to seek new international agreements on terrorism, rather than to go after the Russians.

138. _____ (1978, Spring/Summer). International terrorism: Trends and potentialities. *Journal of International Affairs,* 32, 1: 115–124.

The author argues that the use of terrorist tactics will persist as a mode of political expression, of gaining international attention, and of achieving limited political goals. Although no terrorists have achieved their stated long-range goals, and in that sense have failed, their use of terrorist tactics has won them publicity and occasional concessions. These tactical successes probably will suffice to preclude the abandonment of terrorist tactics. (Includes five graphs.)

139. _____ (1983). Research in terrorism: Areas of consensus, areas of ignorance. In B. Eichelman, David A. Soskis, & W. Reid (eds.), *Terrorism: Interdisciplinary perspectives* (p. 160). Washington, D.C.: American Psychiatric Association.

The author observes that very little terrorism is seen in totalitarian countries, leading some to consider the possibility that terrorism is a product of freedom, particularly of freedom of the press.

140. _____ (1981, May). A strategy for combating terrorism. *The RAND Paper Series,* P-6624. Santa Monica, CA: The RAND Corporation, 8p.

See entry 628.

141. _____ (1980, December). The study of terrorism: Definitional problems. *The RAND Paper Series,* P-6563. Santa Monica, CA: The RAND Corporation, 10p.

Tackles the definitional problems involved in analyzing terrorism. Argues that no precise or widely accepted definition exists. Suggests definitions that would help in the continuing research on terrorism. The paper was first presented at the 1978 meeting of the Institute of Management Sciences and Operations Research Society of America in New York on May 3, 1978.

142. _____ (1982, March). Talking to terrorists. *The RAND Paper Series,* P-6750. Santa Monica, CA: The RAND Corporation, 15p. See entry 629.

143. _____ (1986). Terrorism cannot be eliminated. In Bonnie Szumski (ed.), *Terrorism: Opposing viewpoints* (pp. 191–196). St. Paul, MN: Greenhaven Press.

The author argues that terrorism is as pervasive as poverty, prejudice, and crime and cannot be eliminated. (Includes a cartoon.)

144. _____ (1980, December). Terrorism in the 1980s. *The RAND Paper Series,* P-6564. Santa Monica, CA: The RAND Corporation, 13p.

This is the text of an address to the 26th Annual Seminar of the American Society of Industrial Security in Miami Beach, FL, on September 25, 1980. Author reviews the trends in terrorism over the last ten years; identifies some of the developments in the 1980s; and predicts what to expect in the coming decade.

145. Katz, Elihu (1980). Media events: The sense of occasion. *Studies in Visual Communication,* 6, 34–89.

Western journalism differs from Eastern journalism in its emphasis on negative events, on things that go wrong. If the opening of a factory is news in Eastern Europe, it is the closing of a factory that is news in the West. Free-world journalism is about conflict: nation against nation, man against man, man against nature. A news event, typically, is the story of some conflict. The conflict may be institutionalized, as in parliaments or sports, or it may be spontaneous, as in a terrorist attack or an earthquake. Such stories, more than any other, define the news. (Includes 14 notes and 18 references.)

146. Kemp, Geoffrey (1986). U.S. support of terrorists is necessary. In Bonnie Szumski (ed.), *Terrorism: Opposing viewpoints* (pp. 133–136). St. Paul, MN: Greenhaven Press.

The author argues that in the struggle against terrorism, the United States should consider itself at war. As such, it is absolutely essential for the U.S. to be less fastidious about the rebels it supports. The top priority of the U.S. should be in protecting its own national security even if, in doing this, it must employ its own "terrorists."

147. Kempster, Norma (1991, May 1). U.S. reports decline in terrorism worldwide. *Los Angeles Times,* p. A8.

The number of terrorist incidents in 1990 amounted to 455 compared to 856 acts in 1988. Possible reasons given for this decline were the end of Communism in Eastern Europe, Syria calling for a moratorium on terrorism, and Saddam Hussein being unable to go through with his threats of terrorist attacks on Americans and their interests. This article indicates that the region with the most terrorism in 1990 was Latin America. Reported incidents numbered 162 with the Middle East only supporting 63 that year. This (1991) is the first time in five years that no Westerners were taken hostage in Lebanon. The one significant development was the Iraqi invasion of Kuwait. A large number of citizens supported Hussein and his threats of terrorist attacks against the West, Israel and moderate Arabs in the event of war, but no Iraqi-backed attacks occurred in 1990. The U.S. State Department still had Iraq on its list of nations that support terrorism along with Cuba, Iran, Libya, North Korea, and Syria. It was thought that Syria would be taken off the list after it sent troops to the anti–Iraq military coalition. Saddam Hussein's inability to carry out his threats may show Syria's strong control over many terrorist groups.

148. Kende, Istvan (1986). Terrorism, wars, nuclear holocaust. *International Social Science Journal,* 38, 4: 529–538.

Presents a survey of political and structural violence which pervades contemporary society. Argues that violence breeds more violence; a distinction is drawn between different types of political violence. Author also explores the political nature of nuclear deterrence.

149. Kennedy, Moorhead (1986, September/October). The root causes of terrorism. *The Humanist,* 46, 5: 5–9, 30.

Morehead Kennedy was an acting economic counselor at the American Embassy in Tehran, Iran, when he was taken hostage by Islamic fundamentalists on November 4, 1979. In this article, he examines the root causes of terrorism and scrutinizes who is being held hostage in Lebanon.

150. Kent, Ian, and Nicholls, William (1977). The psychodynamics of terrorism. *Mental Health and Society,* 4, 1–2: 1–8.
Proposes a dynamic and social explanation of terrorism. Argues that terrorist actions are aimed at redress of specific political conditions, and that political terrorism involves the exploitation of mental illness. (Includes ten references.)

151. Kim, Byon-Suh, and Taylor, Robert W. (1978). Violence and change in postindustrial societies: Student protest in America and Japan in the 1960s. In Marius H. Livingston with Lee Bruce Kress & Marie G. Wanek (eds.), *International terrorism in the contemporary world* (pp. 204–219). Westport, CT: Greenwood Press.
This article examines violence as seen in post-industrial societies. Authors examine this issue within a theoretical perspective as well as its expansion in an institutional scale. (Includes two figures and 40 notes.)

152. Kirkpatrick, Jeane J. (1986). Terrorist goals do not justify terrorism. In Bonnie Szumski (ed.), *Terrorism: Opposing viewpoints* (pp. 119–122). St. Paul, MN: Greenhaven Press.
The author calls upon the American public to reject terrorists' pleas for understanding of their political goals. She believes violence in any form is repulsive and unacceptable. (Includes one drawing.)

153. Kleg, Milton (1986, Fall). On teaching about terrorism: A conceptual approach. *Social Science Record,* 24, 1: 31–39.
Author recommends a viable approach to study terrorism in secondary classrooms; emphasizes the use of conceptual mapping, case studies, and springboards to discussion. Numerous examples of conceptual maps are provided.

154. _____, and Mahlios, Marc (1990, October). Delineating concept meaning: The case of terrorism. *Social Education,* 54, 6: 389–392.
There is a consensus that definitional problems are associated with delineating the concept of terrorism. Author presents a model teachers can use in guiding students to reach consensus on the meaning of terrorism; uses terrorism to show procedural steps that involve students in self and small group interviews where definitions are clarified until consensus is reached. Includes references for students and teachers.

155. Knauss, P.R., and Strickland, D.A. (1988). Political disintegration and latent terror. In Michael Stohl (ed.), *The politics of terrorism* (pp. 85–125). New York: Marcel Dekker, Inc.

The aim of this chapter is to explore the connection between terrorism and the fear of anarchy. On the one side, many scholars have claimed that terrorism is effective just insofar as it paralyzes and disorganizes its intended victims and evokes this very fear of chaos. On the other side, terrorism has been considered by the same conventional scholars as being in isolation from political repression and the "normal" fear of the state. (Includes 23 notes and 50 references.)

156. Knutson, Jeanne N. (1984, June). Toward a United States policy on terrorism. *Political Psychology,* 5, 2: 287–294.

Examines current U.S. policy on international terrorism and concludes that the policy is flawed. Advocates a "politically rational, comprehensive strategy, which reaffirms U.S. support for legitimate dissent while increasing security measures and penalties for those who resort to violence."

157. _____ (1984, June). Toward a United States policy on terrorism: An addendum on Northern Ireland. *Political Psychology,* 5, 2: 295–298.

Suggests that the U.S. posture of affirmative neutrality regarding the Northern Ireland conflict should be replaced with policies based on lessons learned from unrests in the U.S. history, particularly in the civil rights movement of the 1960s.

158. Kolinsky, Eva (1988). Terrorism in West Germany. In Juliet Lodge (ed.), *The threat of terrorism* (pp. 57–88). Great Britain: Wheatsheaf Books Ltd.

Political terrorism in West Germany highlights a paradox of the German tradition and political culture. For the opposition to advocate alternatives has been regarded with suspicion in a political environment anxious to defend stability as a precondition of democracy. Yet extraparliamentary opposition has frequently sought the abolition or transformation of "the system" as a prerequisite for effective political action. West German terrorism and the reactions to it have their common roots in a predemocratic tradition of delegitimizing opposition and delegitimizing the political order. The following headings are included in the essay: 1) System Stability, Opposition and Terrorism, 2) In Search of the Lost Revolution: Terrorism from the Left, 3) Back to Hitler with a Vengeance: Terrorism from the Right, and 4) Terrorism and the West German State. (Includes four tables and 34 notes.)

159. Kupperman, Robert H. (1986). Terrorism is international warfare. In Bonnie Szumski (ed.), *Terrorism: Opposing viewpoints* (pp. 33–42). St. Paul, MN: Greenhaven Press.

The author argues that, far from over-reacting to the nature of terrorism, the United States is under-reacting. Author believes that terrorism has become a method of international warfare, and its ultimate aim is to bring down the democracies of the United States and Western Europe. (Includes one image.)

160. _____ (1987). Vulnerable America. In Paul Wilkinson & Alasdaire M. Stewart (eds.), *Contemporary research on terrorism* (pp. 570–580). Aberdeen, MA: Aberdeen University Press.

The mysteries of atomic weaponry are neither as secret nor as difficult to master as we had once hoped. The number of near-nuclear and nuclear powers is expected to grow significantly by the end of the century. As a result, we face the very real danger of a nuclear holocaust triggered by the aggression of rogue states or by catalytic conflict in the Third World. Chemical and biological weapons — less expensive and easier to fabricate — may yet become the poor man's bomb, a means by which radical subnational and national groups can attain the extortion potential of a nuclear device. (Includes one note.)

161. _____, and Trent, Darrell M. (1979). *Terrorism: Threat, reality, response.* Stanford, CA: Hoover Institution Press, 450p.

This book is a comprehensive study of the concept of terrorism. Authors examine national and international nature of terrorism and identify policy issues, especially as they apply to emergency preparedness and response to terrorism. (Includes eight selected readings, notes, bibliography, and index.)

162. Kurz, A. (ed.) (1987). *Contemporary trends in world terrorism.* The Jaffe Center for Strategic Studies. New York/Westport, CT: Praeger, 171p.

The author's associates at the Jaffe Center for Strategic Studies, and particularly those in the Center's Project on Terrorism, made a major contribution to the success of an International Conference on "Current Trends in World Terrorism" held in July 1985 at Tel Aviv University. This book is based on the conference and contains 14 articles by individual authors. (Includes 15 chapters and an index.)

163. Lankiewicz, Donald (1986, Fall). Responding to international terrorism during the critical period: The case of the Barbary pirates. *Social Science Record,* 24, 1: 29–30.

This article focuses on the United States' first experiences with terrorism. Emphasis is placed on historical background, original source materials, and teacher directions for examining this issue. Also details the tributes for peaceful passage, ransom for hostages, and eventual armed conflict with the pirates of the "Barbary Coast" of North Africa between 1783 and 1812. Interesting association of colonial history and terrorism.

164. Laqueur, Walter (1977). *Terrorism.* Boston: Little, Brown and Company, 267p.

This essay grew out of a study of guerrilla warfare, and the conclusion that urban terrorism is not a new stage in guerrilla warfare; it differs from it in essential respects, and is heir to a different tradition. The author aimed at hitherto neglected aspects which are of key importance—the doctrine of systematic terrorism, its common patterns, motives and aims and lastly the efficacy of terrorism. (Includes tables and references).

165. Laufer, David (1988). The evolution of Belgian terrorism. In Juliet Lodge (ed.), *The threat of terrorism* (179–211). Great Britain: Wheatsheaf Books Ltd.

Deep-seated antagonism between the country's two linguistic/ethnic groups of Dutch-speaking Flemings and Francophone Walloons has existed for years and has often erupted into violence. In spite of significant devolution to regional and community councils, extremists from both sides continue to call for secession, albeit with little resonance among the electorate. The linguistic/ethnic debate, however, has remained primarily within the political sector because of factors peculiar to Belgian history and the Belgian psyche. These factors mitigated the tendency toward separatist terrorist violence, whereas the linguistic conflict as a whole stifled the earlier development of an ideologically based terrorist group. (Includes 40 notes.)

166. Leaute, Jacques (1987). Academics and policy makers. In Paul Wilkinson & Alasdaire M. Stewart (eds.), *Contemporary research on terrorism* (pp. 590–594). Aberdeen, MA: Aberdeen University Press.

Author suggests that the academic has to be prepared to make a clear recommendation about terrorism. Academics habitually prefer to balance pros and cons, to examine all ramifications, complexities and implications, and to try to foresee all contingencies. Too many academic advisers have proved useless to decision makers because of their inability to present any clear conclusions. They require, they can always argue, more time to do further research. What is required is an adviser who is fair but clear in recommending choices.

167. Lebow, Richard Ned (1978). The origins of sectarian assassination: The case of Belfast. *Journal of International Affairs,* 32, 1: 43–62.

More than 1,800 people have been murdered in Northern Ireland since 1969. Many of them were killed simply because they belonged to the "other side." This study explores the reasons behind such killing. What are the political and social condition associated with sectarian assassination? Who carries out such killing? What kinds of people are chosen for victims? Answers to these questions should provide insight into the dynamics of intense communal conflict. (Includes one table and 25 footnotes.)

168. Ledeen, Michael (1980). Covert operations can fight terrorism. In Bonnie Szumski (ed.), *Terrorism: Opposing viewpoints* (pp. 218–222). St. Paul, MN: Greenhaven Press.

The author states that Americans feel unjustifiably squeamish toward the use of secret military operations. This feeling must be overcome, author believes, if the United States is successfully to strike back against terrorism. Author believes that methods such as counterterrorism and selective assassinations are necessary in repelling communist-inspired terrorism.

169. Lent, John A. (1977, Winter). Foreign news in the American media. *Journal of Communication,* 27, 1: 46–50.

National interests, crisis reporting, foreign censors, and a shrinking corps of correspondents are said to constrain international coverage in U.S. media. The author considers four factors which might account for the state of foreign news coverage in the United States mass media. (Includes 33 references.)

170. Leventhal, Paul, and Alexander, Yonah (eds.) (1987). *Preventing nuclear terrorism.* Lexington, MA: Lexington Books, 472p.

This two-part book examines the "Report of the International Task Force on Prevention of Nuclear Terrorism" and related issues. The analysis focuses on concern that nuclear weapons would probably be the terrorist's weapon of choice if protective measures are not instituted. Additionally, discussions focus on measures the international community can institute, and response options to deal with terrorists who acquire nuclear weapons.

171. Livingston, Marius H. with Kress, Lee Bruce, and Wanek, Marie G. (eds.) (1978). *International terrorism in the contemporary world.* Westport, CT: Greenwood Press, 522p.

The editors assembled a panel of experts to discuss the international context of terrorism. The contemporary view of international terrorism explicates the political consequences of terrorism as well as some of the legal problems of international terrorism. The authors also deal with some of the historical aspects of international terrorism. (Includes 44 articles and a selected bibliography.)

172. Livingstone, Neil C. (1989). *The cult of counterterrorism: The "weird world" of spooks, counterterrorists, adventurers, and the not-quite professionals.* Lexington, MA: Lexington Books, 439p.

Through this book the author takes the reader into the often cloistered and always shrouded world of counterterrorism. The author argues that it is a world that admits few outsiders and is characterized by its own folkways and rituals, not unlike those of a religious brotherhood. From the Special Forces Club in London to the CIA's training facility, known as "the farm," near Williamsburg, Virginia, or the secluded chateau outside of Paris that houses the elite French counterterrorism unit RAID, the reader is given a tour of the sites and locales that form the backdrop to the war against terrorism. Much of it is uncharted terrain from the standpoint of previous scholarship, or even popular literature.

173. Lodge, Juliet (1988). The European community and terrorism: Four principles to concerted action. In J. Lodge (ed.), *The threat of terrorism* (pp. 229–264). Great Britain: Wheatsheaf books.

The essay examines crises of terrorism within European communities. With specific examples of terrorism, the author discusses European communities' responses to United States' strike on suspected sponsors of terrorism; the "Hague Declaration on Terrorism," and how the European Community responded to the case in study. (Includes 45 notes.)

174. _____ (ed.) (1988). *The threat of terrorism.* Great Britain: Wheatsheaf Books, 280p.

The essays in this book adopt a case study approach with a view to illuminating the nature, incidence and persistence of terrorist activity in the state of question. The targets of both indigenous and international terrorists are examined along with international links of terrorist groups. Government responses to terrorist activity that originate within and outside its territory are scrutinized. The essays produce a snapshot of terrorism over the last decade. The case study approach was chosen to facilitate an analysis of terrorism within specific national settings.

175. _____ (ed.) (1988). *The threat of terrorism.* Boulder, CO: Westview Press.
See entry 174.

176. Lomasky, Loren E. (1991). The political significance of terrorism. In Raymond G. Frey & Christopher W. Morris (eds.), *Cambridge studies in philosophy and public policy.* (pp. 86-115). New York: Cambridge University Press.
Suggests that the distinctiveness of terrorists' attitudes is key to an appreciation and understanding of the political significane of terrorism.

177. Long, David E. (1990). *The anatomy of terrorism.* New York: The Free Press, 228p.
This book confronts the component elements of terrorism — those the author dealt with daily for three years, from 1985 through 1987, as director of regional policy formulation and coordination in the U.S. State Department's Office of Counter Terrorism, and with which his successors are continuing to wrestle. These elements are examined within the following six questions: 1) What is terrorism? 2) Why do people commit terrorist acts? 3) What groups are engaged in terrorism? 4) What are their sources of support? 5) How do terrorists plan and execute their acts? And finally, 6) How can governments organize to combat terrorism?

178. Long, Kenneth J. (1990, Fall). Understanding and teaching the semantics of terrorism: An alternative perspective. *Perspectives on Political Science,* 19, 4: 203-208.
At issue here are the conventional definitions of terrorism. The author recommends using historical case studies to clarify terrorism, educate students about the dynamics of state and state-sponsored terrorism, and challenge the attitudes and beliefs students bring into the situation. An excellent article for classroom use.

179. Lopez, G.A. (1988).Terrorism in Latin America. In Michael Stohl (ed.), *The politics of terrorism* (pp. 497-524). New York: Marcel Dekker, Inc.
This chapter begins with two working assumptions regarding the exam-

ination of political terrorism in Latin America: 1) Terrorism has played a major role in the violence-induced political change and violence-sustained political power of post–1945 Latin America. 2). Varied types of terror, as well as the diverse identities of terrorists, are such that the phenomenon provides more data than explanation for why terror violence has been such a pronounced pattern of political life in Latin America. In light of these considerations, this chapter provides a somewhat selective examination of the patterns of and explanations for insurgent and state terror in Latin America over the past two decades. (Includes three tables, one illustration, six notes, and 53 references.)

180. McCauley, Clark R., and Segal, Mary E. (1987). Social psychology of terrorist groups. In Clyde Hendricks (ed.), *Group processes and intergroup relations: Review of personality and social psychology,* Vol. 9 (pp. 231–256). Beverly Hills, CA: SAGE.

See entry 181.

181. _____, and _____ (1989). Terrorist individuals and terrorist groups: The normal psychology of extreme behavior. In Jo Groebel & Jeffrey H. Goldstein (eds.), *Terrorism: Psychological perspectives* (pp. 39–64). Sevilla, Spain: Publicaciones de la Universidad de Sevilla.

Authors analyze data and theory from three areas of research on the social psychology of terrorist groups: religious conversions to cults; extremity shift to group opinions; and individual extremity shift in obedience studies. Also presents an overview of what is known about terrorist groups and their members. Shows how a social psychological framework can be useful in the analysis of terrorist behavior.

182. McClure, Brooks (1978). Hostage survival. In Marius H. Livingston with Lee Bruce Kress & Marie G. Wanek (eds.), *International terrorism in the contemporary world* (pp. 276–281). Westport, CT: Greenwood Press.

Author suggests that of all the tactics used by political terrorists, kidnapping has probably been the most effective. To support this contention, author shows that during the past four years as much as $80 million in ransoms for hostages has been collected in Latin America alone. Also, the author documents non-financial impacts of kidnappings: scores of prisoners have been released; governments have been embarrassed; relations between nations have been strained; and worldwide publicity for terrorist causes has been realized.

183. McGurn, William (1986). Terrorism is never justified. In Bonnie Szumski (ed.), *Terrorism: Opposing viewpoints* (pp. 90–95). St. Paul, MN: Greenhaven Press.

The author suggests that in many war-related situations, violence can be justified. Acts of terrorism cannot, however, be included among these justifiable situations. The author argues that terrorists knowingly target innocent civilians and therefore transcend all rules of just warfare. (Includes one drawing.)

184. McKinley, M. (1987). The Irish Republican Army and terror international: An inquiry into the material aspects of the first fifteen years. In Paul Wilkinson & Alasdaire M. Stewart (eds.), *Contemporary Research on Terrorism* (pp. 186–229). Aberdeen, MA: Aberdeen University Press.

The purpose of this chapter is to challenge the assertions that there existed in Northern Ireland an international terrorist network as evidenced by the contacts, supply of arms and operations of the paramilitary organizations involved in the conflict, particularly the Irish Republican Army (IRA). The reality, the author argues, is that selectivity in views have served as basis for the generalized proposition. (Includes 219 notes.)

185. Martin, J.M., and Romano, A.T. (1992). *Multinational crime: Terrorism, espionage, drug and arms trafficking.* Newbury Park, CA: Sage, 159p.

This book outlines the phenomenon of multinational systemic crime — i.e., crime by various kinds of organizations that operate across national boundaries. The analysis concentrates on terrorism, espionage, drug trafficking, and arms trafficking.

186. Martin, R.C. (1987). Religious violence in Islam: Towards an understanding of the discourse on Jihad in modern Egypt. In Paul Wilkinson & Alasdaire M. Stewart (eds.), *Contemporary Research on Terrorism.* Aberdeen, MA: Aberdeen University Press, 55–71.

The author explores the Jihad as religious violence. While examining the general doctrine of Jihad in terms of the semiotics of Muslim world views, the author also explores the semantics of the Qur'an, as employed by Muslims in their discourse about Jihad. (Includes 58 notes and appendix.)

187. Maurer, Marvin (1978). The Ku Klux Klan and the National Liberation Front: Terrorism applied to achieve diverse goals. In

Marius H. Livingston with Lee Bruce Kress & Marie G. Wanek (eds.), *International terrorism in the contemporary world* (pp. 131– 152). Westport, CT: Greenwood Press.

This essay examines how terrorist tactics are employed by different groups to achieve diverse goals. The KKK and the NLF are used in this case study. (Includes 90 notes.)

188. Maynes, Charles W. (1991). All political violence is not terrorism. In Bonnie Szumski (ed.), *Terrorism: Opposing viewpoints* (pp. 22– 25). St. Paul, MN: Greenhaven Press.

Following the April 1986 U.S. bombing of Libya, many United States citizens were upset at the lack of support from Western Europe. In the following viewpoint, the author argues this reaction was not from cowardice or disinterest, but rather because the U.S. definition of terrorism is too broad and insupportable. Author believes that the U.S. is taking sides in what are essentially civil wars in the Middle East and Central America and should expect to be attacked for their involvement.

189. Melman, Y. (1986). *The master terrorist: The true story of Abu-Nidal.* New York: Adama Books, 171p.

This book is an interim report on the terrorist group led by Abu Nidal. It is meant to portray a Palestinian terrorist organization and to give as detailed information as possible on the circumstances surrounding its establishment, operational environment and aims. It does not claim to tell the whole story and relate all the facts. (Includes ten chapters, an epilogue, references, and eight appendices.)

190. Melville, Margarita B., and Lykes, M. Brinton (1992, March). Guatemalan Indian children and the sociocultural effects of government-sponsored terrorism. *Social Science and Medicine,* 34, 5: 533–548.

Authors describe and compare the emotional, social, and cultural effects of government-sponsored terrorism on Mayan children in Guatemala and Guatemalan children exiled in Mexico. Study found that the subjects in Guatemalan villages were more fearful than those in Mexican refugee camps.

191. Merari, Ariel, and Friedland, Nehemia (1985). Social psychological aspects of political terrorism. *Applied Social Psychology Annual,* 6: 185–205.

Examines methodological and theoretical obstacles to the study of terrorism. Discusses the role of social psychology in portraying terrorism; examines ways terrorism uses fear. (Includes 45 references.)

192. Mickolus, Edward F. (1980). *Transnational terrorism: A chronology of events, 1968–1979*. Westport, CT: Greenwood Press.
This is a compilation of terrorist incidents, and the organizations believed to be involved.

193. _____ (1978). Trends in transnational terrorism. In Marius H. Livingston with Lee Bruce Kress & Marie G. Wanek (eds.), *International terrorism in the contemporary world* (pp. 44–73). Westport, CT: Greenwood Press.
In the last decade the world has seen the rise of a new type of actor on the global stage: the transnational terrorist. The author argues that numerous groups are engaged in various types of acts to gain publicity and increase public awareness of their causes. Consequently, these groups succeed because they are willing to engage in the assassination of government leaders, sabotage of critical facilities, bombing of embassies and foreign corporations, assaults on military installations, skyjackings, kidnappings of diplomats and businessmen, and the takeover of embassies and holding of their staffs for ransom. (Includes nine tables and 16 notes.)

194. Midlarsky, Manus I., Crenshaw, Martha, and Yoshida, Fumihiko (1980, June). Why violence spreads: The contagion of international terrorism. *International Studies Quarterly,* 24, 2: 262–298.
This study examines the spread of international terrorism from 1968 to 1974. Using Poisson and negative binomial probability models, a diffusion of international terrorism was found in the first segment of the time period (1968–1971) and contagion as a direct modeling process in the second (1973–1974). Accordingly, the theory of hierarchies in which the diplomatic status of a country predicts its degree of imitability was found to operate among Latin American countries during the second portion of the overall period, but not during the first. An inverse hierarchy is suggested as an explanation for the contagion of violence, from Latin America and other third world countries to Western Europe. Autocorrelation functions were used to assess which forms of terrorism were most contagious in which regions. (Includes five formulas, nine tables, and 40 references.)

195. Miller, Abraham H. (1980). *Terrorism and hostage negotiations*. Boulder, CO: Westview Press, 135p.

Author examines incidents of terrorism and the implications of hostage negotiations. Also crucial to this book is an analysis the dilemma posed by media coverage of terrorism, and the problems for governments' policies on terrorism.

196. Mitchell, Thomas H. (1989, Spring). Understanding contemporary terrorism. *International Journal of Social Education,* 4, 1: 99–106.
Article provides reader with contemporary issues related to terrorism and examines progress that has been made to understand its dimensions. Examines causes of terrorism and terrorist strategies; suggests how the subject can be explored in the classroom.

197. Mojekwu, Christopher C. (1978). From protest to terror-violence: The African experience. In Marius H. Livingston with Lee Bruce Kress & Marie G. Wanek (eds.), *International terrorism in the contemporary world* (pp. 177–181). Westport, CT: Greenwood Press.
Africa has been the target and the victim of international terror and violence, notably from the fifteenth century to the present. The author argues that slave raiding and the slave trade in East, North, and West Africa were indeed acts of transnational terrorism; they were acts of terror in which Africa was the target and Africans the victims.

198. Montana, Patrick J., and Roukis, George S. (eds.) (1983). *Managing terrorism: Strategies for the corporate executive.* Quorum Books, 182p.
In reviewing the literature on terrorism, the editors decided that a book about managing terrorism would be useful for the business community. This book is no more than a guide or a perfunctory how-to-do-it manual; it is designed to help corporate executives to assess the potential terrorist threat or crisis, if it should occur; a "survival kit" for corporate executives. (Includes nine articles from different authors, five figures, ten tables, a selected bibliography, and index.)

199. Moodie, Michael (1978). The patriot game: The politics of violence in Northern Ireland. In Marius H. Livingston with Lee Bruce Kress & Marie G. Wanek (eds.), *International terrorism in the contemporary world* (pp. 94–110). Westport, CT: Greenwood Press.
The politics of violence in Northern Ireland is in the eye of the beholder. Those who are committed to the creation of a 32-county Irish republic claim that theirs is an act of patriotism as readily and as self-righteously as those who affirm their loyalty to the British crown.

It is only one of the differences that have divided the Ulster community for the last four centuries and continue to make it a province of the United Kingdom where governing without consensus remains the rule. (Includes 39 notes.)

200. Morris, Eric and Hoe, Allan (with Potter, J.) (1987). *Terrorism: Threat and response.* Macmillan Press, 205p.

This text examines the nature and extent of international terrorism, the threat, and government responses to terrorism. Authors also examine corporate responses to terrorism.

201. Motley, James Berry (1987, Fall). Low intensity conflict: Global challenges. *Teaching Political Science,* 15, 1: 15–23.

Discusses the ability of the United States to deal with low intensity conflicts such as terrorism. Describes necessary preparations and actions for meeting this challenge.

202. Moxon-Browne, E. (1988). Terrorism in France. In J. Lodge (ed.), *The threat of terrorism* (pp. 213–228). Great Britain: Wheatsheaf Books Ltd.

The attitude of successive French governments toward terrorism has appeared to some observers to be somewhat lackadaisical, and this may well be explained by the ambivalent connotations of the concept of "terror" in the French political psyche. This article examines that issue within the context of how France responds to terrorism. (Includes seven notes.)

203. Mullen, Robert K. (1978, Spring/Summer). Mass destruction and terrorism. *Journal of International Affairs,* 32, 1: 63–90.

The concepts of mass destruction and terrorism are ancient; what is relatively new is a frequently expressed view that terrorists will acquire the means and motivations to exercise mass destruction. This paper examines that view in terms of the means of mass destruction which exist in a technologically advanced society, what broad properties characterize such means, the resources required by a terrorist or terrorist group to implement them, and the characteristics of terrorist adversaries who may be considered potential implementers. One objective of this paper is to place the potential for mass destruction terrorism into a perspective tempered by recent and historical events relative to demonstrated terrorists' capabilities and motivations. In so doing, this discussion avoids Shultz's general category of "Establishment Terrorist" (see entry 262), either in the sense of institutional terrorism, or terrorism applied by elements of governments, as in attempts or executions of coups d'état. (Includes 57 footnotes.)

204. Mullins, Wayman C. (1988). *Terrorist organizations in the United States: An analysis of issues, organizations, tactics and responses.* Springfield, IL: Charles C. Thomas, Publisher, 226p.

This book is a multi-faceted examination of terrorism. It traces the roots of terrorism to determine how terrorism can be understood, analyzed and even anticipated on the basis of its purpose, its potential for violence, its available resources, its mode of operation, its anticipated audience and its hoped-for outcome. Author suggests that strategies and tactics can be developed on the basis of these elements. (Includes 19 tables, appendix and index.)

205. Murphy, John F. (1976). *State support of international terrorism: Legal, political, and economic dimensions.* London: Mansell Publishing Limited, 125p.

The author has made every effort to develop a typology of state support and state sponsorship of terrorism that minimizes reference to specific states. Rather the focus is on individuals' particular acts that might be perceived as international terrorism and on states' acts that might be perceived as state support. The thesis of this book is that state support of terrorism is illegal and immoral.

206. Narveson, Jan (1991). Terrorism and morality. In Raymond G. Frey and Christopher W. Morris (eds.). *Cambridge studies in philosophy and public policy* (pp. 116–169). New York: Cambridge University Press.

Argues that "terror may be used for political ends, typically by instilling fear in members of a population by means of random acts of violence, acts that may be visited, without warning, upon anyone; by means of a contractarian account of morality, according to which morality consists of internalized rules, general adherence to which brings about mutually beneficial consequences." Suggests that violators of such rules often put themselves into a Hobbesian "state of nature" and consequently outside the protection of such rules.

207. Netanyahu, Benjamin (1986). Terrorism can be eliminated. In Bonnie Szumski (ed.), *Terrorism: Opposing viewpoints* (pp. 183–190). St. Paul, MN: Greenhaven Press.

The author denies that terrorism is an inevitable part of living in the modern world. Author suggests that by following Israel's example to allow terrorism no leniency, the United States can eradicate terrorists and reduce incidents of violence directed at its interests. (Includes one cartoon.)

208. Netanyahu, Benzion (1986). Terrorists' causes are lies. In Bonnie Szumski (ed.), *Terrorism: Opposing viewpoints* (pp. 51–57). St. Paul, MN: Greenhaven Press.

The author argues that terrorist causes are pretense, designed to delude and gain sympathy from a naïve public. Author asserts that terrorists do not fight for freedom, but fight to instill their own form of despotism. (Includes one drawing.)

209. Nidal, Abu (1986). The Palestinian goal justifies terrorism. In Bonnie Szumski (ed.), *Terrorism: Opposing viewpoints* (pp. 113–118). St. Paul, MN: Greenhaven Press.

This article is an excerpt from an interview in the German publication *Der Spiegel*. The avowed terrorist Abu Nidal explains why violent, armed struggle is necessary to achieve the goal of Palestinian liberation.

210. Nimmo, Dan, and Combs, James E. (1989). *Nightly horrors: Crisis coverage in television network news.* Knoxville, TN: University of Tennessee Press, 216p.

This book is a study of how the three major networks reported six major disasters in their evening news programs, from 1978 to 1982. The crises studied are: The People's Temple tragedy in Jonestown, Guyana; the nuclear disaster at Three Mile Island; the 1979 crash of a DC-10 (American Airlines Flight 191) in Chicago; the Mount St. Helens eruptions; the Iranian hostage crisis; and the 1982 Tylenol poisonings. Chapter 5 is particularly valuable to students of terrorism in the media. In some ways, this book is the study of television news in crisis coverage, the nature of television news, and the content of crisis reporting in television news. (Includes six chapters, an introduction, 26 tables of data, four footnoes, and 115 references.)

211. Nordland, Rob, and Wilkinson, Ray (1986, April 7). Inside terror, Inc. *Newsweek*, pp. 25–28, 33.

Explains how governments systematically finance and in other ways support terrorist acts. Most of the analysis focuses on Libya and Syria and how they support terrorist groups.

212. Norton, A., and Greenberg, M.H. (eds.) (1979). *Studies in nuclear terrorism.* Boston, MA: G.K. Hall, 465p.

This is an analysis of fear associated with nuclear terrorism, the problem of nuclear acquisition by terrorists, and how nations can cope with the potential threat of nuclear terrorism. (Includes 20 articles, two appendices, glossary, selected bibliography, and index.)

213. O'Ballance, Edgar (1978). Terrorism in the Middle East. In Marius H. Livingston with Lee Bruce Kress & Marie G. Wanek (eds.), *International terrorism in the contemporary world* (pp. 160–164). Westport, CT: Greenwood Press.

This paper excludes, except by way of brief reference, what may be thought of as battlefield or urban guerrilla warfare, as expounded by Mao Tse-tung and other authorities, to consider only terrorism with a political motive. The hostage system, murder, torture, and terrorism in all forms are not new to the Middle East; they have been carried out for a variety of reasons, and particularly for political ends.

214. O'Brien, C.C. (1983). Terrorism under democratic conditions: The case of the IRA. In Martha Crenshaw (ed.), *Terrorism, legitimacy, and power: The consequences of political violence* (pp. 91–104). Middletown, CT: Wesleyan University Press.

The author defines terrorism in terms of the political context in which it occurs, seeing terrorism as unjustified violence against a democratic state that permits effective and peaceful forms of opposition. Author concludes that the use of violence for political ends within democratic societies should always be classified as terrorism and dealt with as such. (Includes three footnotes.)

215. Olson, Peter A. (1988, Summer). The terrorist and the terrorized: Some psychoanalytic considerations. *Journal of Psychohistory,* 16, 1: 47–60.

Author develops a speculative and theoretical framework to assist in understanding the intrapsychic and group dynamic depth psychology matrix for the motivations behind a terrorist act. Also summarizes what is known about the childhood and adolescent development of terrorists and the effects on child development in countries where terrorism and terror are a day-to-day reality.

216. O'Neill, Bard E. (1978, Spring/Summer). Toward a typology of political terrorism: The Palestinian resistance movement. *Journal of International Affairs,* 32, 1: 17–42.

The analysis of Palestinian acts of violence is part of a larger comparative effort which seeks to create an intellectually rigorous typology of political terrorism. As such, it is but one of several case studies designed to flesh out a heuristic typology proposed by Professor Richard Shultz (see entry 262). If successful, the collective enterprise should provide scholars with a cross-cultural classification scheme that will facilitate subsequent steps in the process of scientific inquiry—i.e., hypothesis generation, hypothesis testing, and theory building and validation. Shultz has suggested seven variables that may be used to distinguish categories of terrorism: causes, environment, goals, strategy, means, organization, and participation. Each of these will be addressed in turn. First, however, some historical comments about the background of Palestinian resistance are required in order to place the problem in better perspective for the reader. (Includes 48 footnotes.)

217. Oots, Kent L., and Wiegele, Thomas C. (1985). Terrorist and victims: Psychiatric and physiological approaches from a social science perspective. *Terrorism,* 8, 1: 1–32.

Author presents a model of terrorist contagion based on biomedical approaches to aggression, violence, and terrorism. Research into the personality, family background, ideologies, and language of terrorists and an understanding of the role of the media in terrorist acts and the biochemical stress responses of terrorists, victims, and audiences are the basis for an epidemiologically based neurophysiological model of terrorist contagion. Argues that the violence-accepting or -rejecting attitude of potential terrorists determines their response to frustration and arousal caused by denial of a political goal. Discusses how to apply research to the stages of stress response among hostages and stress inoculation.

218. Oppenheimer, Martin (1986). Terrorism is sometimes justified. In Bonnie Szumski (ed.), *Terrorism: Opposing viewpoints* (pp. 86–89). St. Paul, MN: Greenhaven Press.

The author argues that terrorism is merely a label applied by governments to actions of legitimate protest. If governments were just and humane, there would be no terrorism. Author's conclusion is that terrorism is sometimes justified.

219. Paisley, Ian, Bradford, Nora, and Taylor, John (1986). IRA terrorism is not justified. In Bonnie Szumski (ed.), *Terrorism: Opposing viewpoints* (pp. 105–112). St. Paul, MN: Greenhaven Press.

In January 1982, three spokespeople for the Unionists party of Northern

Ireland spoke before the National Press Club in Washington, DC. Their speeches make up this article. All three emphasize the terror, instability, and fear the IRA generates in Northern Ireland. Author concludes that IRA terrorism is not justified. (Includes one drawing.)

220. Parry, Albert (1976). *Terrorism: From Robespierre to Arafat.* New York: The Vanguard Press, Inc., 615p.

This book is about the kind of terror that strikes at the body politic, involving not random individuals, but whole masses of society — entire nations and continents, their economic and political structures, and their body of mores and morals. (Includes 29 illustrations, appendix, bibliography, notes, and index.)

221. Passe, Jeff (1986, Fall). Teaching upper grade elementary school children about terrorism: It can be done. *Social Science Record,* 24, 1: 26–28.

Author provides practical guidelines on how to handle terrorism in the upper elementary classroom. Article includes a flow chart showing fourth graders' analysis of the hostage crisis. Argues that such teaching promotes the conceptual and thinking skills needed in the social studies curriculum.

222. Pearlstein, Richard M. (1991). *The mind of the political terrorist.* Wilmington DE: Scholarly Resources Inc., 237p.

The author explores the mind of the political terrorist and attempts to identify, analyze, explain, and illustrate the interrelationship between psychoanalytic and psychodynamic rewards of political terrorism.

223. Peleg, I. (1988). Terrorism in the Middle East: The case of the Arab-Israeli conflict. In Michael Stohl (ed.), *The politics of terrorism* (pp. 525–548). New York: Marcel Dekker, Inc.

Terrorism is seen as the systematic use of violence for political purposes against innocent civilians. The author's definition of terrorism is comprised of four distinguishing elements: the objectives (of terrorism) are always political, the means are always violent (rather than, say, legal or electoral), the target is always the innocent civilian (although others may be targeted as well), and the process is always systematic and nonrandom (even though tactically the target for a specific operation may be selected randomly). Terrorism is not a mindless, senseless, irrational form of violence; it is a planned strategy, a form of rational behavior, or, as Brian Jenkins (see entry 141) put it succinctly, "a means to an end." (Includes two tables and 33 notes.)

224. Perdue, William D. (1989). *Terrorism and the state: A critique of domination through fear.* New York: Praeger, 226p.

This book is a clarification of the institutional forces that are at the base of political economy of terrorism. From this critical and holistic perspective, the author suggests that the relevant literature must logically include works on ideology, colonialism, imperialism, dependency, models of development, state organization, and social change. With a few sterling exceptions, such topics are routinely absent from the specialized literature on terrorism. But it is not enough to remain formally academic. Throughout this work, an attempt was made to give fair hearing to certain of the victims and resisters of institutional terror.

225. Phelps, Thomas (1986, Fall). A victimologist looks at terrorism. *Social Science Record,* 24, 1: 10–13.

Defines state terrorism and reviews the 12-point anti-terrorism program of Amnesty International, lists the psychological needs of victims, and catalogs the various methods of torture used in state terrorism.

226. Pluchinsky, Dennis A. (1987). Middle Eastern terrorist activity in Western Europe in 1985: A diagnosis and prognosis. In Paul Wilkinson & Alasdaire M. Stewart (eds.), *Contemporary research on terrorism* (pp. 164–178). Aberdeen, MA: Aberdeen University Press.

The author discusses the factors which make Western Europe an attractive operational area for Middle East terrorist groups. This analysis is followed with a diagnosis and prognosis concerning Middle Eastern terrorist activity. (Includes two figures and 11 notes.)

227. Pollack, Benny, and Hunter, Graham (1988). Dictatorship, democracy and terrorism in Spain. In Juliet Lodge (ed.), *The threat of terrorism* (pp. 119–144). Great Britain: Wheatsheaf Books Ltd.

Between 1968 and May 1986, according to Ministry of the Interior figures, 667 violent deaths resulted from terrorist activity in Spain. The overriding motivation behind the vast majority, however, has been an intense nationalism. Such nationalist motivation has allowed for one particular organization to achieve the indisputable, and unenviable, position of being clearly at the top of the terrorist league in Spain. Since 1968 Euzkadi Ta Azkatasuma (ETA) has been responsible for three times as many deaths as the aggregate total of all other terrorist organizations in Spain. Author suggests that the number of victims of ETA terrorism continues to grow. (Includes three tables and 49 notes.)

228. Post, Jerrold M. (1987). Group and organizational dynamics of political terrorism: Implications for counterterrorist policy. In Paul Wilkinson & Alasdaire M. Stewart (eds.), *Contemporary research on terrorism* (pp. 307–317). Aberdeen, MA: Aberdeen University Press.

The author examines the question, What will deter terrorists from their acts of violence? The question contains a premise which all too often is left implicit. For the purposes of this discussion, the author wanted to make that premise explicit and rephrase the question as it should be asked. Based on a clear understanding of the psychological framework of terrorists, the author asks: What acts will impact upon terrorists in such a way as to deter them from their acts of violence?

229. _____ (1986, April). Hostilite, conformite, fraternite: The group dynamics of terrorist behavior. *International Journal of Group Psychotherapy,* 36, 2: 211–224.

Author describes two major categories of terrorists: (1) anarchic-ideologues, "who wish to destroy the world of their fathers"; and (2) nationalist-separatists, "who carry on the mission of their forerunners." Suggests that uniformity exists between terrorists despite their divergent views or beliefs.

230. _____ (1990). Terrorist psycho-logic: Terrorist behavior as a product of psychological forces. In Walter Reich (ed.), *Origins of terrorism: Psychologies, theologies, states of mind* (pp. 25–40). New York: Cambridge University Press, 289p.

Argues that psychological forces drive terrorists to commit acts of violence. Suggests that a specific logic characterizes terrorists' reasoning processes. "The principal argument of this essay is that individuals are drawn to the path of terrorism in order to commit acts of violence, and their special logic, which is grounded in their psychology and reflected in their rhetoric, becomes their justification for their violent acts."

231. Purnell, Susanna W., and Wainstein, Eleanor (1981, November). *The problems of U.S. businesses operating abroad in terrorist environments.* RAND Report R-2842-DOC.

See entry 694.

232. Quainton, A.C.E. (1983). Terrorism and political violence: A permanent challenge to governments. In Martha Crenshaw (ed.), *Terrorism, legitimacy, and power: The consequences of political violence* (pp. 52–64). Middletown, CT: Wesleyan University Press.

Author examines the challenges which institutions and individuals face as they approach the 21st century. High on the list of such challenges is the threat which political violence and terrorism represent to the creation of a stable, peaceful, and democratic world order. (Includes five footnotes.)

233. Ramirez, J. Martin (1989). Terrorism in Spain: The case of ETA. In Jo Groebel and Jeffrey H. Goldstein (eds.), *Terrorism: Psychological perspectives* (pp. 153-161). Sevilla, Spain: Publicaciones de la Universidad de Sevilla.

Author presents a review of the past and present situation of a clandestine Basque organization (ETA), known for its violent tactics and responsible for most of the terrorist acts in Spain.

234. Rapoport, David (1987). Why does religious messianism produce terror? In Paul Wilkinson and Alasdaire M. Stewart (eds.). *Contemporary research on terrorism* (pp. 72-88). Aberdeen, MA: Aberdeen University Press.

A most striking development in recent years has been the use of theological concepts to justify terrorist activity, a phenomenon which the author has called "holy terror." The most notorious instance has occurred among the Sharia where the revival of Jihad (holy war) doctrines has produced some remarkable incidents and a striking willingness, even eagerness, to die, a disposition created by the belief that one who is killed while fighting in a Jihad is guaranteed a place in paradise. (Includes 35 notes.)

235. _____, and Alexander, Yonah (eds.) (1982). *The morality of terrorism: Religious and secular justifications.* New York: Pergamon Press, 377p.

This book is part of the author's ongoing analysis of the link between terrorism and religious violence, and secular justifications of violence.

236. Redlick, Amy Sands (1979). The transnational flow of information as a cause of terrorism. In Yonah Alexander, David Carlton & Paul Wilkinson (eds.), *Terrorism: Theory and practice* (pp. 73-95). Boulder, CO: Westview Press.

Author suggests that developments in transportation and communications have made cultural interactions of communities an important dimension of international relations. Because technological improvements tend to augment the speed, scope, and range of contacts between societies, they have affected significantly the global flow of information. Today, a continuous stream of information about terrorism is dispensed by radio, television, newspapers, literature, and journals on an international scale, enabling terrorists to observe and imitate other groups. (Includes 45 notes.)

237. Reich, Walter (ed.) (1990). *Origins of terrorism: Psychologies, theologies, states of mind.* New York: Cambridge University Press, 289p.

This book examines the origins of terrorist behavior and the logic of terrorism. Each chapter helps improve the reader's understanding of terrorist behavior and the limits and opportunities of psychological inquiry of terrorism.

238. _____ (1990). Understanding terrorist behavior: The limits and opportunities of psychological inquiry. In Walter Reich (ed.), *Origins of terrorism: Psychologies, theologies, states of mind* (pp. 261–279). New York: Cambridge University Press.

Examines the opportunities and limits of research on the psychology of terrorism. Several aspects of terrorism are examined; however, emphasis is placed on the psychology of the terrorists as it pertains to their developments, motivations, personalities, decision-making patterns, behaviors in groups, and psychopathologies. Suggests ways to avoid problems.

239. Reinares, Fernando (1987). The dynamics of terrorism during the transition to democracy in Spain. In Paul Wilkinson & Alasdaire M. Stewart (eds.), *Contemporary research on terrorism.* Aberdeen, MA: Aberdeen University Press, 121–129.

Author argues that despite all of the self-justification, the practical reality of terrorism has developed into a relentless attack on those forces working towards a peaceful and pluralist re-organization of society. This study covers the time period from 1968 to 1980. (Includes three tables of data and 15 notes.)

240. Robertson, K.G. (1987). Intelligence, terrorism and civil liberties. In Paul Wilkinson & Alasdaire M. Stewart (eds.), *Contemporary research on terrorism* (pp. 549–569). Aberdeen, MA: Aberdeen University Press.

It has become commonplace in the literature on terrorism that intelligence is indispensable to successful counterterrorism, but despite some useful efforts several key issues remain to be explored. This chapter focuses on four questions: How different in nature is terrorism from the other threats faced by democratic states? What is intelligence? How can intelligence help in responding to terrorism? And finally, what are the tensions between the role of intelligence in countering terrorism and civil liberties in democratic states? (Includes 32 notes.)

241. Rosenthal, Uriel, Charles, Michael T., and 't-Hart, Paul (eds.) (1989). *Coping with crises: The management of disasters, riots and terrorism.* Springfield, IL: Charles C. Thomas, Publishers, 485p.

This book attempts to expand knowledge in the area of crisis management. It focuses on high-profile events which have occurred in recent history and are thus familiar to a large segment of the world population. Provides a basis for thinking about enhancing the reader's capacity to anticipate, prevent, and cope with crises.

242. _____, and _____ (1989). Managing terrorism: The South Moluccan hostage takings. In Uriel Rosenthal, Michael T. Charles, and Paul 't-Hart (eds.), *Coping with crises: The management of disasters, riots and terrorism* (pp. 367–393). Springfield, IL: Charles C. Thomas, Publishers.

Examines the decision-making process in the South Moluccan (the Netherlands) hostage takings of 1977. Focuses on the events in De Punt and Bovensmilde in May-June 1977. Issues examined are learning from history, managing administrative complexity, managing a protracted crisis, making decisions on the use of force, and managing the aftermath.

243. Rothenberg, Elliot. (1986). Terrorists should be given stricter penalties. In Bonnie Szumski (ed.), *Terrorism: Opposing viewpoints* (pp. 209–214). St. Paul, MN: Greenhaven Press.

The author argues that terrorism, which includes the deliberate killing of innocent human beings, is a heinous crime. Author suggests that terrorists who are caught should automatically be given the death penalty.

244. Rubenstein, Richard E. (1987). *Alchemists of revolution: Terrorism in the modern world.* New York: Basic Books, Inc., 258p.

This text is a thorough examination of terrorism in the modern world. Emphasis is placed on the causes of terrorism, the political imagery associated with terrorism, and the relationship between terrorism, social revolutions, and national liberation movements. (Includes five parts with 13 chapters.)

245. Rubin, B. (ed.) (1989). *The politics of terrorism: Terror as a state and revolutionary strategy.* Lanham, MD: University Press of America, Inc., 236p.

Author examines terrorism as a political strategy employed by states and revolutionaries. Discussion includes analysis of the political uses of terrorism in volatile regions of the Middle East, Peru, and South Africa. Interesting to this discussion is a contemporary survey of the politics of terrorism.

246. Rubin, Jeffrey Z., and Friedland, Nehemia (1986, March). Theater of terror. *Psychology Today,* 20, 3: 18-28.

Authors discuss the motivation of terrorists and the effect of their actions on the public. Argues that terrorist acts are a carefully scripted "performance" designed to grasp public attention. Authors say that such attention also evokes emotions from the public which accords terrorism symbolic significance. It is recommended that all negotiations during terrorism events be conducted out of the view of the public and the mass media. This would decrease public exposure and would prevent public emotions from being evoked by terrorism. The 1985 *Achille Lauro* ship hijacking is used as an illustration.

247. Ryan, Alan (1991). State and private: Red and White. In Raymond G. Frey & Christopher W. Morris (eds.), *Violence, terrorism, and justice* (pp. 230-255). Cambridge Studies in Philosophy and Public Policy. New York: Cambridge University Press.

The author "considers whether we must, while invoking a generally utilitarian standpoint, distinguish state from individual violence, as well as Red terror, that is committed in the name of order." The author believes that terrorism is marked by two distinguishing characteristics: "they use methods that deprive their victims of the power of a graduated, rational response, and they express, through their nature, the unwillingness to abide by restraint."

248. Said, Edward W. (1987, April). *The essential terrorist.* Information Papers Series No. 3. Washington, D.C.: General Union of Palestinian Students, 13p.

This article in this pamphlet was first published in the June 14, 1986, issue of *The Nation,* as a review of *Terrorism: How the West Can Win,* edited by Benjamin Netanyahu. Author argues that the concept "terrorism" has attained an extraordinary status in American public discourse, thereby replacing "Communism" as public enemy number one. Consequently, events in the Middle East are often characterized within the perspective of terrorism.

249. Salmony, Steven E., and Smoke, Richard (1988). The appeal and behavior of the Ku Klux Klan in object relations perspective. *Terrorism,* 11, 4: 247–262.

Authors suggest that the actions of the Ku Klux Klan (KKK) exemplify a psychosocial pathology, and explain how it can be analyzed with the object relations theory.

250. Sandler, Todd, Atkinson, Scott E., Cauley, Jon, Soom Im, Erik Ik, Scott, John, and Tschirhart, John (1987). Economic methods and the study of terrorism. In Paul Wilkinson & Alasdaire M. Stewart (eds.), *Contemporary research on terrorism* (pp. 376–389). Aberdeen, MA: Aberdeen University Press.

The purpose here is to report on the use of economic methods in the study and understanding of terrorism; in determining the best means of thwarting it. They believe that the use of economic methodology can provide valuable insights for the following issues: a) how best to deter terrorism when terrorists are apt to substitute their operational modes; b) how to form international agreements designed to eliminate safe havens; c) how to manage an incident involving hostages held for ransom; d) how to assess the net benefits associated with a countermeasure and; e) how to assign resources to thwarting terrorism in the face of limited budgets. (Includes 40 notes.)

251. Sassoli, M. (1987). International humanitarian law and terrorism. In Paul Wilkinson & Alasdaire M. Stewart (eds.), *Contemporary research on terrorism* (pp. 466–474). Aberdeen, MA: Aberdeen University Press.

Unlike other crimes, terrorism and terrorist acts are not only a challenge but also a twofold threat to the law of a state: a) *a direct threat,* in that they jeopardize the life and physical integrity of individuals, most of whom — whether in truth or merely in the eyes of the terrorists — represent the State and its polity, but who sometimes are ordinary citizens implicated merely by accident; and b) *an indirect threat,* in that in combating terrorist acts, the aggressed state runs the risk of departing from the law — possibly under the influence of public opinion. Thus, terrorists may themselves create the conditions which to their mind justify their deeds. Author argues that it is not surprising that terrorists are, quite consciously, natural allies of people in favor of capital punishment. (Includes 34 notes.)

252. Schechterman, Bernard (1986, December). Religious fanaticism as a factor in political violence. *International Freedom Foundation,* 1, 3: 1–6.

Examines the context in which religious fanaticism takes place. It is also an analysis of individual and universal tendencies of political violence.

253. _____, and Slann, M. (eds.) (1990). *Violence and terrorism 90/91* (annual editions, each on a different topic). Guilford, CT: The Duskin Publishing Group, Inc., 244p.

This is a collection of articles by reputable journalists and academicians who have written extensively about terrorism. In all, 78 articles are included in this volume and are divided into seven sections: 1) the concept of terrorism (six articles); 2) the causes and scope of terrorism (14 articles); 3) the terrorists (14 articles); 4) terrorism and the media (five articles); 5) tactics, strategies, and targeting (16 articles); 6) countering terrorism (18 articles); and 7) trends and projections of terrorism (five articles). Includes a topic guide, an appendix, and a two page appendum summarizing worldwide terrorism since World War II.

254. Schelling, Thomas C. (1991). What purposes can international terrorism serve? In Raymond G. Frey & Christopher W. Morris (eds.), *Violence, terrorism, and justice,* (pp. 18–32). Cambridge Studies in Philosophy and Public Policy. New York: Cambridge University Press.

Analysis is confined to international terrorism: "terrorism committed by nations of one country, or by members of nationalist groups or organizations, against governments, institutions, or people in another country." Examines the purposes of international terrorism.

255. Schiller, D. Th. (1987). The police response to terrorism: A critical overview. In Paul Wilkinson & Alasdaire M. Stewart (eds.), *Contemporary research in terrorism* (pp. 536–569). Aberdeen, MA: Aberdeen University Press.

There is the obverse side to the issue of terrorism, and questions abound: How useful are military units in maintaining internal security? How well are even elite formations like paratroopers or marine commandos suited to fight an enemy whose tactics include the use of disguises, hidden weapons, time-bombs, and the absence of uniforms and bases, defended positions and the like? This article examines police response to airport attacks in London in December 1985. (Includes eight notes.)

256. Schlagheck, D.M. (1988). *International terrorism: An introduction to the concepts and actors.* Lexington, MA: Lexington Books, 165p.

This book was written for students in a variety of courses, and it focuses on the recurring questions about terrorism, politics, and violence using case illustrations. As supplementary reading in an introductory or intermediate international relations course, in a comparative politics course, or in a more specialized course focusing on political violence or terrorism, this book helps to illuminate the basic concepts and issues in international terrorism. It is useful as specialized reading in a world politics course, or to establish the framework for a terrorism seminar.

257. Schmid, Alex P. (1983). *Political terrorism: A research guide to concepts, theories, data bases, and literature.* New Brunswick, NJ: Transaction Books, 585p.

This is an extensive reference guide for the beginning student/researcher in terrorism. Also provides a bibliography and a world directory of terrorist organizations.

258. _____ (1988). Politically-motivated violent activists in the Netherlands in the 1980s. In Juliet Lodge (ed.), *The threat of terrorism* (pp. 145–178). Great Britain: Wheatsheaf Books, Ltd.

There is at present no domestic terrorism in the Netherlands, and international terrorism has also largely bypassed Holland. Together with the Danes, the Dutch are in an exceptional position both within the EEC and within NATO. Nevertheless, the non-terrorism of the Netherlands deserves analysis as it might throw some light on the causes of terrorism elsewhere in Western Europe. Author has achieved that objective through this work. (Includes one table and 85 notes.)

259. Scott, John Anthony (1986, Fall). On violence in history: A tale of one city and two Thomases. *Social Science Record,* 24, 1: 23–25.

Author urges teachers to address the root causes of international and state terrorism through the literary device of a dialogue. Criticizes the shallow analysis of wars offered in textbooks.

260. Seton-Watson, Christopher (1988). Terrorism in Italy. In Juliet Lodge (ed.), *The threat of terrorism* (pp. 89–118). Great Britain: Wheatsheaf Books Ltd.

Author analyzes the scope of terrorism in Italy. Through this analysis, author provides the reader with various ideological perspectives about terrorism, state responses, public opinion, and the international links of such acts of violence. (Includes 45 notes.)

261. Shultz, George P. (1986). The U.S. must retaliate against terrorist states. In Bonnie Szumski (ed.), *Terrorism: Opposing viewpoints* (pp. 197–203). St. Paul, MN: Greenhaven Press.

The author argues that Americans engage in far too much self-flagellating over terrorist claims of political and social injustice. Terrorists are murderers and lawbreakers, author asserts; suggests that the United States should take forceful and organized action against them. (Includes one cartoon.)

262. Shultz, Richard (1978). Conceptualizing political terrorism: A typology. *Journal of International Affairs,* 32, 1: 7–16.

Throughout history, the strategies and tactics of political terrorism have maintained a trenchant position in the political calculus within and between nations. However, since World War II, the practice of political terrorism has undergone a frightful proliferation at the national and transnational levels. Given this proliferation, and given the immense complexity of political terrorism, it would seem fruitless to attempt to analyze this process without first developing a systematic typology. In the case of the study or analysis of political terrorism, such developments have generally not been undertaken. While an intense study has ensued this post-war proliferation of political terrorist incidents, the literature has been primarily descriptive, prescriptive and very emotive in form. Very few studies have approached the issue from a more analytical, theoretical, and objective position. In addition, one is hard pressed to locate studies aimed at developing typologies that lend themselves to the rigorous analysis of the various forms political terrorism has taken, to depict common linkages and specific differences. This article seeks to take the initial steps in constructing a more flexible and useful typology of political terrorism. (Includes one figure and 18 footnotes.)

263. Simpson, Peter (1986). Just war theory and the IRA. *Journal of Applied Philosophy,* 3, 1: 73–88.

The Irish Republican Army (IRA) contends that its violent actions are sanctioned by traditional just war doctrine. The author examines the extent to which this is true, concluding that violence for the sake of Irish unity or violence committed outside the borders of Northern Ireland is unacceptable.

264. Sloan, Stephen (1978). International terrorism: Academic quest, operational art and policy implications. *Journal of International Affairs,* 32, 1: 1–6.

Confronted with a growing recognition of the threat by the public, policymakers and law enforcement authorities are hard pressed to "do something" in the face of a new and often grimly imaginative threat to the public order. The politics of concern call for bold programs to meet a new challenge. Such concern may lessen after an effective military response, as illustrated by the operations of Entebbe or Mogadishu. At such times, the mass media often proclaims that "the war on terrorism" has been initiated and the public slips back into a false sense of security based on the impression that the proper response has been found and that terrorism is now under control. This sense of security often remains until another incident confronts a global audience who prefer "the resolution" of a conflict by "concrete" action to the uncertainty that some day they may become the victims of terrorism.

265. _____ (1981). *Simulating terrorism.* Norman, OK: University of Oklahoma Press, 160p.

The text examines aspects of terrorism, from simulation to the execution of acts of violence. (Includes 15 chapters, two appendices, notes, bibliography, and index.)

266. Sobel, L.A. (1975). *Political Terrorism, Vol. 1.* New York: Facts on File, Inc., 309p.

This book documents specific acts of political violence that are characterized as terrorism. These incidents occurred between 1960 and 1970. The contents of this book are larngerly from the reports printed by Facts on File in its weekly coverage of world events. The entries document terrorism in the Middle East, Latin America, United States, and other areas.

267. _____ (1978). *Political Terrorism, Vol. 2.* (1974–1978). New York: Facts on File, Inc., 279p.

This book documents specific acts of terrorism and the actions taken against the perpetrators of each terrorist act. The entries over specific areas of the Middle East, Latin America, and the United States. The list also includes incidents of terrorism in more than 28 other countries.

268. Soskis, David A. (1983). Behavioral scientists and law enforcement personnel: Working together on the problem of terrorism. *Behavioral Science and the Law,* 1, 2: 47–58.

Argues that behavioral scientists work with law enforcement personnel on the problem of terrorism in three general contexts: clinical help for victims, training and consultation for hostage negotiation, and profiling and institutional consultation. Says the problems encountered by behavioral scientists working in this area have usually involved difficulties in maintaining an effective consultant role, overidentification with the law enforcement identity, or inappropriate media statements. (Includes 16 references.)

269. _____, and Linowitz, Jan R. (1988). Terrorism. In John G. Howells (ed.), *Modern perspectives in psychosocial pathology: Modern perspective in psychiatry, 11* (pp. 318–331). New York: Brunner/Mazel, Inc.

Examines terrorism, terrorist incidents and what clinicians can learn from them. The clinician's role is examined as it relates to primary, secondary, and tertiary intervention.

270. Spates, C.R., Little, P., Stock, H.V., and Goncalces, J.S. (1990). Intervention in events of terrorism. In L.J. Hertzberg, G.F. Ostrum, & J.R. Fields (eds.), *Violent behavior, vol. 1: Assessment & intervention* (pp. 185–199). Costa Mesa, CA: PMA Publishing Corp.

This chapter provides an overview of the incidence of terrorism, and examination of the theories regarding terrorism. Analysis suggests the likelihood that all forms of terrorism will further escalate in the years ahead.

271. Sterling, Claire (1981). *The terror network: The secret war of international terrorism.* New York: Holt, Rinehart and Winston, Reader's Digest Press, 355p.

The text examines the secret war of international terrorism with specific examples of incidents of terrorism. These include acts perpetrated by the PLO in Europe; the IRA; terror in Basqueland; anarchy in Turkey; Cuba's roles; and Qaddafi's role.

272. Stohl, Michael (1988). National interests and state terrorism in international affairs. In Michael Stohl (ed.), *The Politics of terrorism* (pp. 273–292). New York: Marcel Dekker, Inc.

The concentration on insurgent terrorism has many consequences, but in this chapter the author is interested only in the effects on our understanding of terrorism in general and its impact on the study of state terrorism in particular. The following characterizations of terrorism are representative "truths" of the current literature. (Includes one table and 62 notes.)

273. _____ (1987). Outside of a small circle of friends: State, genocide, mass killings and the role of bystanders. *Journal of Peace Research,* 24, 2: 151–166.

This paper examines the circumstances and the structural conditions which have allowed mass killings and genocide to be built into current state systems. Author also explores the literature of "bystander apathy" to suggest bystander non-involvement in the international system of states. Suggests how to move from non-involvement to the "small circle of friends" involvement in mass killings. (Includes one table, three notes, and 67 references.)

274. _____ (ed.) (1988). *The politics of terrorism* (3rd ed.). New York: Marcel Dekker, Inc., 622p.

Author provides the reader with an introduction to the concept and practice of terrorism embedded within a firm understanding of politics and social structure. The assembled chapters explore the major theories, typologies, concepts, strategies, tactics, ideologies, practices, implications of, and responses to contemporary political terrorism. From the exploration and consideration of these analyses of political terrorism, readers should become cognizant of the importance of historical, structural, and environmental constraints relevant to any analysis of terrorism. The chapters in this work deal with 1) Some Characteristics of Political Terrorism in the 1960s; 2) The Urban Context of Political Terrorism; 3) Political Disintegration and Latent Terror; 4) Societal Structure and Revolutionary Terrorism: A Preliminary Investigation; 5) The Theoretical Utility of Typologies of Terrorism: Lessons and Opportunities; 6) Terror in the United States: Three Perspectives; 7) Governance by Terror; 8) National Interests and State Terrorism in International Affairs; 9) Terrorism at Home and Abroad: The U.S. Government View; 10) Ethnic and Ideological Terrorism in Western Europe; 11) Terrorism in Sub-Saharan Africa; 12) Terrorism in Latin America; 13) Terrorism in the Middle East: The Case of the Arab-Israeli Conflict; and 14) Political Terrorism in the United States: Historical Antecedents and Contemporary Trends, and Conclusion.

275. _____ (1988). Responding to the terrorist threat: Fashions and fundamentals. In Michael Stohl (ed.), *The politics of terrorism* (pp. 579–599). New York: Marcel Dekker, Inc.

Rather than presenting a summary of the preceding chapters in this volume, this concluding chapter discusses four issue areas that remain quite controversial in the study of terrorism: 1) the interrelationship among political terrorism, the media, and civil liberties; 2) counterterrorism policies; 3) the threat that terrorists will go nuclear; and 4) the existence of an international terrorist network and the role of the Soviet Union in the problem of terrorism. This discussion is presented to encourage discourse and to illuminate the complexity of the issues connected to the problem of political terrorism, rather than for the purpose of proposing easily adopted solutions. (Includes 47 references.)

276. Storr, Anthony (1978). Sadism and paranoia. In Marius H. Livingston with Lee Bruce Kress & Marie G. Wanek (eds.), *International terrorism in the contemporary world* (pp. 231–239). Westport, CT: Greenwood Press.

This chapter discusses human aggression and relates it to terrorism. (Includes 14 notes.)

277. Suarez-Orozco, Marcelo M. (1991, Spring). The heritage of enduring a "dirty war": Psychological aspects of terror in Argentina, 1976–1988. *Journal of Psychohistory,* 18, 4: 469–505.

Examines the mechanism used by the Argentine population to cope with state terrorism following the military takeover in 1976. Found that a great majority of Argentines developed conscious and unconscious strategies to cope with state terrorism.

278. Sundberg, Jacob. (1978). The antiterrorist legislation in Sweden. In Marius H. Livingston with Lee Bruce Kress, & Marie G. Wanek (eds.), *International terrorism in the contemporary world* (pp. 11–122). Westport, CT: Greenwood Press.

During the 1960s a policy of involvement gradually succeeded the neutral and more prudent Swedish policy of the 1950s. The Greek coup d'état of August 21, 1967, particularly incensed leading socialist circles and created a strong reaction. Efforts were made to cultivate the birth of a Greek resistance movement, partially directed by the dethroned Greek politician Professor Andreas Papandreou. He was invited to direct his fight against the Greek regime from Sweden. He cooperated with Anthony Brillakis, head of the Greek Communist party, to establish terrorist activities in Greece. (Includes 29 notes.)

279. Sundiata, I.K. (1978). Integrative and disintegrative terror: The case of Equatorial Guinea. In Marius H. Livingston with Lee Bruce Kress & Marie G. Wanek (eds.), *International terrorism in the contemporary world* (pp. 182–194). Westport, CT: Greenwood Press.

In the spring of 1975 exile sources reported the execution of over 300 people, including former members of the government. Communication with the outside world was severely limited. It has been charged that those seeking refuge in the neighboring countries of Gabon and Cameroon are not safe but are kidnapped, returned, and executed. (Includes 41 notes.)

280. Szumski, Bonnie (ed.) (1986). *Terrorism: Opposing viewpoints.* St. Paul, MN: Greenhaven Press, 240p.

This is a collection of viewpoints on terrorism expressed by 34 authors. Basic to the text is its illumination of viewpoints on what constitutes terrorism, its causes, and whether it is justified. The essays examine the role of superpowers in terrorism and consider whether terrorism can be eliminated.

281. Targ, H.R. (1988). Societal structure and revolutionary terrorism: A preliminary investigation. In Michael Stohl (ed.), *The politics of terrorism* (pp. 127–151). New York: Marcel Dekker, Inc.

This chapter makes two assumptions about revolutionary terrorism. The first is that revolutionary terrorism is merely one form of behavior by individuals or groups in support of fundamental change in a given society. The hypothesis examined in this chapter suggests that terrorism is a form of political action in historical settings not conducive to mass action for systematic transformation. The second assumption is that, for reasons analyzed in the following sections, revolutionary terrorism is social, not individual, pathological behavior in that it occurs in social structures and historical settings where the forces for social change are at their weakest. (Includes three tables, two figures, notes, and 12 references.)

282. Taylor, Robert W. (1987). Liberation theology, politics and violence in Latin America. In Paul Wilkinson & Alasdaire M. Stewart (eds.), *Contemporary research on terrorism* (pp. 45–54). Aberdeen, MA: Aberdeen University Press.

This chapter examines the marriage between liberation theology, politics and violence in Latin America; it suggests a philosophical justification for the liberation movement. (Includes 37 notes.)

283. Teichman, Jenny (1989). How to define terrorism. *Philosophy,* 64: 505–517.

Author explains that "the philosophical interest of terrorism is due partly to the fact that the term is notoriously difficult to define," and partly to the disagreement about the justification of terrorism. The paper is devoted to the problems of definition, and the moral question of terrorism. Author offers definitions of terrorism. (Includes seven footnotes.)

284. Terrorism: What is behind it and why? (1987, January 8). *AWAKE,* 68, 1: 6-10.

This article analyzes the motives behind much of terrorism. It focuses and identifies the main targets of terrorism, and what terrorism accomplishes. More important is the analysis which suggests that the United States seems a society vulnerable to terrorism. The author argues that this vulnerability is fueled by the instant impact of news events. The media of communication, particularly television, are said to multiply the power of terrorism. "The terrorist wants international publicity for his cause—and thanks to the media, he gets it." (Includes two pictures.)

285. Thackrah, R. (1987). Terrorism: A definitional problem. In Paul Wilkinson & Alasdaire M. Stewart (eds.), *Contemporary research on terrorism* (pp. 24-41). Aberdeen, MA: Aberdeen University Press.

In the field of terrorism there is no agreement about any single definition, but there is considerable agreement about the main elements which definitions should contain. Based on the discussion in this chapter, the author has tentatively come to the following definition: Terrorism is an organized system of extreme and violent intimidation to create instability within democracies. International terrorists seek to launch indiscriminate and unpredictable attacks on groups (police, army, multinational, business, etc.) or nations to change the political and economic balance of the world. (Includes 50 notes.)

286. Tharp, Paul A., Jr. (1978, Spring/Summer). The laws of war as a potential legal regime for the control of terrorist activities. *Journal of International Affairs,* 32, 1: 91-100.

The authors explore both the rights and duties imposed by the laws of war upon combatants, drawing analogies from the existing rules which might be applicable to the types of activities which are labeled as terrorism. The author also discusses some of the political "escape clauses" which have been suggested as ways to temper a code of law with political reality and humanitarian concerns. (Includes 24 footnotes.)

287. Thompson, James (1991, January-March). Kuwait Airways hijack: Psychological consequences for survivors. *Stress Medicine,* 7, 1: 3-9.

Examines the psychological reactions of survivors of an airplane hijacking. Details some of the most common complaints by survivors. Outlines stages of responses to the hijacking and the release of survivors.

288. Toloyan, Khachig (1987). Martyrdom as legitimacy: Terrorism, religion and symbolic appropriation in the Armenian diaspora. In Paul Wilkinson & Alasdaire M. Stewart (eds.), *Contemporary research on terrorism* (pp. 89–103). Aberdeen, MA: Aberdeen University Press.

This chapter argues against any explicit causal relation between Armenian religion and terrorism. More than most, Armenian terrorism is best understood as a cultural, and not simply a political, phenomenon. This study focuses on the culturally privileged concepts and discourses that are essential to what Richard Martin (see entry 186), writing on Islam, has called world-view formation. (Includes 14 notes.)

289. _____ (1989). Narrative culture and the motivation of the terrorists. In John Shotter & Kenneth J. Gergen (eds.), *Texts of identity: Inquiries in social construction series* vol. 2 (pp. 99–118). London: SAGE Publications.

Examines the mediating factors that precipitate terroristic violent acts. Addresses specific issues: terrorists' self-image and motivation; cultural construction of individual motives; and Armenian political culture and Armenian terrorists.

290. Totten, Michael (1986, Fall). Nuclear terrorism: The possibilities, probable consequences, and preventive strategies. *Social Science Record,* 24, 1: 14–16.

Explores the possibility of terrorism acts against nuclear power stations; suggests specific strategies for reactor security, public policy, and course of actions to increase public safety.

291. Totten, Sam (1986, Fall). Introduction to teaching about terrorism. *Social Science Record,* 24, 1: 3–5.

Discusses historical and conceptual framework for understanding contemporary terrorism. Includes quotations from government officials, syndicated columnists, and scholars regarding terrorism and its effect on society.

292. Townshend, C. (1987). Terror in Ireland: Observations on Tynian's *The Irish Invincibles and Their Times.* In Paul Wilkinson &

Alasdaire M. Stewart (eds.), *Contemporary research on terrorism* (pp. 179–185). Aberdeen, MA: Aberdeen University Press.

This article is a review and analysis of the book *The Irish National Invincibles and Their Time* by Patrick Joseph Percy Tynan. (Includes 16 notes.)

293. Trela, J., and Hewitt, Christopher (1986, November). Age and terrorism victimization. Paper presented at the Annual Scientific Meeting of the Gerontological Society (39th, Chicago, IL, November 19–23), 24p.

While research has examined how age-related factors structure the probability of experiencing a particular event or suffering a particular kind of injury, one issue which has not been empirically addressed is the age structure of victimization from terrorist activity and civil strife. Authors explore the relationship between age and terrorist victimization; data on fatalities resulting from political violence were analyzed from Northern Ireland (1965–1985), Spain (1975–1985), and Italy (1970–1981). The results suggest that all three countries shared an age-sex profile of victims that was disproportionately young and male. Concludes that the rate of victimization of the elderly appears to be low in countries where terrorist groups focused on combatants and somewhat higher in countries where terrorism was indiscriminate.

294. Tucker, H.H. (eds.) (1988). *Combating the terrorists: Democratic responses to political violence.* Facts on File, New York, 203p.

This volume of studies on contemporary terrorism gives compelling testimony to the fantastic proliferation of terror organizations and political chaos created by terrorist crimes. It has the special merit of describing some comparatively successful responses to the destabilizing pressures to which Western nations are being subjected. The Italian experience is especially illuminating because Italy has been one of the hardest hit targets and it is one of the more skillful in suppressing the campaign against its government and society. There is much to be learned in this book about terror groups and countering terrorism in West Germany, Northern Ireland, Spain, the European Community and the United States.

295. Tugwell, M. (1987). Terrorism and propaganda: Problem and response. In Paul Wilkinson & Alasdaire M. Stewart (eds.), *Contemporary research on terrorism* (pp. 409–418). Aberdeen, MA: Aberdeen University Press.

Propaganda and terrorism are identical insofar as they both seek to influence a mass audience in a way that is intended to benefit the sponsor. But while terror has a singular purpose—inducing fear and uncertainty—propaganda can and does serve every imaginable purpose from religion to politics to commerce. Terrorism is, as the nineteenth-century anarchists claimed, "propaganda by deed"; in Brian Jenkins' more recent formulation, it is theater. Terrorism may be other things as well, but there is no doubt that there are close links between these subjects; indeed, terror might be seen as a sub-species of propaganda. (Includes 22 notes.)

296. U.S. Department of State (1987, October 27). Iran's use of international terrorism. *Special Report* No. 170, Bureau of Public Affairs, 1–4.

This is a chronology and overview of the extent of Iranian involvement in terrorism, and the proportion of terrorist acts perpetrated by Iran.

297. Ustinov, G. (1986). Afghan rebels are terrorists. In Bonnie Szumski (ed.), *Terrorism: Opposing viewpoints* (pp. 167–174). St. Paul, MN: Greenhaven Press.

The author, writing in Soviet newsmagazine *New Times,* describe how Afghan counter-revolutionaries terrorize the civilian population in an attempt to regain control of the government. (Includes two photographs.)

298. Vanden, H.V. (1987). State policy and the cult of terror in Central America. In Paul Wilkinson & Alasdaire M. Stewart (eds.), *Contemporary research on terrorism* (pp. 256–269). Aberdeen, MA: Aberdeen University Press.

Terrorist bands were considered beyond the pale and were thought to be composed of the lunatic fringe of deviant political movements. Although often convenient for state policy makers, this explanation tends to view political terrorism as an activity that, like anarchism, is directed against states if not against society itself. The author argues that terrorism is not only practiced by fringe groupings such as Black September (Palestinian) or Sendero Luminoso (Peruvian), but by major state actors as well. (Includes 50 notes.)

299. Wagenlehner, Gunther (1978). Motivation for political terrorism in Germany. In Marius H. Livingston with Lee Bruce Kress & Marie G. Wanek (eds.), *International terrorism in the contemporary world* (pp. 195–203). Westport, CT: Greenwood Press.

This essay examines what the author believes are motivations for terrorism in Germany. The analysis focuses on political terrorism practiced by the Red Army Faction.

300. Wanek, Marie G. (1978). Symposium summary. In Marius H. Livingston with Lee Bruce Kress & Marie G. Wanek (eds.), *International terrorism in the contemporary world* (pp. 1–18). Westport, CT: Greenwood Press.

This chapter is a synthesis of the different perspectives on terrorism that were articulated at a three-day symposium at Glassboro State College in 1976. The contents of this chapter reflect primarily the papers included in this book, but some materials have been taken from other papers presented at the symposium.

301. Warner, B.W. (1987). Extradition law and practice in the crucible of Ulster, Ireland and Great Britain: A metamorphosis? In Paul Wilkinson & Alasdaire M. Stewart (eds.), *Contemporary research on terrorism* (pp. 475–509). Aberdeen, MA: Aberdeen University Press.

This article outlines the Irish and British positions on the extradition of fugitive political offenders. It also examines the practical application of these positions following the renewal of civil conflict after 1969. The effect of the "flanking movement" contained in the extra-territorial legislation of 1976 is detailed. Other suggested solutions to the extradition problem such as an All-Ireland Court are mentioned in passing. Finally, the author suggests that Ireland's signing of the European Convention for the Suppression of Terrorism provides some signposts as to the future direction of extradition among the parties. (Includes 179 notes.)

302. Waugh, William L. (1990). *Terrorism and emergency management.* New York: Marcel Dekker, Inc., 209p.

The author argues that terrorist violence can cause catastrophic destruction on a level comparable to that caused by major natural and technological disasters. Indeed, the destruction may be more than similar when terrorists use chemical, biological, or radiological weapons or their violence results in structural failures, widespread power outages, or disruption of communication or transportation networks. For these reasons, the author suggests that the problem of terrorism may best be addressed in a broader fashion than is now common. In short, the emergency management model may provide a framework that will encourage such a broad view and suggest a wide range of policy options.

303. Webster, William H. (1984, March). The FBI vs. domestic terrorism. *USA Today,* 112, 2466: 10–13.

Describes the efforts of the Federal Bureau of Investigation to combat domestic terrorism, contingency plans, and special training in hostage rescue. Psycholinguistics is being used to deduce information about unknown terrorists; 95 terrorist suspects were arrested in 1982, resulting in 84 convictions.

304. Weinberg, Leonard, and Eubank, William L. (1987). Italian women terrorists. *Terrorism.* 9, 3: 241–262.

Provides a biographical analysis of Italian women arrested for planning political acts of violence and terrorism in Italy between 1970 and 1984. Compares their roles with those of their male counterparts.

305. Wheeler, Jack (1986). Afghan rebels are freedom fighters. In Bonnie Szumski (ed.), *Terrorism: Opposing viewpoints* (pp. 159–166). St. Paul, MN: Greenhaven Press.

The author discusses some of the atrocities the Soviets have committed against the Afghan people, and explains that the Mujaheddin are holy warriors, fighting to repel an evil, heartless regime. (Includes one cartoon.)

306. Wilkinson, Paul (1988). British policy on terrorism: An assessment. In Juliet Lodge (ed.), *The threat of terrorism* (pp. 29–56). Great Britain: Wheatsheaf Books Ltd.

This essay is an analysis of British policy on terrorism. Discusses British approach to terrorism before and after 1970. (Includes 30 notes.)

307. _____ (1987). Kidnap and ransom. In Paul Wilkinson & Alasdaire M. Stewart (eds.), *Contemporary research on terrorism* (pp. 390–392). Aberdeen, MA: Aberdeen University Press.

Author argues that political kidnappers almost invariably pose political demands, the most popular being the release of fellow terrorists from jail. Thus they involve the government directly in the negotiations and openly challenge its authority. Author says government has a due to protect all its citizens and to uphold the law. Consequently, it must balance the individual's interest in securing safe release against the public interest, which may be seriously harmed by the encouragement of further attacks.

308. _____ (1983). The Orange and the Green: Extremism in Northern Ireland. In Martha Crenshaw (ed.), *Terrorism, legitimacy and power: The consequences of political violence* (pp. 105–123). Middletown, CT: Wesleyan University Press.

The author argues that those who resort to terrorism in a democratic society, brutally blotting out the rights of their fellow citizens, are reprehensible and should be unequivocally condemned. The men of violence on both sides of the sectarian divide must be deterred or subdued if democratic politics and reconciliation in Northern Ireland are to have a chance. In resolving this problem of order, the British government therefore deserves the fullest support of the Opposition at Westminster and of democratic allies in Ireland and America, for their moral and political support and cooperation in security matters are vital to the defeat of terrorism in the North. (Includes 21 footnotes.)

309. _____ (1987). Pathways out of terrorism for democratic societies. In Paul Wilkinson & Alasdaire M. Stewart (eds.), *Contemporary research in terrorism* (pp. 453–465). Aberdeen, MA: Aberdeen University Press.

Author defines terrorism as coercive intimidation, or more fully as the systematic use of murder, injury and destruction, or threat of same, to create a climate of terror, to publicize a cause and to coerce a wider target into submitting to the terrorist's aims. International terrorism, the author suggests, must be viewed as terrorism exported across international frontiers or used against foreign targets in the terrorists' country of origin. There is no case of purely domestic terrorism, but there are, of course, many campaigns in which the political violence is concentrated in a single national territory or region (e.g., the Irish Republican Army [IRA], and the Basque and Corsican terrorists). (Includes ten notes.)

310. _____ (1979). Social scientific theory and civil violence. In Yonah Alexander, David Carlton & Paul Wilkinson (eds.), *Terrorism: Theory and practice* (pp. 45–72). Boulder, CO: Westview Press.

Author argues that there appears to be no substantial theoretical literature in social science that specifically addresses terrorism as a phenomenon. Author says that some general theories of violence have yielded hypotheses about terrorism which, though hotly disputed, are of considerable academic value. The chapter examines some of the more influential of these theories and their underlying assumptions. (Includes 46 notes.)

311. _____, and Stewart, Alasdaire M. (eds.) (1987). *Contemporary research on terrorism*. Aberdeen, MA: Aberdeen University Press, 625p.

The editors assembled experts who discuss the different perspectives of terrorism. Thirty-six separate articles are presented under the following six topics: 1) Definitional and Conceptual Aspects; 2) Moral and Religious Aspects; 3) Trends and Patterns in the History of Terrorism; 4) Behavioral Aspects; 5) Terrorism and the Media; and 6) National and International Responses. (Includes selected bibliography and an index.)

312. Wilson, Michele, and Lynxwiler, John. (1988). Abortion clinic violence as terrorism. *Terrorism*. 11, 4: 263–273.

Examines and compares instances of abortion clinic violence (1982–1987), with official and academic definitions of terrorism. Authors conclude that abortion clinic violence fits the classification of "limited political" or "subrevolutionary" terrorism, even though the FBI has not included such acts as terrorism.

313. Winkler, Carol (1989). Presidents held hostage: The rhetoric of Jimmy Carter and Ronald Reagan. *Terrorism,* 12, 1: 21–30.

See entry 736.

314. Wolf, John B. (1976, July-September). An analysis framework for the study and control of agitational terrorism. *The Police Journal.* XLIX, 30: 165–171.

The following headings are included in the article: 1) Categories Extracted from the Analytical Syntheses; 2) Categories Included in the Analytical Framework; 3) Computer-Assisted Analysis; 4) Analytical Projections; 5) Analytical Frameworks and Public Order.

315. _____ (1976, Winter). Controlling political terrorism in a free society. *ORBIS: A Journal of World Affairs,* 1289–1308.

The following are some headings included in the article: 1) Strategic Considerations; 2) Tupamaro Tactics and the Police Officer; 3) Police Education and Integrity; 4) Special Police Operations Programs; 5) Improved Court-Management Procedures and Policies; 6) The Official Hostage Policy of the United States Government; 7) Responsibility of the Press and Media; 8) Cabinet Committee Working Group; 9) An Eye on the Future.

316. _____ (1981). *Fear of fear: A survey of terrorist operations and controls in open societies.* New York: Plenum Press, 219p.

The following chapters are presented: 1) The Global Terrorist Coalition; 2) Urban Terrorist Operations; 3) Organization and Management Practices of Urban Terrorist Groups; 4) Terrorist Manipulation of the Democratic Process; 5) Prisons, Courts, and Terrorism; 6) Controlling Political Terrorism in a Free Society; 7) Approaches to Antiterrorism; 8) Antiterrorism in Western Europe; 9) Antiterrorist Intelligence: Limitations and Applications; and 10) A Framework for the Study and Control of Terrorism. (Includes six appendixes, a selected bibliography, and index.)

317. _____ (1977, Oct.-Dec.). A global terrorist coalition: Its incipient state. *The Police Journal.* LI, 4: 328–339.

The following are some headings included in the article: 1) Palestinian Terrorist Organizations; 2) A Common Terrorist Ideology; 3) Combined Terrorist Operations; 4) Tactical and Logistical Aspects of Combined Terrorist Operations; 5) Patterns of Terrorist Cooperation; 6) The Tupamaro Model; and 7) Libya's Role as a Subversive Center.

318. _____ (1978). Organization and management practice of urban terrorist groups. *Terrorism: An International Journal,* 1, 2: 169–186.

The following are some headings included in the article: 1) Articulating the Goals of a Terrorist Organization; 2) Target-Assessment Techniques; 3) Terrorist Command Councils; 4) Aspects of Terrorist Recruitment and Discipline; 5) The 26th-of-July Movement in Havana; 6) A Critique of the Terrorist Style of Organization; and 7) Recent Trends in the Organization of Terrorist Groups in the United States.

319. _____ (1977, July-September). Prisons, courts and terrorism: The American and West German experience. *The Police Journal,* LI, 3: 221–230.

The following headings are included in the article: 1) The Islamic Guerrillas in America; 2) Statewide Correctional Alliance for Reform; 3) Arrest and Escape of Joanne Chesimard; 4) New World of Islam; 5) Holmesburgh Prison and "Bubbles" Price; 6) Symbionese Liberation Army; 7) New World Liberation Front; 8) Trial of the "San Quentin Six"; 9) Baader-Meinhof "Annex"; 10) Prison Escape Schemes; 11) Inmate Communication Systems; 12) Future Considerations; and 13) Recommendations for Prisons.

320. _____ (1975, April-June). Terrorist manipulation of the democratic process. *The Police Journal.* XLVIII, 2: 102–112.

The following headings are included in the article: 1) Terrorism and Revolution; 2) Strategic Considerations; 3) Law-Enforcement Liaison Shortcomings; 4) Intelligence Networks; 5) Nature of the Democratic Response; 6) British Approach to Small-Scale Terrorism; 7) Democratic States and Repression.

321. _____ (1977, July-September). Urban terrorist operations. *The Police Journal,* LI, 3: 221–230.

The author examines urban terrorist operations with emphasis on the advantages and disadvantages of such operations. Concludes with analysis of urban terrorist strategies and modern warfare.

322. Wright, Fred, and Wright, Phyllis (1982, Summer). Violent groups. *Group,* 6, 2: 25–34.

Authors analyze empirical studies and theoretical formulations to determine and construct the characteristics of violence-prone groups. Groups analyzed include the Weather Underground, the Black Liberation Army, and the Charles Manson Group. Discusses leadership characteristics, group norm-forming, and group control processes. (Includes 25 references.)

323. Wright, Robin (1986). Terrorists act to achieve freedom. In Bonnie Szumski (ed.), *Terrorism: Opposing viewpoints* (pp. 47–50). St. Paul, MN: Greenhaven Press.

The author argues that the United States has a history of reacting to each individual act of terrorism. Instead, it should attempt to pursue and correct terrorism's cause—a frustrating lack of political and personal freedom for people in many countries. Terrorists are not bloodthirsty murderers, she argues, but people motivated by dreams of freedom and independence, not unlike America's founders.

324. Young, Marlene A. (1989). Crime, violence, and terrorism. In Richard Gist and Bernard Lubin (eds.), *Psychosocial aspects of disaster* (pp. 140–159). New York: John Wiley & Sons.

Examines the impact of criminal violence and the aftermath of victimization. Suggests intervention techniques for individual and community victims of violence.

325. Zinam, Oleg (1978). Terrorism and violence in the light of a theory of discontent and frustration. In Marius H. Livingston with Lee Bruce Kress & Marie G. Wanek (eds.), *International terrorism in the contemporary world* (pp. 240–265). Westport, CT: Greenwood Press.

Violence and terror have existed since time immemorial. Yet those who believe in the perfectibility of human nature are puzzled by the observation that violence, organized crime, and terrorism are on the rise despite a remarkable improvement in human conditions. Author argues that the increase in violence is proportionately greater in the most prosperous and technologically advanced countries. (Includes six figures, 68 notes, and a selected bibliography.)

Chapter 3

Terrorism in the Electronic Media

326. Adams, William C. (1985, August-September). The Beirut hostages: ABC and CBS seize an opportunity. *Public Opinion,* 45–48.
Author examines coverage of the 1985 Beirut hostage crisis by two American television networks: ABC and CBS. The article emphasizes the volume of coverage, the dimension of content, and the story angle taken by each network in its reports.

327. _____ (ed.) (1982). *Television coverage of international affairs.* Norwood, NJ: Ablex Publishing, 253p.
Thirteen studies examine television coverage of international affairs. The analyses focus on Third World leaders' methods of promoting various domestic interests.

328. _____ (ed.) (1981). *Television coverage of the Middle East.* Norwood, NJ: Ablex, 167p.
Eight chapters by ten distinguished scholars provide an extraordinary analysis of how the Middle East is portrayed in U.S. television news. (Includes 22 tables and 189 references.)

329. _____, and Joblove, Michael (1982). The unnewsworthy holocaust: TV news and terror in Cambodia. In William C. Adams (ed.), *Television coverage of international affairs* (pp. 217–226). Norwood, NJ: Ablex Publishing.
Examines what network television news covered about human rights violations in Cambodia. Argues that the "genocidal policies" of Cambodia's forces of the Khmer Rouge were insufficiently reported. (Includes one table and four references.)

330. Alali, A. Odasuo, and Eke, Kenoye K. (eds.) (1991). *Media coverage of terrorism: Methods of diffusion.* Newbury Park, CA: SAGE, 152p.

What is terrorism? When is an act of political violence an act of terrorism? When is it a legitimate instrument of struggle for a people determined to escape a political cul-de-sac? What is the proper role of the media, especially television, in their coverage of terrorism? This book considers these and other questions concerning the media, terrorism, and the relationship between the two. Led by Alali and Eke, seven distinguished scholars provide excellent analyses of specific aspects of the media's role in the diffusion of news on terrorism. They investigate the characterization and labeling of political violence and its perpetrators; examine case studies on the different forms that media coverage of terrorism take; and review the journalist's role. The book also offers visual researchers issues and methods they can use to examine the media. (Includes nine chapters, 18 tables of data, 201 references, and one appendix.)

331. Alexander, Yonah (1979). Terrorism and the media: Some considerations. In Yonal Alexander, David Carlton & Paul Wilkinson (eds.), *Terrorism: Theory and practice* (pp. 159–174). Boulder, CO: Westview Press.

In spite of various national and international efforts to deal with the dangers of terrorism, the author argues that the level of non-state violence is often defined within the following ten factors: disagreement about who is a terrorist, lack of understanding of the causes of terrorism, the support of terrorism by some states, the existence of an international network of terrorism, the politicization of religion, double standards of morality, loss of resolve by governments, weak punishment of terrorists, flouting of world law, and the roles of the mass media. While all these factors deserve serious and thorough study, the author focuses on the interaction of terrorism and the media, specifically as related to the police handling of incidents. (Includes 39 notes.)

332. _____ (1980). Terrorism and the media: Some observations. *Terrorism: An International Journal,* 3, 179–80.

The author suggests that two major problems should be considered in connection with this modern brand of criminality. First is the fact that to terrorists, extensive coverage by the media is the major reward and the media willingly or unwillingly become tools in the terrorist strategy. Conversely, it is possible that advertising terrorism increases the effectiveness of its message through repetition and imitation. The second concern is the vital importance of protecting the "people's right to know" and of a free press in an open society. Recognizing the seriousness and the complexity of the problem and the fact that research in this area is limited, the author decided to address the issues resulting from the interaction of terrorism, the media, and the police. The implication is that any research undertaken in this connection should take into account 12 major observations and considerations that have been identified by the author. Each point is identified and explained.

333. _____ (1977). Terrorism and the media in the Middle East. In Yonah Alexander & Seymour M. Finger (eds.), *Terrorism: Interdisciplinary perspectives* (pp. 166-206). London: McGraw-Hill Book Company (UK) Limited.

This article examines the role of the media in reporting about the Middle East. Particular attention is paid to how Egypt is portrayed in the media, and how organizations such as the PLO and Fatah are portrayed in the media. The author also examines the impact of such coverage. (Includes 102 notes.)

334. _____ (1979). Terrorism, the media, and the police. In Robert Kupperman & Darrel M. Trent (eds.), *Terrorism* (pp. 331-348). Stanford, CA: Hoover Institution Press.

The author suggests that the level of non-state violence appears to be on the increase as a result of diverse conditions summarized by the following ten factors: disagreement about who is a terrorist, lack of understanding of the causes of terrorism, the support of terrorism by some states, the existence of an international network of terrorism, the politicization of religion, double standards of morality, loss of resolve by governments, weak punishment of terrorists, flouting of world law and the roles of the mass media. While these factors deserve serious and thorough study, this analysis focuses on the interaction of terrorism and the media, specifically as related to current criminal justice processes. (Includes 43 notes.)

335. _____ (1978, Spring/Summer). Terrorism, the media and the police. *Journal of International Affairs,* 32, 1: 101-114.

In spite of various national and international efforts to deal with the dangers of terrorism, the author suggests that the level of non-state violence remains high. The reasons for this condition are diverse and also defined by at least ten factors: dissagreement about who is a terrorist, lack of understanding of the causes of terrorism, the support of terrorism by some states, the existence of an international network of terrorism, the politicization of religion, double standards of morality, loss of resolve by governments, weak punishment of terrorists, flouting of world law and the roles of the mass media. While all these factors deserve serious and thorough study, this essay focuses on the interaction of terrorism and the media, specifically as related to current criminal justice processes. (Includes 43 footnotes.)

336. _____ (ed.) (1987). *The 1986 annual on terrorism.* Hingham, MA: Kluwer Academic Publishers.
See entry 5.

337. _____, Carlton, David, and Wilkinson, Paul (eds.) (1979). *Terrorism: Theory and practice.* Boulder, CO: Westview Press, 280p.
See entry 6.

338. _____, and Picard, Robert G. (eds.) (1991). *In the camera's eye: News coverage of terrorist events.* New York: Brassey's (U.S.), Inc., 156p.
The editors assembled a panel of distinguished scholars to develop a book that addresses specific issues of terrorism in news media coverage of events. Implicit is how media coverage of terrorism constructs reality. Also, there are chapters that capture perspectives in journalism and terrorism, and that evaluate media performance in terrorist incidents. The book contains ten chapters that focus on the meanings that are constructed by news media coverage of terrorism, the ways in which media cover different terrorist acts and perpetrators, and how the mass media perform during coverage of terrorism. (Includes 12 tables of data, 215 notes, 91 references, and 100 selected bibliography.)

339. Alter, Jonathan (1985, July 8). The network circus: TV turns up the emotional volume. *Newsweek,* p. 21.
This article focuses on the three networks (ABC, CBS, and NBC) and how they cover terrorism. The networks are accused of having made clowns out of themselves during the Beirut crisis. The author argues that "the networks fought bitterly for the honor of being manipulated most often by the Shiites." Additionally, the author's analysis implies that American journalists paid for or were paid for stories. Even though each network denied the accusations, they claimed that they couldn't "vouch for their competition." One interesting observation is how the terrorists played favorites with reporters. For example, the author says that the Shiites favored ABC's Charles Glass. But when NBC's anchorman Tom Brokaw arrived in Lebanon he was treated as

a mere "member of the pack." The author observes that he was not accorded the same "courtesy" as his ABC counterpart; ABC had a clear advantage in this coverage of terrorists. Additionally, the hostage holders allowed ABC to deliver the hostages' mails and were given an exclusive interview with the TWA pilot. The author supports this argument by indicating that when a temporary pool coverage was attempted, ABC was reluctant to accept this arrangement and stayed one step ahead of the other networks. And because ABC was constantly scooping NBC and CBS, many people wondered if foul play was involved. This article does illustrate how television coverage of crisis situations can be both beneficial and detrimental. Also, media coverage of terrorism never provides the whole picture, especially when "the terrorists are allowed to act as executive producers." Lastly, the author argues that television coverage of terrorism often preys upon the emotions of its audience. Visually, television can humanize or dehumanize any situation; it often works to the advantage of the terrorist. (Includes one cartoon.)

340. Altheide, David L. (1987, June). Format and symbols in TV coverage of terrorism in the United States and Great Britain. *International Studies Quarterly,* 3, 161–176.

A conceptual scheme for understanding how TV news formats shape the reports that are broadcast in the United States and the United Kingdom is examined in this explanatory, comparative study of TV news coverage of a terrorist incident in London's Hyde Park in 1982. While ideological positions clearly flow from most news reports, the analysis suggests that news practices and perspectives also contribute to the visual and thematic emphasis of reports. News formats of the even type associated with regular evening newscasts in both countries focused on visuals of the aftermath and tactics of terrorism, while topic type formats associated with interviews and documentary presentations included materials about purposes, goals, and rationale. These variations in format produce consistent differences in message content in both countries, suggesting that an organizational media logic is relevant for understanding information control about terrorism and other events. Implications are noted for theoretical understanding about ideology and social control. In particular, the author believes that future research attention should be directed to regulation and control of news formats, and the implications for a mass audience, leadership styles, and international affairs.

341. _____ (1985, Summer). Impact of format and ideology on TV news coverage of Iran. *Journalism Quarterly,* 62: 346–351.

This article is an analysis of production formats and their compatibility with ideological processes and how they underlie and contribute to news content. Television news formats are analyzed according to event characteristics such as accessibility, visual quality, drama and action, audience relevance, encapsulation and thematic unity. This content analysis of the Iranian hostage crisis covers the period November 4, 1979, to January 24, 1981. The analysis reveals that cultural stereotypes and images, including political and ideological value judgments, can find their way into news content without intending to do so. (Includes two tables of data and 15 references.)

342. _____ (1981). Iran v. U.S. TV news: The hostage story out of context. In William C. Adams (ed.), *Television coverage of the Middle East* (pp. 128-159). Norwood, NJ: Ablex.

This chapter examines format, mode of emphasis, themes, topics, and visual images of reports about a specific hostage crisis to determine the degree to which news reports reflect reality. Analyses of 375 reports in network evening news from November 1979 to June 1980 suggest the important diplomatic role mass media operatives play. (Includes four tables and nine references.)

343. _____ (1982, Autumn). Three-in-one news: Network coverage of Iran. *Journalism Quarterly,* 59, 482-486.

Contrary to the often repeated claims by ABC, CBS and NBC that they are competing with each other, there is an increasing amount of evidence to suggest that in terms of the news programming offered to their respective audiences, the networks are quite similar, and indeed, offer few divergent points of view or topics of focus. This article reports a study of media coverage by the three major television networks of the Iranian hostage crisis during an eight month period (November 4, 1979–June 7, 1980). The results of the study indicate that: 1) there are no significant differences among the three major networks, indicating a consonance or correspondence of coverage; 2) network reporting fluctuates together – as one network increases or decreases coverage, so do the other two; 3) the number of reports decreased for all networks overall during the period except for the time when the U.S. launched a rescue attempt; 4) the number of reports by one network could be relied upon to predict the number by the other two; 5) coverage of current aspects, such as the health of the Shah of Iran, was far greater than of historical aspects; and 6) historical, cultural, and religious contexts which gave rise to the crisis were covered far less than the volatility and instability of the current government of Iran. In summary, the author suggests that the same message and emphasis are presented to the

American viewers by the three major networks; there are only minor variations in coverage. This is attributed to similarities in organization and format. (Includes three tables of data and 14 references.)

344. Andrews, Kate (1989, Summer). Airline disaster highlights need for ethical coverage. *Journalism Educator,* 44, 2: 50–51, 76.
See entry 563.

345. Aner, Kerstin (1983, October-December). La violence et les medias [Violence and the media]. *Revue Internationale de Criminologie et de Police Technique,* 36, 4: 72–83.
See entry 564.

346. Association for Education in Journalism and Mass Communication (1991, August). Proceedings of the Annual Meeting of the Association for Education in Journalism and Mass Communication (74th, Boston, MA, August 7–10). Part X: United States Coverage of International News, 459p.
Fifteen papers of this proceedings discuss how the United States media cover international news. Discussion includes TV news, newspapers, news magazines.

347. _____ (1990, August). Proceedings of the 1990 Annual Meeting of the Association for Education in Journalism and Mass Communication. (73rd, Minneapolis, MN, August 1–4). Part VI: Foreign and International Media Studies, 339p.
Includes 11 papers from proceedings that discuss foreign and international media studies. Includes cultural analysis, content analysis, and other media theories.

348. Atwater, Tony (1991). Network evening news coverage of the TWA hostage crisis. In A. Odasuo Alali & Kenoye K. Eke (eds.), *Media coverage of terrorism: Methods of diffusion* (pp. 63–72). Newbury Park, CA: SAGE.
This critical analysis of television coverage of terrorist activity suggests that journalists risk providing a platform for terrorist causes when the events are covered continuously and extensively. The success of a terrorist operation is highly contingent on the amount of publicity it receives; therefore, it is the journalist's responsibility to use discretion to avoid becoming a tool in the terrorist strategy. The comprehensive study of the TWA hostage crisis addressed these issues and all stories

107

broadcast between June 14, 1985, and June 30, 1985, were included in this analysis. Story topic, origin, topical emphasis, and actual news time covered by the three major networks that the hijacking of the TWA flight was the dominant news event during the period studied and the coverage was continuous and extensive. The topics that were most covered included the plight of the hostages and U.S. government reaction to the situation, and less dramatic yet important topics such as the history of Lebanon and probable cause for the hijacking took a back seat to the drama of the hostages. As in the Iranian hostage crisis, journalists neglected to inform the public of factors that instigated the hijacking, choosing to dazzle the audience with tear-jerking drama instead of acting as interpreters and educators.

349. _____, and Green, Norma F. (1988, Winter). News sources in network coverage of international terrorism. *Journalism Quarterly,* 65, 4: 967–971.

Relatively little attention in the literature on media coverage of terrorism has been devoted to examining sources televised in network coverage of terrorist incidents. To provide empirical evidence on how network news personalizes coverage of international terrorism, the authors provide a content analysis of network evening news coverage of the TWA hijacking in June 1985. They found that relatives and hostages were most frequent sources in this terrorist incident. This study was among the first to use the "sound bite" concept as the unit of analysis in investigating network coverage of international terrorism. Five major research questions were addressed in this study: 1) Which sources were the primary characters used in personalizing network evening news coverage of the TWA hijacking? 2) To what extent were networks similar or different in the types of sources televised during the TWA hijacking? 3) In what settings were televised news sources most often presented, e.g. news conference, on-site interview? 4) What was the ratio of official to unofficial televised sources in network coverage of the TWA hijacking? and 5) What was the ratio of domestic to non-domestic televised sources in network coverage of the incident? (Includes three tables of data and 16 references.)

350. _____, and _____ (1988, July). Televised news sources in network coverage of international terrorism. Paper presented at the Annual Meeting of the Association for Education in Journalism and Mass Communication (71st, Portland, OR, July 2–5), 27p.

Authors conducted a content analysis of videotaped reports relating to the TWA airliner hijacking in June 1985 to examine how United States network news personalizes coverage of international terrorism. Video-tapes of the TWA hostage incident from "ABC World News Tonight," "CBS Evening News," and "NBC Nightly News" during the period of June 14 through June 30, 1985, were analyzed according to the televised news source — defined as the videotaped "sound bite" of the newsmaker as seen and heard in the context of a network news report. Authors identified a total of 790 "sound bites" that were broadcast in 244 stories during the 17-day incident, with CBS televising the largest percentage of news. Results show that the sources televised during the TWA hijacking were most frequently unofficial, domestic sources. Over half of these sources were either hostages or relatives and friends of hostages, suggesting that network coverage of terrorism tends to relate a "human" drama in which hostages and their families are portrayed as the central characters. (Includes five tables of data and 30 footnotes.)

351. Avallone, Franco (1982). Analisi psicologico-sociale del compart-amento comunicativo del rotocalco televisivo sul terrorismo [Social-psychological analysis of communicative function of television pro-grams on terrorism]. In RAI Radiotelevisione Italiana, *Terrorismo e TV,* 1.

This analysis suggests that the media perform a socio-psychological as well as communicative functions in their representations of terrorism on television.

352. Bandura, Albert (1990). Mechanisms of moral disengagement. In W. Reich (ed.), *Origins of terrorism: Psychologies, ideologies, theol-ogies, states of mind.* Woodrow Wilson Center Series (pp. 161-191). New York: Cambridge University Press.

See entry 16.

353. Barnhurst, Kevin G. (1991). The literature of terrorism: Implica-tions for visual communications. In A. Odasuo Alali & Kenoye K. Eke (eds.), *Media coverage of terrorism: Methods of diffusion* (pp. 112-137). Newbury Park, CA: SAGE.

Author argues that even though research on the press and terrorism has analyzed visual presentation using a variety of measurements, none has been thorough. Also, author says that since specific aspects of the visual form of news reports are used to define sensationalism, visual researchers can contribute to the study of terrorism and prominent news play by applying their detailed knowledge of form to analyze an important dimension of the complex and baffling phenomenon of ter-rorism. (Includes 47 references.)

354. Barton, Richard L., and Gregg, Richard B. (1982, Spring). Middle East conflict as a TV news scenario: A formal analysis. *Journal of Communication,* 32, 2: 172–185.

Analysis of CBS coverage of a Middle East conflict suggests that two dominant, mutually supporting patterns of meaning – prediction and affirmation of network authority – are created by the interaction of conventional and organic formal elements of news. The authors argue that studies employing the methods of content analysis to examine the nature of news reporting are satisfying in some respects but disappointing in others. (Includes two figures and 15 references.)

355. Bassiouni, M. Cherif (1982, Spring). Media coverage of terrorism: The law and the public. *Journal of Communication,* 32, 2: 128–143.

When does the public's right to know interfere with their protection? This is an examination of First Amendment issues and a proposal for media self-regulation. The author's analysis of empirical data relating to individual international terrorism suggests that its impact derives not from its numbers but from its ancillary effects. Most of the data reported in this study were extracted from a study by the United States Central Intelligence Agency's National Foreign Assessment Center. (Includes 33 references.)

356. _____ (1981). Terrorism, law enforcement, and the mass media: Perspectives, problems, proposals. *Journal of Criminal Law and Criminology,* 72, 1: 801–851.

See entry 355.

357. Behm, A.J. (1991). Terrorism, violence against the public, and the media: The Australian approach. *Political Communication and Persuasion,* 8: 233–246.

See entry 571.

358. Bell, J. Bowyer (1978, May-June). Terrorist scripts and live-action spectaculars. *Columbia Journalism Review,* 47–50.

This article is adapted from *A Time of Terror: How Democratic Societies Respond to Revolutionary Violence* (Basic Books, Inc., May, 1978). What the producers of terrorist spectaculars have managed to do is to raise the level of attraction to a peak beyond former riot rituals, to a level comparable at times to coverage of more conventionally global events, like the World Cup final or the Olympics. Each of the following steps is identified and discussed: 1) a terrorist-spectacular first should be staged in an ideologically satisfactory locale with more than adequate technological facilities; 2) the terrorist drama must offer the reality or prospect of violence; 3) the third component of the successful terrorist-spectacular under optimum conditions is movement — the change of scenery that allows the cameras to follow the actors (terrorists, hostages, security people) from one site to the next — coupled with the passage of time.

359. Bering-Jensen, Henrick (1990). The silent treatment for terrorists. In Bernard Schechterman & M. Slann (eds.), *Violence and Terrorism 90/91* [Annual Editions] (pp. 122–123). Guilford, CT: The Dushkin Publishing Group, Inc.
   See entry 360.

360. _____ (1988, November 21). The silent treatment for terrorists. *Insight,* 34–35.
   Author presents the dilemma democratic governments face in media coverage of terrorism. The case of Great Britain's crackdown on access to the media by terrorists is amplified. Argues that the broadcast ban in Great Britain is similar to the one in effect in the Republic of Ireland since the 1970s.

361. Blaisse, Mark (1992). Reporters' perspectives. In David L. Paletz & Alex P. Schmid (eds.), *Terrorism and the media* (pp. 137–169). Newbury Park, CA: Sage Publications, Inc.
   See entry 572.

362. Bogart, Leo (1968, Summer). The overseas newsman: A 1967 profile study. *Journalism Quarterly,* 45, 293–306.
   Today's foreign correspondent differs strikingly from his 19th-century predecessors. He is an "organization man," working as part of a team. This is the picture emerging from a survey of 206 OPC members. The emergence of television as a highly important source of foreign news coverage for the American public does not appear to be reflected in a commensurate growth of broadcast news staffs relative to the whole corps of overseas newsmen. It is interesting to note that magazines are close runners-up to newspapers in the number of full-time correspondents employed, and are the leading employers of stringers and free-lancers. (Includes 31 tables of data.)

363. Bormann, Ernest G. (1982). A fantasy theme analysis of the television coverage of the hostage release and the Reagan inaugural. *Quarterly Journal of Speech,* 68, 2: 133–145.

The author employs the fantasy theme analysis to examine the rhetoric of TV coverage of the Iranian hostage release and the Reagan inaugural address. A comparative analysis of both suggests how television creates social reality; it also characterizes Reagan's speech as fantasy.

364. Bremer, L. Paul, III (1990). Terrorism and the media. In Bernard Schechterman & M. Slann (eds.), *Violence and terrorism 90/91* [Annual Editions] (pp. 108–110). Guilford, CT: The Dushkin Publishing Group, Inc.
See entry 574.

365. _____ (1987). Terrorism and the media. Washington, D.C.: U.S. Department of State, Bureau of Public Affairs, Office of Public Communication, Editorial Division.
See entry 574.

366. Brown, William J. (1987, May). Mediated communication flows during a terrorism event: The TWA Flight 847 hijacking. Paper presented at the International Communication Association, Montreal.
See entry 576.

367. _____ (1990, Spring). The persuasive appeal of mediated terrorism: The case of the TWA Flight 847 hijacking. *Western Journal of Speech Communication,* 54, 2: 219–236.
Analyzes the effects of terrorism as a persuasive form, rather than a dysfunctional sociological act. Analyzes the 1985 TWA Flight 847 hijacking to determine the rhetorical functions of terrorism and evaluates the persuasive appeals of mediated narrative; applies theory to analysis of terrorist spokesman.

368. Burgess, Parke G. (1973). Crisis rhetoric: Coersion vs. force. *Quarterly Journal of Speech,* 59: 61–73.
See entry 28.

369. Burnet, Mary. (1971). *The mass media in a violent world (1970 Symposium proceedings).* Paris, France: UNESCO.
This symposium was designed to address definitional issues related to violence, and the relationship between mass mediated violence and real-life violence. Experts from 18 countries examined these issues with the ultimate objective of encouraging reason over violence as a means of settling disputes. All these perspectives are captured in this book,

using the dramatic context of violence in media entertainment as its backdrop. Because of media influence of these processes, experts suggest that media can also be a catalyst in understanding and the resolution of conflict.

370. Carpini Delli, Michael X., and Williams, Bruce A. (1987, March). Television and terrorism: Patterns of presentation and occurrence, 1969 to 1980. *The Western Political Quarterly,* 40, 1: 45-64.

This article documents how network coverage of terrorism makes it difficult for viewers to form accurate conclusions about the nature and frequency of terrorism. The authors suggest that agenda setting may be the main role of the electronic media. The media are thus critical in shaping the political priorities of both the general public and public officials. Case studies using 1969 to 1980 as test period found that all three major networks (ABC, CBS, and NBC) were similar in their pattern of coverage. More air time was given to events close to home or in areas that are considered important to the United States; the Middle East featured prominently. Coverage of hostage-taking and hijackings was overplayed. Whereas bombings are the most prevalent demonstration of terrorism, they were significantly downplayed. The authors suggest that this is because hijackings and hostage-taking are more attractive to the viewing audience. The authors suggest that the networks pay closer attention to the long-term, scientific basis of news coverage. (Includes seven tables of data and 48 references.)

371. Casey, William J. (1986, November). Conquering the cancer of terrorism. *USA Today* (Magazine), 115, 2498: 10-12.

See entry 31.

372. Catton, William R. (1978). Militants and the media: Partners in terrorism. *Indiana Law Journal,* 53, 705-715.

The official position has been that the presence of media creates an unequal balance in potrayals of terrorist incidents. Consequently, terrorists take advantage of this imbalance thereby jeopardizing First Amendment rights for the media. The author examines these issues within the context of the U.S. Constitution.

373. Clark, Dennis (1978). Terrorism in Ireland: Renewal of a tradition. In Marius H. Livingston with Lee Bruce Kress & Marie G. Wanek (eds.), *International terrorism in the contemporary world* (pp. 77-83). Westport, CT: Greenwood Press.

See entry 34.

374. Clawson, Patrick (1987, Winter). Why we need more but better coverage of terrorism. *ORBIS,* 30, 4: 701–710.
See entry 582.

375. Clutterbuck, Richard (1981). *The media and political violence* (2d. ed.). London: The Macmillan Press.
What is the power and role of the media in political violence? The author examines the context within which media, particularly television, influence public demonstrations. Of particular interest is the impact media coverage has on the violence in Northern Ireland. The author balances this issue with the question of whether journalistic standards and parliamentary legislative actions are appropriate ways to regulate media coverage of political violence.

376. Cohen, Akiba A., Adoni, Hanna, and Drori, Gideon (1983, Winter). Adolescents' perceptions of social conflicts in television news and social reality. *Human Communication Research,* 10, 2: 203–225.
Author examined 492 ninth-grade and 425 twelfth-grade Israeli adolescents to determine differential perception of social conflicts in society and of their presentation by television news, with the assumption that television presents a distorted picture of social conflicts. Study focuses on three conflicts (school integration, labor disputes, and political terrorism). Among its findings is that the older subjects typically differentiated between the realms of reality to a greater degree than the younger subjects. (Includes 54 references.)

377. Cooper, H.H.A. (1977). Terrorism and the Media. In Yonah Alexander & Seymour M. Finger (eds.), *Terrorism: Interdisciplinary perspectives* (pp. 141–156). London: McGraw-Hill Book Company (UK) Limited.
This essay is a comprehensive analysis of the role of the media in terrorist incidents. As background to this discussion, the author examines what is viewed as the purpose of terrorism and public opinion about the media. Tries to determine whether the media are propagandizing terrorism or performing the role of analyst and social commentator. Also, the author examines the investigative reporting that is related to terrorism. (Includes 12 notes.)

378. Cooper, Thomas (1988, July). Terrorism and perspectivist philosophy: Understanding adversarial news coverage. Terrorism and the news media research project. Boston, MA: Emerson College, 10p. (ED 312696).
See entry 379.

379. _____ (1991). Terrorism and perspectivist philosophy: Understanding adversarial news coverage. In Yonah Alexander & Robert G. Picard (eds.), *In the camera's eye: News coverage of terrorist events* (pp. 10–29). New York: Brassey's (U.S.), Inc.

This analysis seeks to determine the differences in meaning attached to terrorist events by individuals and nations with adversarial relationships, and how these perspectives affect the importance and meaning attached to acts of political violence. Cooper uses the coverage by the U.S. and Soviet Union of the Chernobyl reactor disaster in 1986, Gorbachev's reaction following Chernobyl, the downing of the K.A.L. airliner in 1983, and the Berlin disco explosion in 1986 as examples of such perspectivist approach. The author argues that perspectivism, based on the adversarial biases of international media organizations, motivates news agencies to align themselves with their own government's perspective while depicting the rival country as a villian. Also, the author contends that in order to offset this type of media coverage between the U.S. and the Soviet Union, an exchange of cultural understanding must continue in order to permit a shift from "adversary" toward "colleague" journalism. (Includes 32 notes and 61 references.)

380. Covert, Lorrie Schmid (1984). A fantasy-theme analysis of the rhetoric of the Symbionese Liberation Army: Implications of bargaining with terrorists. Dissertation, University of Denver.

See entry 585.

381. Cox, Robert (1981). The media as a weapon. *Political Communication and Persuasion,* 1, 297–300.

It was a routine story in the violent early years of the seventies, the darkest decade in Argentina's history: an Army colonel had been kidnapped by the People's Revolutionary Army (ERP) and the terrorists were threatening to kill him if their demands for the release of captured guerrillas were not met. Successive deadlines had run out and the terrorists had announced their "final" terms. The colonel was to be killed (the terrorists used the term "execute") at midnight if the demands were not met. The author presents the argument that the media failed in their duty by not reporting truthfully and not commenting fairly on the terror used to fight terrorism. Rather, the Argentine media allowed themselves to be used to cripple the minds of the public.

382. Crelinsten, Ronald D. (1987). Power and meaning: Terrorism as a struggle over access to the communication structure. In Paul Wilkin-

son & Alasdaire M. Stewart (eds.), *Contemporary research on terrorism* (pp. 419–450). Aberdeen, MA: Aberdeen University Press.
See entry 46.

383. _____ (1992). Victims' perspectives. In David L. Paletz & Alex P. Schmid (eds.), *Terrorism and the media* (pp. 208–238). Newbury Park, CA: Sage Publications, Inc.
See entry 588.

384. Czerniejewski, Halina J. (1977, April). Terrorism and news: In search of definable boundaries. *The Quill,* p. 12.
The question of news judgment is one often raised when media coverage of terrorism appears to exceed the expectations of the law enforcement community. The author suggests specific guidelines which will help news organizations deal with their coverage of terrorist acts. The author says these guidelines are not aimed at encroaching upon news judgment and the selection of news.

385. Dobkin, Bethami A. (1992a, Spring). Paper tigers and video postcards: The rhetorical dimensions of narrative form in ABC news coverage of terrorism. *Western Journal of Communication,* 56, 2: 143–160.
Author identifies ways in which news coverage of acts of terrorism aids media organizations and incumbent governments. An analysis based on ABC news coverage of terrorist incidents broadcast between Reagan's 1981 inauguration and the 1986 U.S. bombing of Libya examines ABC's use of the romantic quest as a narrative frame for terrorist acts. Examines narratives such as the casting of top government officials as paper tigers, the formation of video postcards of hostages to mobilize viewer emotions, and speculation about the desirability of military intervention. The overarching melodramatic imperative that structures news narratives privileges military responses to foreign adversaries but does not enhance understanding of political crises.

386. _____ (1992b). *Tales of terror: Television news and the construction of terrorist threat.* New York: Praeger, 133p.
This is an analysis of more than 200 evening newscasts of ABC during the first six Reagan years. Author concludes that mass media coverage of terrorism encourages panic about terrorism as well as support for specific U.S. policy objectives. This research contributes to the ongoing debate about media responsibility/irresponsibility in coverage of terrorism. (Includes seven chapters, a bibliography, and an index.)

387. Dominick, Joseph R. (1973). Crime and law enforcement in prime-time television. *Public Opinion Quarterly,* 37, 2: 241–250.

A content analysis of one week of dramatic and comedy television programs indicate that crime and violent crimes were prevalent in two-thirds of the programs examined. The study indicates that while real life crimes against property and against family members were under-represented in television programs; 60 percent of television crimes comprise armed robbery.

388. Dowling, Ralph E. (1988, March). The contribution of speech communication scholarship to the study of terrorism: Review and preview. Paper presented at the Conference on Communication in Terrorist Events: Functions, Themes, and Consequence (Boston, MA, March 3–5), 41p.

Author notes that existing research into terrorism shows great promise but argues that despite widespread recognition of terrorism's communicative dimensions, few studies have been done from within the discipline of speech communication. Author defines the discipline of speech communication and rhetorical studies, reviews the few existing rhetorical studies of terrorism, and goes on to show the ways in which a rhetorical perspective would alter and improve research carried out from other perspectives. Concludes that the rhetorical perspective has much to offer the future interdisciplinary study of terrorist phenomena. (Includes a 119-item bibliography of basic sources in rhetoric and the rhetoric dimensions of terrorism.)

389. _____ (1989, February). The media and the terrorists: Not innocents, but both victims. Paper presented at the Annual Meeting of the Western Speech Communication Association (Spokane, WA, February 18–21), 21p.

See entry 592.

390. _____ (1982). The rhetorical genre of terrorism: Identification and policy implications. Paper presented at the Annual Meeting of the Western Speech Communication Association (Denver, CO, February 19–23), 26p.

Author suggests that rhetorical critics must examine terrorism to determine what contributions they can make to the understanding of rhetoric and to the evaluation of proposed responses to the terrorist threat. Not only must the rhetorical acts of crusader terrorists be viewed as rhetoric, but they must also be considered a rhetorical genre. This genre, with the appropriate recurring forms, arises from the constraints imposed by the nature and purposes of terrorists and can be called the "terrorist-spectacular." Argues that although access to the media is the purpose of the terrorists, the long-term goal of the terrorist groups is to change the world according to some grand design. Another goal of terrorism is to demonstrate to terrorists their own worthiness and thus to claim a sort of moral victory over their enemies. Given the importance of rhetorical purposes served by terrorist spectaculars, the author suggests that the prevention of terrorism be realized through voluntary restraint or self-regulation by the news media. This study suggests approaches to terrorism prevention. (Includes 51 notes.)

391. _____ (1986, Winter). Terrorism and the media: A rhetorical genre. *Journal of Communication,* 36, 1: 12–24.
The author's purpose is to identify the situational demands influencing political terrorists, the recurrent forms of a terrorist genre, the rhetorical purposes of terrorists, and the probable results of proposed responses to terrorism. The author argues that terrorists are so restrained by situation and purpose that their acts form a distinct rhetorical genre; they send distinct messages to their audience. Suggests that their failure to persuade or conquer makes this important for long-term objectives. (Includes 31 references.)

392. _____ (1988, September). The terrorist and the media: Partners in crime or ritual and harmless observers? Paper presented at the "Media and Modern Warfare" Conference (New Brunswick, Canada, September 30), 34p.
See entry 595.

393. _____, and Nitcavic, Richard G. (1989, November 20). Visions of terror: A Q-methodological analysis of American perceptions of international terrorism. Paper presented at the Annual Meeting of the Speech Communication Association (75th, San Francisco, CA, November 18–21, 1989), 33p. (ED 312698)
See entry 61.

394. Eke, Kenoye K., and Alali, A. Odasuo (1991). Introduction: Critical issues in media coverage of terrorism. In A.O. Alali & Kenoye K. Eke (eds.), *Media coverage of terrorism: Methods of diffusion* (pp. 3–11). Newbury Park, CA: Sage Publications, Inc.
See entry 596.

395. Elkin, Michael (1987, September 10). Terrorism on TV — Who are the real hostages? *Miami Jewish Tribune,* 17–18.

Author discusses some of the most heinous acts of violence in the world that receive detailed news coverage. Two questions are posited: 1) Is the coverage a good thing? and 2) Are the media giving terrorists exactly what they want — lots of publicity — and possibly giving sympathetic treatment to the goals or motivations of terrorists?

396. _____ (1990). Terrorism on TV — Who are the real hostages? In Bernard Schechterman & M. Slann (eds.), *Violence and Terrorism 90/91* [Annual Editions] (pp. 116–120). Guilford, CT: The Dushkin Publishing Group, Inc.

See entry 395.

397. Elliot, Deni (undated). Family ties: A case study of coverage of families and friends during the hijacking of TWA Flight 847. Terrorism and the News Media Research Project, Paper No. 7, Louisiana State University.

This paper examines the way American news media covered families and friends of the TWA Flight 847 hostages, and how these people dealt with the event and the media.

398. _____ (1988). Family ties. A case study of families and friends during the hijacking of TWA Flight 847. *Political Communication and Persuasion,* 5: 67–75.

See entry 397.

399. Elliot, Philip, Murdock, Graham, and Schlesinger, Philip (1982). Lo stato e il terrorismo alla televisione Britannica. In RAI Radiotelevisione Italiana, *Terrorismo e TV, Vol. 2.* Rome: RAI, Verifica de Programmi Transmessi.

This research presents three perspectives on how television mediates terrorism. These perspectives are that of officials and authorities, that of terrorism as a legitimate political violence, and that of those who oppose the state perspective. Each perspective adds to the debate about the legitimacy of terrorism, state action, and media mediation of the opposing factions.

400. Farnen, Russell F. (1990, March-April). Terrorism and the mass media: A systemic analysis of a symbiotic process. *Terrorism,* 13, 2: 99–143.

Author describes both the media's and terrorism's roles, techniques, and expectations in the media-terrorist interactive system, as illustrated by the Italian Red Brigade's kidnapping and murder of Aldo Moro. Author observes that the public role of the mass media in most Western societies is to inform and educate citizens in the ways of democracy. By contrast, the goal of organized terrorism is to upset these orderly processes and achieve private, usually unpopular political and informational goals. Along the way, the terrorists and the media engage in mutual use and abuse. Author offers suggestions on ways to publicize terrorism for informational rather than exploitive purposes.

401. Foreign Policy Association (1986). International terrorism: In search of a response. *Great decisions '86* (pp. 35–44). New York: Foreign Policy Association.

See entry 85.

402. Francis, Richard (1983). La politique de la BBC en matiere de presentation de la violence [BBC policy regarding the presentation of television violence]. *Revue Internationale de Criminologie et de Police Technique,* 36, 4: 91–99.

Like most media operatives, the British Broadcasting Corporation (BBC) has developed guidelines for portayals of violence on television. This paper describes these guidelines, noting that the BBC uses specific factors to determine how stories about terrorism and other forms of violence and accidents are covered.

403. Friedlander, Robert A. (1982). Iran: The hostage seizure, the media, and international law. In Abraham H. Miller (ed.), *Terrorism: The media and the law* (pp. 51–66). Dobbs Ferry, NY: Transnational Publishers, Inc.

On November 4, 1979, more than 60 American nationals were seized by young Iranian militants and held hostage at the U.S. Embassy in Tehran. According to the author, the seizure of the Embassy personnel not only symbolized a major breakdown of international law, but also starkly revealed America's powerlessness to deal with an act of state-encouraged terrorism within a foreign jurisdiction. (Includes 91 footnotes.)

404. Gallup Organization (1986). The people and the press; Part 2. An ongoing Times Mirror Investigation of public attitudes towards the news media. Los Angeles, CA: Times Mirror.

See entry 603.

405. Gerbner, George (1991). Symbolic functions of violence and terror. In Yonah Alexander & Robert G. Picard (eds.), *In the camera's eye: News coverage of terrorist events* (pp. 3–9). New York: Brassey's (U.S.), Inc.
See entry 95.

406. _____ (1988, July). Symbolic functions of violence and terror. Terrorism and the news media research project. Association of Education in Journalism and Mass Communication, 8p. (ED 312725)
See entry 95.

407. _____, et al. (1978, Summer). Cultural indicators: Violence profile no. 9. *Journal of Communication,* 28, 3: 176–207.
See entry 97.

408. _____, and Gross, Linda (1979). Living with television: The violence profile. In H. Newcomb (ed.), *Television: The critical view* (pp. 71–91). New York: Oxford University Press.
See entry 96.

409. _____, and _____ (1976). Living with television: The violence profile. *Journal of Communication,* 26, 2: 172–199.
See entry 96.

410. Gerrits, Robert P.J.M. (1992). Terrorists' perspectives: Memoirs. In David L. Paletz & Alex P. Schmid (eds.), *Terrorism and the media* (pp. 29–61). Newbury Park, CA: Sage Publications, Inc.
See entry 98.

411. Gifford, C.A., and Cohen, L. (1987, August). Television, censorship and South Africa. Paper presented at the Annual Meeting of the Association for Education in Journalism and Mass Communication (70th, San Antonio, TX, August 1–4), 32p.
Author observes that television network news has often been accused of inciting and prolonging incidents of public violence, whether riots or terrorism, and in South Africa this type of thinking has led to increasingly stringent restrictions on both domestic and foreign media covering the violent unrest there. This study determined a chronology of events and analyzed the content of United States network television's coverage of South Africa from January 1982 through August 1986, to

determine the impact of varying degrees of censorship on the amount and kind of reporting coming from South Africa. Data show that in the short term, at least, the coverage actually increased during the two states of emergency that included curbs on the media. Author observes that the curb failed to silence the critics; in the longer term, however, the coverage has declined, but this may be due to factors other than censorship.

412. Graber, Doris A. (1979). Evaluating crime-fighting policies: Media images and public perspectives. In Ralph Baker and Fred A. Myer, Jr. (eds.), *Evaluating alternative law-enforcement policies* (pp. 179–199). Lexington, MA: Heath Lexington Books.
   See entry 609.

413. Graham, Katharine (1986). The media must report terrorism. In Bonnie Szumski (ed.), *Terrorism: Opposing viewpoints* (pp. 75–81). St. Paul, MN: Greenhaven Press.
   The author admits that the media have been irresponsible in their reporting of terrorism in the past. However, she believes censoring a free press is not the answer. Author asserts that in a democratic society, an unhampered press is essential.

414. Green, L.C. (1985). Terrorism and its responses. *Terrorism,* 8, 1: 33–77.
   See entry 611.

415. Groebel, Jo (1989). The problems and challenges of research on terrorism. In Jo Groebel and Jeffrey H. Goldstein (eds.), *Terrorism: Psychological perspectives.* Series of psychobiology (pp. 15–38). Sevilla, Spain: Publicaciones de la Universidad de Sevilla.
   See entry 105.

416. _____, and Goldstein, Jeffrey H. (eds.) (1989). *Terrorism: Psychological perspectives.* Series of psychobiology. Sevilla, Spain: Publicaciones de la Universidad de Sevilla.
   See entry 106.

417. Grossman, Larry (1986, June). The face of terrorism. *The Quill,* 17: 38–41.
   This is an excerpt from remarks made by the author at a luncheon sponsored by media practitioners. Author argues that even though televi-

sion coverage encourages terrorists, lack of coverage would be a victory for terrorism. He suggests that "it is always better to cover it than to cover it up." The following are some questions addressed by the author: Should television refrain from covering terrorist episodes as they happen? What kinds of special restraints should television exercise when covering terrorist events? Can television ever avoid becoming part of the story? Should television permit itself to become a platform for terrorist propaganda? Should television broadcast interviews of hostages when they are in captivity?

418. Haig, Alexander M. (1985, March 9). TV can derail diplomacy. *TV Guide,* 33, 10: 4–8.

What problems does the freedom of the press bring to the United States? How do these problems affect the U.S. government? Should there be a fine line between the media and diplomats? Is it up to the U.S. government to change these flaws? A free press is perhaps the most important safeguard the American people have against pranksters, scandals, malfeasance and imprudence; however, it is necessary to add that along with freedom comes responsibility. It is not a secret that the governments with which we deal rely on American television for information, just as the American public does. If misleading reports get on the air, sensible negotiations can be derailed. While acknowledging the medium's achievements, the author believes its immaturity hurts such efforts for mediating. He points to the fact that television's impact is immediate — worldwide, across the nation and in Washington, D.C. It should be clear that the action of television news, to focus on personalities or to sensationalize some stories, is not completely a defect of television reporting. It is not the messenger's fault that the news is unpleasant, it is the person who leaks detrimental and dangerous stories that is guilty. As a public official the author learned from having lived under the scrutiny of the television camera's lense for some decades. First, that one cannot spend all of one's time managing the press. Second, sadly, television has a way to go before it can cover diplomacy maturely. The government should not change these flaws, they will ultimately change on their own. When the press crosses that certain line the public rises up and reacts.

419. Harris J. (1983). *The new terrorism.* New York, NY: Simon & Schuster.

Author examines the role of the media in terrorist crises. Argues that while such coverage has led to calls for stricter government controls, terrorism is a legitimate news event that must be covered.

420. Heisey, D. Ray (1986, Fall). Reagan and Mitterand respond to international crisis: Creating versus transcending appearances. *Western Journal of Speech Communication,* 50, 4: 325–335.

Argues that acceptance of political reality shapes presidential foreign policy rhetoric. Examines the rhetorical responses of presidents Reagan and Mitterand to the terrorist bombing in Beirut and to acts of military intervention by the United States and France in Grenada and Chad.

421. Herman, Edward S. (1982). *The real terror network: Terrorism in fact and propaganda.* Boston, MA: Southend Press.

U.S. news media have been accused of emphasizing news about terrorism only if it affects American interests. This book examines the ways and the angles that Western media use to emphasize terrorist actions that challenge Western interests.

422. Hertsgaard, Mark (1985, December). TV, terrorism, and the White House. *American Film,* XI, 3: 38, 79–80.

Author examines the problems created for the White House by television coverage of the TWA hostage crisis. Author shows how White House staffers arranged photo opportunities to make President Ronald Reagan look good, and to control news broadcast of the crisis. Article includes analysis of confrontation between the Justice Department and the major news networks.

423. Heumann, J. (1980, Summer/Fall). U.S. network television: Melodrama and the Iranian crisis. *Middle East Review,* 51–55.

Central to this article is the question, Did the national network news organizations do an adequate job of informing the American public about what was happening in Iran before, during and after the American Embassy in Tehran was taken over? The author provides a persuasive response to this question. (Includes footnotes.)

424. Hewitt, Christopher (1992). Public's perspectives. In David L. Paletz & Alex P. Schmid (eds.), *Terrorism and the media* (pp. 170–207). Newbury Park, CA: Sage Publications, Inc.

See entry 615.

425. Hickey, Neil (1976, August 7). The medium in the middle. *TV Guide,* 10–13.

Author examines the argument about television coverage of terrorism, considering the opinion of experts who suggest that television coverage incites terrorists and the opposing view that censorship would make things even worse. The author suggests eight guidelines for television coverage of terrorism: 1) minimize the "how-to" aspects of terrorist acts so as not to encourage other terrorists; 2) downplay and omit the names of terrorist groups that claim credit for violent acts; 3) limit live coverage of kidnappings, skyjackings and other crimes involving hostages; 4) give proper emphasis to the inhuman and barbarous aspects of terrorist acts; 5) refrain from routinely interviewing terrorist leaders on camera; 6) give air time to terrorist acts only in realistic proportion to their objective news value; 7) emphasize the low likelihood of success in terrorist activities; and 8) provide documentaries and thoughtful analysis on the range of problems facing a community or country to reduce violence/terrorism.

426. _____ (1976, July 31). Terrorism and television. *TV Guide,* p. 4.
Article examines the relationship between terrorism and television news, and how television newspersons handled specific terrorist incidents. In one incident, the Baarder-Meinhof terrorist kidnapping of a West Berlin politician in February 1975, an editor describes how terrorists effectively hijacked a local television network.

427. Hocking, Jennifer J. (1992). Governments' perspectives. In David L. Paletz & Alex P. Schmid (eds.), *Terrorism and the media* (pp. 86–104). Newbury Park, CA: Sage Publications, Inc.
See entry 616.

428. Hoge, James W. (1982). The media and terrorism. In A.H. Miller (ed.), *Terrorism: The media and the law* (pp. 89–105), Dobbs Ferry, NY: Transnational Publishers.
Terrorist stories, depending on proximity, raise special but related questions. The first is a *strategic* question: Whether to cover the incident and, if so, how much emphasis to put on the story? The second is a *tactical* question: How to go about obtaining as much information as possible without further endangering hostages and officials? This article uses specific examples of terrorism to examine media's responsibilities in covering acts of terrorism. These examples suggest that media coverage of terrorism should be expanded not restricted. Author argues for voluntary media guidelines over enforced censorship. (Includes ten footnotes.)

429. Holden, Robert T. (1986, January). The contagiousness of aircraft hijacking. *American Journal of Sociology,* 91, 4: 874–904.
See entry 618.

430. Holz, Josephine, Cardinal, Eric, and Kerr, Dennis (1987, May 14–17). The *Achille Lauro:* A study in terror. Paper prepared for the 42nd annual conference of the American Association of Public Opinion Research. Hershey, PA.

This is an analysis of an NBC News Special on June 17, 1986, that examined the events surrounding the hijack of the Italian cruiseliner *Achille Lauro* in October 1985. The sample for this study consisted of adults recruited nationwide. The study found that terrorists are not humanized by news coverage; the sample was mixed as to whether viewers perceive greater risk and fear as a result of news coverage, and some believe that viewers identify with the victims of terrorism rather than with the terrorist.

431. Inciardi, James A. (1991). Narcoterrorism: A perspective and commentary. In R.J. Kelly and D.E.J. MacNamara (eds.), *Perspectives on deviance: Dominance, degradation and denigration* (pp. 89–103). Cincinnati, OH: Anderson Publishing Co.

Author captures in this chapter recent discussions of terrorism and drug trafficking have linked the two phenomena, often suggesting that they embody a conspiracy having both strategic and tactical goals.

432. Irvin, Cynthia L. (1992). Terrorists' perspectives: Interviews. In David L. Paletz & Alex P. Schmid (eds.), *Terrorism and the media* (pp. 62–85). Newbury Park, CA: Sage Publications, Inc.

See entry 621.

433. Iyengar, Shanto (1991). *Is anyone responsible? How television frames political issues.* Chicago, IL: University of Chicago Press, 195p.

Author examines television's role in defining our notion of political accountability: the way we understand the causes — and solutions — of major national problems. Covers areas that are essential to the media critic.

434. Jaehnig, Walter B. (1978). Journalists and terrorism: Captives of the libertarian tradition. *Indiana Law Journal,* 53, 4: 717–744.

See entry 622.

435. _____ (1982). Terrorism in Britain: The limits of free expression. In Abraham H. Miller (ed.), *Terrorism: The media and the law* (pp. 106–129). Dobbs Ferry, NY: Transnational Publishers.

This analysis examines the triangular media–law enforcement–government relationships in coverage of terrorism. Specific incidents of violence which result from the dispute between England and Northern Ireland are used to examine media self-regulation by the British Broadcasting Corporation. Against this backdrop is the 1974 Prevention of Terrorism Act and the 1979 agreement with London's Metropolitan Police regarding "sensitive" programming.

436. _____, Weaver, David H., and Fico, Frederick (1981, Winter). Reporting crime and fearing crime in three communities. *Journal of Communication,* 31, 1: 88–96.
See entry 133.

437. Jenkins, Brian M. (1981, February). Fighting terrorism: An enduring task. *The RAND Paper Series,* P-6585. Santa Monica, CA: The RAND Corporation, 8p.
See entry 625.

438. _____ (1981, June). The psychological implications of media-covered terrorism. *The RAND Paper Series,* P-6627. Santa Monica, CA: The RAND Corporation, 9p.
See entry 626.

439. _____ (1983). Research in terrorism: Areas of consensus, areas of ignorance. In B. Eichelman, D. Soskis & W. Reid (eds.), *Terrorism: Interdisciplinary perspectives* (p. 160). Washington, D.C.: American Psychiatric Association.
See entry 139.

440. _____ (1981, May). A strategy for combating terrorism. *The RAND Paper Series,* P. 6624. Santa Monica, CA: The RAND Corporation, 8p.
See entry 628.

441. _____ (1982, March). Talking to terrorists. *The RAND Paper Series,* P-6750. Santa Monica, CA: The RAND Corporation, 15p.
See entry 629.

442. Johnpoll, Bernard (1977). Terrorism and the media in the United States. In Yonah Alexander & Seymour M. Finger (eds), *Terrorism:*

Interdisciplinary Perspectives (pp. 157–165). London: McGraw-Hill Book Company (UK) Limited.

The author argues that no evidence exists to support the contention that the media in the United States or in most of the Western democratic nations overplayed terrorist activities. A careful perusal of American newspapers and radio wire-service logs would indicate that such coverage was kept to a minimum — possibly underplayed at times. (Includes nine notes.)

443. Jonathan Institute (1984, October). Lost in the terrorist theater. *Harper's Magazine,* 269, 163: 43–58.

See entry 631.

444. Jones, Juanita B., and Miller, Abraham H. (1979). The media and terrorist activity: Resolving the First Amendment dilemma. *The Ohio Northern University Law Review,* 6: 70–81.

The analysis in this article revolves around First Amendment freedoms and the invaluable role of a free press in a democratic society, and how they conflict with the basic human concern for saving lives. To support this contention, the authors give examples of terrorist activities and media reaction to such activities. In one particular episode involving the Hanafi Muslims, the press broadcast suggested that the police negotiators were preparing for assault, even though they were attempting to deliver food to the hostage takers. The author argues that gunfire might have erupted had the police not been able to convince Hanafi members that the press reports were incorrect. To deal with this problem and others like it, the authors suggest a cooperative arrangement under which the media would be allowed to participate in intensive training on how police negotiators learn how to engage suspects in conversations. The article also cites cases where the media were denied access to courtrooms, prisons, and ongoing terrorist operation areas, and relates how lower courts and the U.S. Supreme Court have ruled in these cases. For the most part, the government feels that press access and the public's right to know are incompatible to hostage negotiations. Lastly, the authors discuss some guidelines for regulation, and argue that the police are simply asking the "media [to] exercise responsible judgement, and that reporters in their zeal to pursue a story remember that their right to a story is not as important as a victim's right to survive." (Includes 41 references.)

445. Joyce, Edward M. (1986, Winter/Spring). Reporting of hostage crises: Who's in charge of television? *SAIS Review,* 6, 1: 169–176.

The author argues that television coverage of hostage crises has brought a new dimension to an old problem. Thanks to the technology of modern news reporting, a story unfolds hour by hour, day by day in full public view, bringing home to the American people as never before the helplessness and humiliation of their government in the face of apparently irrational, inhuman terrorist demands. Television seems such a ubiquitous feature of these episodes that the public has come to associate the attentions of the media apparatus to some degree with the motivation of the hostage-takers. Inevitably, allegations are made that television itself is a major contributor to the problem. It is claimed that television coverage of such incidents abets the terrorists' desires for publicity and manipulates the public's reactions. Many charge that, instead of being a mere observer, recorder, and disseminator of events around the world, television should be considered an active participant in them and a shaping force in determining the political response to them. Guidelines for coverage of terrorism and hostage-takings were drafted independently by a number of prominent news organizations, including UPI, the *Louisville Times and Courier-Journal, The Chicago Sun-Times,* and CBS News. The guidelines all attempt to shape responsible coverage while recognizing that there can be no specific self-executing rules for coverage of stories where the facts and circumstances will inevitably vary. (Includes seven footnotes.)

446. Kamen, Jeff (1990, December 17). A matter of live coverage and death. *Channels,* 10: 6.

The author argues that television news coverage of hostage-takers can endanger hostages, illustrating the point with an analysis of the hostage incident outside a hotel bar on September 17, 1990, in Berkeley, California.

447. Karkashian, J.E. (1977). Problems of international terrorism: Statement. Washington, DC: Department of State, Bureau of Public Affairs, Office of Media Services.

See entry 633.

448. Katz, Elihu (1980). Media events: The sense of occasion. *Studies in Visual Communication,* 6, 84–89.

See entry 145.

449. Kellner, Douglas (1992). *The Persian Gulf TV war.* Boulder, CO: Westview Press, 460p.

Examines television coverage of the Persian Gulf war, from its inception as a crisis to the war. Discusses how aspects of terrorism (i.e., environmental terrorism) were woven into television coverage of the crisis. Terroristic coverage was achieved through many dimensions, such as creating "fear of Iraq" in the minds of viewers, and projecting specific "racism against Arabs."

450. Kelly, James (1986, May 19). Caught by the camera: NBC's interview with a terrorist stirs up controversy. *Time,* 127, 20: 90.
    Author discusses NBC's exclusive interview with Abul Abbas, a Palestinian suspected in the murder of cruise ship passenger Leon Klinghoffer. Suggests that NBC's exclusive did not pass the test of whether the information from the interview was vital to grant protection to a fugitive. The controversy surrounding this interview is well documented here.

451. Kelly, Michael J. (1989). The seizure of the Turkish Embassy in Ottawa: Managing terrorism and the media. In Uriel Rosenthal, Michael T. Charles & P. 't-Hart (eds.), *Coping with crises: The management of disasters, riots, and terrorism* (pp. 117–138). Springfield, IL: Charles C. Thomas, Publishers.
    See entry 635.

452. Kent, Ian, and Nicholls, William (1977). The psychodynamics of terrorism. *Mental Health and Society,* 4, 1–2: 1–8.
    See entry 637.

453. Kidder, Rushworth M. (1986, May 16). Unmasking terrorism: Manipulation of the media. *The Christian Science Monitor.* 18–20.
    See entry 638.

454. _____ (1990). Unmasking terrorism: Manipulation of the media. In Bernard Schechterman & M. Slann (eds.), *Violence and terrorism 90/91* [Annual Editions] (pp. 111–115). Guilford, CT: The Dushkin Publishing Group, Inc.
    See entry 638.

455. Klein, Maurice M. (1989). Terrorists and the media: A social learning approach. In Jo Groebel and Jeffrey H. Goldstein (eds.), *Terrorism: Psychological perspectives.* Series of psychobiology (pp. 85–117). Sevilla, Spain: Publicaciones de la Universidad de Sevilla.
    See entry 638.

456. Krauthammer, Charles (1985, July 15). Looking evil dead in the eye. *Time,* 126, 2: 80.
See entry 642.

457. Larson, James F. (1986, Autumn). Television and U.S. foreign policy: The case of the Iran hostage crisis. *Journal of Communication,* 36, 4: 108–127.
A number of general propositions about TV and foreign policy provide the backdrop against which U.S. television network news coverage of Iran between 1972 and 1981 — and especially during the hostage crisis — can be interpreted. Iran is both a compelling case study and a major landmark in our understanding of the structural relationship between television news and U.S. foreign policy. One focal point of such a study is the 444-day crisis involving U.S. hostages in Tehran, beginning with their seizure on November 4, 1979. This study explores what the Iran experience either modifies or confirms about our knowledge of the relationship between television and U.S. foreign policy. (Includes one figure, one table of data, and 36 references.)

458. Lent, John A. (1977, Winter). Foreign news in the American media. *Journal of Communication,* 27, 1: 46–50.
See entry 169.

459. Levy, Rudolfo. (1985, Oct.-Dec.). Terrorism and the mass media. *Military Intelligence,* 34–38.
It is evident that terrorists have expended considerable effort to manipulate the media in all five of its basic functions (Informational, Judgmental, Educational, Interactional, and Recreational). Carlos Marighella, Brazilian philosopher, author, and leader of a terrorist organization until his death in 1969, described media manipulation strategy as an aggressive psychological warfare technique which attempts to place the government in the position of always having to defend itself. According to Marighella's Manual of the Urban Guerrilla, terrorist media manipulation strategy is divided into three phases: 1) Phase I, primary; 2) Phase II, secondary; and 3) Phase III, final.

460. Long, Kenneth J. (1990, Fall). Understanding and teaching the semantics of terrorism: An alternative perspective. *Perspectives on Political Science,* 19, 4: 203–208.
See entry 178.

461. Marcellini, Mario and Avallone, Franco (1978). *Il ruolo dell' informazione in una situazione di emergenza — 16 Maezo 1978: il rapi-*

mento di Aldo Moro [The role of information in an emergency situation – March 16, 1978: The kidnapping of Aldo Moro]. Rome: RAI Radiotelevisione Italiana, Verifica Programmi Trasmessi.

This is a content analysis of broadcast news reports of Italian and foreign press about the kidnap of Aldo Moro, president of the Christian Democratic Party, on March 16, 1978, by the Red Brigade.

462. Martin, L. John (1985). The media's role in international terrorism. *Terrorism: An International Journal,* 8, 2: 127–146.

Terrorism, like propaganda, is a form of persuasive communication. Like propaganda, it is a pejorative term. Some have referred to it as propaganda of the deed. It is hard to define because its definition depends on whether one agrees with the message and the political alignment of those who perpetrate political violence. Consequently, acts of violence by those we agree with are not labeled terrorism. After considering various definitions and examples of what is and is not terrorism, this paper looks at the symbiotic relationship that exists between terrorism and mass media. Each exploits the other and terrorism has no meaning without media coverage in this age of mass communications. Terrorists use mass media for both tactical and strategic purposes, the author argues. While the mass media do, generally, cover terrorism at a rate of at least nine incidents per day worldwide, according to a pilot study undertaken for this paper, the press uses the term "terrorist" sparingly, preferring such neutral terms as guerrilla, rebel, and paramilitary, or using no value-laden adjectives at all. (Each country in the study, except Egypt, did have its pet terrorists.) This raises the question of the effectiveness of terrorism; the press gives terrorists publicity but often omits the propaganda message that terrorists would like to see accompanying reports of their exploits, thus reducing terrorism to mere crime or sabotage. (Includes one table, 67 notes, and 21 references.)

463. _____, and Drazin, Joseph (1991). Broadcast gatekeepers and terrorism. In Yonah Alexander & Robert G. Picard (eds.), *In the camera's eye: News coverage of terrorist events* (pp. 121–130). New York: Brassey's (U.S.) Inc.

The author interviewed seven television journalists (two editors, two producers, two correspondents, and one anchorman) to determine how they viewed terrorism as a news event. Journalists from ABC, CNN, and PBS constituted this pool. Twelve topics were examined, yielding different responses, yet a degree of unanimity emerged in the belief that media coverage of terrorism serves society. (Includes 14 references and 12 notes.)

464. Mazur, Allan (1982, June). Bomb threats and the mass media: Evidence for a theory of suggestion. *American Sociological Review,* 47, 2: 407-411.
See entry 653.

465. Media Guideline Document (1982). National Advisory Committee on Criminal Justice Standards and Goals, Report of the Task Force on Disorders and Terrorism, 1976. In Abraham H. Miller (ed.), *Terrorism: The media and the law* (pp. 153-160). Dobbs Ferry, NY: Transaction Publishers, Inc.
See entry 654.

466. Media reporting of terrorism implicated as accessory to crimes. (1977, July). *Gallup Opinion Index,* No. 144, pp. 410-418.
See entry 655.

467. Meeske, Milan D., and Javaheri, Mohamad H. (1982, Winter). Network television coverage of the Iranian hostage crisis. *Journalism Quarterly,* 59, 641-645.
The goal of this study was to analyze the networks' (ABC, CBS and NBC) coverage of the story by answering the following questions: What difference in coverage can be noted among the three American networks? Was there bias toward either the Iranian or United States government in the networks' coverage? The data provide adequate answers to these questions. (Includes two tables and 11 footnotes.)

468. Midgley, Sarah, and Rice, Virginia (eds.) (1984). *Terrorism and the Media in the 1980s* (Conference Proceedings). Washington, D.C.: The Media Institute and Institute for the Studies in International Terror.
See entry 657.

469. Miller, Abraham H. (1980). *Terrorism and hostage negotiations.* Boulder, CO: Westview Press, 135p.
See entry 195.

470. _____ (1979). Terrorism and the media: A dilemma. *Terrorism* 3, 79-89.
The issue of the media and terrorism is a complex one. It raises interesting issues: concerns for First Amendment freedoms and concerns

with the invaluable role of the press in a democratic society are pitted against humanitarian concerns for saving lives. This is not an abstract conflict; it continually manifests itself in real-life situations where human life is imminently at stake. The author suggests that the problem admits neither easy answers nor complex solutions but rather complex choices. The exercise of any one of these choices will leave some constituencies dissatisfied. (Includes 15 notes.)

471. _____ (1983). Terrorism and the media: Observations from the American and British experiences. In P.J. Montana & G.S. Roukis (eds.), *Managing terrorism: Strategies for the corporate executive* (pp. 91–107). Quorum Books.

This chapter explores the relations between law enforcement and the media during terrorist incidents. Author argues that among the by-products of contemporary terrorism has been conflict between law enforcement and the media. This is especially true in situations where law enforcement and the media confront each other when terrorist operations are in progress. For their part, the media have been concerned about getting firsthand, on-the-spot coverage of news as it is being made. That kind of coverage calls for relatively free access to the scene where news occurs. In contrast, ongoing terrorist scenes usually elicit a police response of control and containment. (Include 23 notes.)

472. _____ (1982). Terrorism, the media, and law enforcement: An introduction. In Abraham H. Miller (ed.), *Terrorism: The media and the law* (pp. 1–10). Dobbs Ferry, NY: Transaction Publishers, Inc. See entry 661.

473. _____ (1982). Terrorism, the media, and the law: A discussion of the issues. In Abraham H. Miller (ed.), *Terrorism: The media and the law* (pp. 13–50). Dobbs Ferry, NY: Transnational Publishers, Inc.

This chapter examines the problems in news gathering and media portrayal of terrorism. The author also deals with the media as uncritical reflector of government opinion; examines the differences in perspectives between local law enforcement and the media; deals with some of the legal controls on the media, and how such controls may create problems for democracies. Included in this discussion is how the police view the media and the areas of disagreement. While legislative response to media coverage has been debated, the author's discussion of these issues illuminates reader understanding of terrorism in the news media. (Includes 73 footnotes.)

474. _____ (ed.) (1982). *Terrorism: The media and the law*. Dobbs Ferry, NY: Transnational Publishers, Inc., 221p.

There are clear indications that balancing of conflicting social values and social responsibilities against one another is always difficult. Under the stress and drama of a terrorist operation in progress where life is at risk, such balance appears impossible. The editor assembled works in this volume that illustrate how the consequence of not finding that balancing point can be the loss of life. Authors believe that only through strong dialogue, based on mutual respect and understanding, can the media and law enforcement begin even to attempt to resolve these issues. It is to this end that the papers presented here were conceived and written. (Includes two appendices, bibliography, and index.)

475. Montgomery, Louise F. (1991). Media victims: Reactions to coverage of incidents of international terrorism involving Americans. In Yonah Alexander & Robert G. Picard (eds.), *In the camera's eye: News coverage of terrorist events* (pp. 58–64). New York: Brassey (U.S.), Inc.

An analysis of media victims in terrorism coverage offers prescriptive measures for television, radio, newspaper, and magazine reporters and editors on how to improve coverage. Author's analysis of 61 respondents (21 victims of incidents of international terrorism, 34 family members, and six others involved in the incidents) reveals how profoundly they were affected by the media. Includes recommendations for improving media coverage of incidents of international terrorism. (Includes one note.)

476. Moreland, Richard L., and Berbaum, Michael L. (1982). Terrorism and the mass media: A researcher's bibliography. In Abraham H. Miller (ed.), *Terrorism: The media and the law* (pp. 191–215). New York: Transnational Publishers.

See entry 665.

477. Mosse, Hilde L. (1978). The media and terrorism. In Marius H. Livingston with Lee Bruce Kress & Marie G. Wanek (eds.), *International terrorism in the contemporary world* (pp. 282–286). Westport, CT: Greenwood Press.

Do media reports about terrorism create specific impressions? Author suggests that one would be unable to understand terrorism without being aware of the role played by the mass media in violence conditioning. Although it is a background role, the author believes that the activities of the media have a far-reaching implication and sometimes are of crucial importance. (Includes six notes.)

478. _____ (1977, December). Terrorism and the media. *New York State Journal of Medicine,* 77, 14: 2294–2296.

Author discusses F. Wertham's work on the mass media, which indicates that television mainly provides audiovisual conditioning to violence. Natural and spontaneous actions of children have been moved toward cynicism, callousness, and indifference. Argues that the magnetic pull of violence has led to increased terrorism in the schools.

479. Murphy, Patrick V. (1982). The police, the news media, and the coverage of terrorism. In Abraham H. Miller (ed.), *Terrorism: The media and the law* (pp. 76–86). Dobbs Ferry, NY: Transnational Publishers, Inc.

This paper discusses the practical problems the police encounter when dealing with the news media during terrorist events. Although the subject is a vivid one, of the many concerns of American police leadership today, it probably takes low priority. Teenage vandalism, convenience-store robberies, newly formed and sometimes insurgent police unions, and the fiscal crunch affecting all municipal services appear to be more pressing problems than media coverage of terrorist events. (Includes four footnotes.)

480. National News Council, The (1982). Paper on terrorism. In Abraham H. Miller (ed.), *Terrorism: The media and the law* (pp. 133–147). Dobbs Ferry, NY: Transaction Publishers, Inc.

See entry 669.

481. Nimmo, Dan, and Combs, James E. (1989). *Nightly horrors: Crisis coverage in television network news.* Knoxville, TN: University of Tennessee Press, 216p.

See entry 210.

482. O'Neill, Michael J. (1986). *Terrorist spectaculars: Should TV coverage be curbed?* New York: Priority Press Publications, 109p.

A critical analysis of how terrorism is covered on television. The author suggests that television coverage of terrorism may have encouraged more airplane hijackings and that terrorists are basically assured of a segment in the evening newscast. Also, the author examines the dilemmas posed by television coverage of terrorism; television, he argues, is overwhelmingly the dominant medium in terrorism coverage. (Includes seven chapters and notes.)

483. O'Sullivan, John (1986). Media publicity causes terrorism. In B. Szumski (ed.), *Terrorism: Opposing viewpoints* (pp. 69–74). St. Paul, MN: Greenhaven Press.

The author enunciates the belief that terrorists need and do thrive on media attention. This article suggests that the mass media exaggerate terrorist situations, thereby causing public apprehension and panic. (Includes one drawing.)

484. Paddock, Alfred H. (1984). Psychological operations, special operations, and U.S. strategy. In Frank R. Barnett, Hugh B. Tovar & Richard H. Schultz (eds.), *Special operations in U.S. strategy* (pp. 231–251). New York: National Strategy Information Center.

See entry 675.

485. Paletz, David L., and Boiney, John (1992). Researchers' perspectives. In David L. Paletz & Alex P. Schmid (eds.), *Terrorism and the media* (pp. 6–28). Newbury Park, CA: Sage Publications, Inc.

See entry 676.

486. _____, and Schmid, Alex P. (eds.) (1992). *Terrorism and the media*. Newbury Park, CA: Sage Publications, Inc., 250p.

See entry 678.

487. _____, and Tawney, Laura L. (1992). Broadcast organizations' perspectives. In David L. Paletz & Alex P. Schmid (eds.), *Terrorism and the media* (pp. 105–110). Newbury Park, CA: Sage Publications, Inc.

Based on the assumption that the media may be influencing the behavior of terrorists, the reactions and responses of government officials, and the views of the public, the authors sought to ascertain the codes or guidelines used by media organizations in covering or depicting terrorists and acts and incidents of terrorism. A questionnaire was sent to 80 broadcast organizations around the world. With approximately a 40 percent response rate, five levels of guidelines emerged: 1) no rules for covering terrorism (no guidelines, codes, or even approaches); 2) no rules, but philosophies or general policies about how to cover terrorism; 3) no rules for terrorism, but general programming rules for covering of violence and civil disorders; 4) standardized guidelines; and 5) detailed rules, codes, guidelines. Concludes that the need to maintain credibility takes precedence in crisis coverage.

488. _____, and Vinson, C. Danielle (1992). Introduction. In David L. Paletz & Alex P. Schmid (eds.), *Terrorism and the media* (pp. 1-5). Newbury Park, CA: Sage Publications, Inc.
See entry 679.

489. _____, Ayanian, John Z. and Fozzard, Peter A. (1981). Terrorism on TV news: The IRA, the FALN, and the Red Brigades. In William C. Adams (ed.), *Television coverage of international affairs* (pp. 143-165). Norwood, NJ: Ablex.

This is a content analysis of stories broadcast during evening news by ABC, CBS, and NBC, from July 1, 1977, to June 30, 1979, about activities by the IRA, the FALN, and the Red Brigades. The study also presents a detailed profile of each terrorist group. This analysis, which includes explanations, offers specific suggestions and recommendations for media operatives to consider in their coverage of terrorist incidents.

490. Palmerton, Patricia R. (1989, November). The reign of confusion: ABC and the "Crisis in Iran." Paper presented at the Annual Meeting of the Speech Communication Association (75th, San Francisco, CA, November 18-21, 1989), 31p. (ED 314767)

With approximately 50 percent of ABC's actual broadcast transcripts, the author examines the news series entitled "Crisis in Iran: America Held Hostage," broadcast between November 8, 1979, and December 7, 1979. With a rhetorical critical analysis, the author argues that confusion was the predominant characteristic in ABC's description of events in Iran. For example, the author says, "President Jimmy Carter and the Ayatollah Khomeini were portrayed by ABC as potentially able to bring order to the situation but failed to do so." On the other hand, most Americans were described as "frustrated" and "outraged," and "their reactions shown as contrasting sharply with the Carter Administration's measured approach, which was portrayed as being based on principles and high morals." The analysis suggests that ABC's coverage was "a test of strength, image, and power of the United States"; that the event had more than symbolic value for the United States; and that the event also had more symbolic value than for their pragmatic effects. Media labeling of events was also a unit of analysis in this study. The author suggests that attempts to label events based upon preconceived ideas, expectations, and limited knowledge prevented Americans from seeing the realities of this situation. (Includes 85 notes.)

491. _____ (1988, Spring). The rhetoric of terrorism and media response to the "Crisis in Iran." *Western Journal of Speech Communication,* 52, 2: 105–121.

This paper examines television news coverage of the first days of the 1979 Iranian hostage crisis. Critical analysis of this coverage shows a pattern which reinforces the terrorist strategy by focusing causation for the crisis on institutional targets, and suggesting that military intervention would re-establish control. This study supports the argument that the rhetorical impact of terrorism occurs in large measure through the response of others to the terrorist action, in particular, media portrayals of terrorist events. (Includes 45 endnotes.)

492. _____ (1985). Terrorism and institutional targets as portrayed by news providers. Paper submitted to the Speech Communication Association, Mass Communication Division.

This study examines how the news media portray terrorism aimed at government institutions and representatives. The analysis includes "CBS Evening News" coverage of the taking of American hostages in Iran from 1979 to 1981. Results indicate that news reports suggest the United States' actions were responsible for what happened to the hostages.

493. _____ (1983). Terrorism and the media: A call for rhetorical criticism. Paper presented to the Speech Communication Association, Mass Communication Division.

The author analyzes the interaction between the media and terrorism. Concludes that because terrorism is a rhetorical endeavor, the rhetoric of terrorism is created in part by the response of the news media.

494. Pearlstein, Richard M. (1991). Tuned-in Narcissus: The gleam in the camera's eye. In Yonah Alexander & Robert G. Picard (eds.), *In the camera's eye: News coverage of terrorist events* (pp. 49–57). New York: Brassey's (U.S.), Inc.

See entry 680.

495. Peretz, D. (1982). *Reporting Lebanon the Christian way: The media in the United States on Lebanon: Part I, A media source guide, issues for the '80s.* New York: Council on International and Public Affairs, 14p.

This guide provides journalists with a critical analysis of U.S. media coverage of Lebanon and the underlying issues which make it such a difficult story to cover. Central to this guide is an article, "Reporting

Lebanon the Christian Way," which details specific examples of over-simplification, misinformation, and biased selectivity on the part of the media in their coverage of the missile crisis in Lebanon during 1981. The guide also contains annotated listings of universities and research centers and non-academic information sources on the Middle East. Includes names and addresses of U.S.-based scholars informed about Lebanon.

496. Pfaff, William (1990). Terrorists call the shots—On front page. In Bernard Schechterman & M. Slann (eds.), *Violence and terrorism 90/91* [Annual Editions] (p. 121). Guilford, CT: The Dushkin Publishing Group, Inc.
   See entry 682.

497. _____ (1986, September 19). Terrorists call the shots—On front page. *Miami Herald.*
   See entry 682.

498. Picard, Robert G. (undated). The conundrum of news coverage of terrorism. Terrorism and the News Media Research Project, paper No. 1, Louisiana State University.
   See entry 684.

499. _____ (1991c). Journalists as targets and victims of terrorism. In Yonah Alexander & Robert G. Picard (eds.), *In the camera's eye: News coverage of terrorist events* (pp. 65–71). New York: Brassey's (U.S.), Inc.
   See entry 685.

500. _____ (1991a). The journalist's role in coverage of terrorist events. In A. Odasuo Alali & Kenoye K. Eke (eds.), *Media coverage of terrorism: Methods of diffusion* (pp. 40–48). Newbury Park, CA: Sage Publications, Inc.
   This analysis deals with the roles journalists assume when covering terrorist events. The author identifies four rhetorical traditions used by journalists in conveying news and how these affect the meanings attached by audiences. These rhetorical traditions are: 1) the information tradition which emphasizes factual information and documentation of events; 2) sensationalism tradition which is presented in ways to emphasize alarm or threat; 3) feature story tradition which gives a personal perspective by focusing on individuals as heroes or villains; and

4) didactic tradition which stresses explanation and education on how and why (authorities fall into this category). Picard further defines journalists as rhetorical amplifiers and arbitrators; that is, they gain audience attention by providing the platform by which messages are conveyed, interpreted, and compared to government versus terrorist descriptions of terrorist events. The author further suggests that journalists create rhetoric whenever they report terrorist events and that the rhetorical tradition employed determines the nature of the rhetorical message received by the audience. (Includes one table of data and 22 references.)

501. _____ (1993). *Media portrayals of terrorism: Functions and meaning of news coverage.* Ames, IA: Iowa State University Press, 147pp.
See entry 687.

502. _____ (1991b). News coverage as the contagion of terrorism: Dangerous charges back by dubious science. In A. Odasuo Alali & Kenoye K. Eke (eds.), *Media coverage of terrorism: Methods of diffusion* (pp. 49-62). Newbury Park, CA: Sage Publications, Inc.
See entry 688.

503. _____, and Sheets, Rhonda S. (1986). *Terrorism and the news media research bibliography.* Columbia, S.C.: Association for Education in Journalism and Mass Communication.
See entry 693.

504. _____, and Sheets, Rhonda S. (1986). *Terrorism and the news media research bibliography.* Boston, MA: Terrorism and the News Media Research Project, Emerson College.
This is a bibliography on terrorism and the news media. Places special emphasis on how terrorism is treated in the news.

505. Quester, George H. (1986). Cruise ship terrorism and the media. *Political Communication and Persuasion,* 4: 355-370.
This article focuses on the number of hostages, the range and endurance of the transportation vehicle, the possibilities of disappearing into the unknown, "de facto torture" in the physical situation of the hostages, ease of the media access, and the novelty of terrorist attacks on cruise ships. The author argues that "the factor of the number of human beings involved as potential hostages doesn't hand the terrorist

so much to an advantage." Basically, despite extensive media coverage, the public would not find the story of a hijacked cruise ship highly compelling. Terrorists failed to realize that modern surveillance systems make it difficult for a ship to disappear. The author argues that because cruise ships are designed to serve everyone, they do not allow for a "de facto torture." The author suggests that because cruise ships are not easily accessible, the media would be caught off guard because television cameras are one of the most valuable assets for any venture in terrorism and hostage taking. (Includes four references.)

506. Rabbie, J.M. (1989). Terrorism and the media: A social psychological approach. In Jo Groebel and Jeffrey H. Goldstein (eds.), *Terrorism: Psychological perspectives.* Series of psychobiology (pp. 119–133). Sevilla, Spain: Publicaciones de la Universidad de Seville.

See entry 696.

507. Rabe, Robert L. (1982). The journalist and the hostage: How their rights can be balanced. In Abraham H. Jiller (ed.), *Terrorism: The media and the law* (pp. 69–75). Dobbs Ferry, NY: Transnational Publishers, Inc.

The author examines the contagion belief in media coverage of terrorist incidents. Author suggests that when terrorist activities are glorified with extensive news coverage, an event is projected as an attraction for others to emulate. When this happens, terrorism has truly made television a pawn in the great game of propaganda. (Includes nine footnoes.)

508. Rada, S.E. (1985, Fall). Trans-national terrorism as public relations. *Public Relations Review,* 11, 3: 26–33.

The author suggests that modern terrorism and public relations share a symbiotic, if different, relationship with the mass media. Both share the objectives of commanding attention, delivering a message, and influencing public opinion. Though some of the similarities are compelling, are they sufficient to equate terrorism with public relations? Public relations is a process that may be invoked by anyone for any purpose. But in spite of some similarities between terrorist techniques with the media and persuasive public relations campaigns, what ultimately separates the two is the social responsibility of the practitioner and the social utility of the end. Terrorism seeks legitimacy through self-definition, not through the mandate of society, the author asserts. (Includes 19 references.)

509. RAI Radiotelevisione Italiana, Verifica dei Programmi Tranmessi (1982). *Terrorismo e TV: Italia, Gran Bretagna, Germania Occidentale* [Terror and TV: Italy, Great Britain, West Germany], 2 vols., Rome: RAI.

This two-volume study examines how terror and terrorism are portrayed on television in Italy, Great Britain, and West Germany. The analysis include descriptive and comparative studies of terrorism and the news media.

510. Rath, Claus, and Jacobsen, Dagmar (1982). Produzione di immagini sul terrorismo alla televisione tedesca occidentale [Production of images on terrorism in the TV of West Germany]. In RAI Radiotelevisione Italiana, *Terrorismo e TV,* Vol. 2. Rome: RAI, Verifica dei Programmi Trasmessi.

Examines research on television portrayal of terrorism as broadcast in West Germany from May to October 1981. The analyses of these programs suggest a perspective for determining the image of terrorism as presented on television.

511. Revzin, Philip (1977, March 14). A reporter looks at media role in terror threats. *The Wall Street Journal,* p. 16.

See entry 699.

512. Ronci, Donatella (1982). Terrorismo e sistema politico nel rotocalco televisivo. In RAI Radiotelevisione Italiana, *Terrorismo e TV,* VOL. 1, *Italia. Immagini del terrorismo nel rotocalco televisivo.* Rome: RAI, Verifica del Programmi Trasmessi.

Examines the relationship between terrorism, information, and power. Explains how institutional structures and power are represented when media mediate portrayals.

513. Rosenfeld, S.S. (1975, November 21). How should the media handle deeds of terrorism? *Washington Post,* p. A19.

The author examines how the media should handle terrorism. While the author acknowledges the dilemma of his loyalty to his profession, he suggests that journalists should not cover terrorists if the purpose of coverage is to send messages for them. While the author is not talking about legislative censorship, he urges his colleagues to limit their coverage of terrorists. The author recommends that reporters stay away from the psychotic violence aspects of coverage and rather report on what he calls "transnational terror."

143

514. Rosenthal, A.M. (1987, January 27). The next hijacking. *The New York Times,* p. A25.

Examines the proposition that the media may be responsible for escalation of terrorist events. Argues that terrorism is caused more by weak-willed governments than by the media.

515. Rubin, Jeffrey Z., and Friedland, Nehemia (1986, March). Theater of terror. *Psychology Today,* 20, 3: 18–28.

Terrorists may explode on the scene in Tehran, Beirut or Latin America, but they soon take the show on the road via television or transportation technology, as with the hijacking of a TWA jet in Athens and the abortive takeover of the Italian liner *Achille Lauro.* For today's terrorists, all the world is indeed a stage, which may be an apt metaphor to help us come to grips with and perhaps devise methods of dealing with political terrorism. A political terrorist's first job is to get and hold the attention of the audience, the authors argue. We typically think of terrorists as having short-term goals, such as obtaining the release of prisoners or some governmental admission of guilt, but their most important objective is to attract an audience and delilver a message. (Includes eight images.)

516. Sanoff, Alvin P. (1986, April 28). TV brings home terror's message. *U.S. News & World Reports,* 100, 160: 29.

Suggests that the televised image of terrorism mobilizes public perception and support for attacks against those suspected of terrorist acts against U.S. citizens. The Libyan raid by the Reagan administration is an example that dominates this discussion.

517. Scanlon, Joseph (1984). Domestic terrorism and the media: Live coverage of crime. *Canadian Police College Journal,* 8, 2: 154–178.

Author analyzes two cases of hostage-takings in Canada and the role of the media in reporting these incidents. Author suggests that these cases indicate why police must pay particular attention to media coverage of terrorism.

518. Schlesinger, Philip (1981). Terrorism, the media, and the liberal-democratic state: A critique of the orthodoxy. *Social Research,* 48: 74–99.

This article is a study of how the media report terrorism in Western democracies. The paper is divided into three sections. The first section attempts to define terrorism in relation to the idea of legitimate political activity and the role of media in assigning legitimacy. In the second section the ideas of official and semi-official governmental view of terrorism and media coverage of terrorism are discussed. For this section, the United Kingdom control over media is examined. The essay concludes with a section devoted to encouraging further study into entire western area. A comparison between specific governmental systems in relation to their control of media and the causes of political violence within those governmental systems is the key to understanding and establishing an effective terrorism coverage policy for the media. (Includes 49 references.)

519. _____, Murdock, Graham, and Elliot, Philip. (1983). *Televising terrorism: Political violence in popular culture.* London: Comedia Publishing.

The authors say television examines terrorism from different perspectives. This book analyzes the different ways television covers terrorism and the problems it poses for liberal democracies.

520. Schmid, Alex P. (1992). Editors' perspective. In David L. Paletz & Alex P. Schmid (eds.), *Terrorism and the media* (pp. 111-136). Newbury Park, CA: Sage Publications, Inc.

See entry 708.

521. _____, and de Graaf, Janny (1982). *Violence as communication: Insurgent terrorism and the Western news media.* SAGE Publications, Inc., 283p.

This book is the first extended study to examine the relationship between insurgent terrorism and the Western news media in a comprehensive way. There have been a few studies that deal with individual cases (such as the press reaction to the Moro abduction in Italy) or with particular aspects, but no attempt was made to link the rise of modern insurgent terrorism to the rise of the mass media, as this work attempts to do. Given the paucity of previous research in the field, this study cannot be anything more than exploratory. Nevertheless, the authors have aimed at developing a framework for analysis that differs significantly from the existing approaches to explain the recent rise in terroristic activity. (Includes five chapters, one appendix, notes, selected bibliography, and 16 tables of data and diagrams.)

522. Shaheen, Jack G. (1984). *The TV Arab.* Bowling Green, Ohio: Bowling Green State University Popular Press.

Portrayals of Arabs during eight seasons of television shows are examined. Author identifies four myths about Arabs: they are all very wealthy, they are barbaric and uncultured, they are sex maniacs, and they revel in acts of terrorism.

523. Signorielli, Nancy, and Gerbner, George (1988). *Violence and terror in the mass media: An annotated bibliography.* Westport, CT: Greenwood Press, 233p.
See entry 711.

524. Silj, Alessandro. (1982). *Stampa, radio e TV di fronte al processo Moro, ai casi La Torre, Delcogliano, Cirillo e ad altre storie di terrorismo* [Press, radio and television before the Moro trial, the cases of La Torre, Delcogliano, Cirillo, and other stories of terrorism]. Rome: RAI Radiotelevisione Italiana, Verifica dei Programmi Trasmessi.
See entry 713.

525. Sloan, Stephen (1978). International terrorism: Academic quest, operational art and policy implications. *Journal of International Affairs,* 32, 1: 1–6.
See entry 264.

526. Sommer, Michael, and Sommer, Heidi (1982). The project of media coverage of terrorism: A summary of national surveys and other investigations, 1977–79. In Abraham H. Miller (ed.), *Terrorism: The media and the law* (pp. 161–187). Dobbs Ferry, NY: Transaction Publishers, Inc.
See entry 716.

527. Spates, C.R., Little, P., Stock, H.V., and Goncalces, J.S. (1990). Intervention in events of terrorism. In L.J. Herzberg, G.F. Ostrum & J.R. Fields (eds.), *Violent behavior, Vol. 1: Assessment & intervention* (pp. 185–199). Costa Mesa, CA: PMA Publishing Corp.
See entry 270.

528. Surlin, S.H., et al. (1987, May). TV Network news: A Canadian-American comparison. Paper presented at the Joint Meeting of the Canadian Communication Association, the International Communication Association, and the Quebec Communication Research Association (Montreal, Quebec, Canada), 24p.
This study investigates the difference between television news pro-

gramming in Canada and the United States in three areas: ownership (public versus private), lanaguage (French versus English), and nation of origin (Canada versus the United States), in order to determine basic differences in the network television news content that Canadian viewers may experience, depending on their news source. Content analysis of randomly constructed network newscasts from the final three weeks of October 1985 indicate that: 1) regardless of which television news they watch, Canadian and American viewers do not receive in-depth reports of events; 2) Canadians viewing American network news will be exposed to virtually nothing about events in Canada; 3) in both countries, international news reporting tends to follow the same general criteria for newsworthiness (armed conflict, terrorism, etc.); 4) politics and economics receive disproportionate attention in the news; 5) news reporters and network anchors are predominantly male; and 6) ownership has no impact on news agenda, or issue of coverage. (Includes data tables.)

529. Terrell, Robert, and Ross, Kristina (1991). The voluntary guidelines' threat to U.S. press freedom. In Yonah Alexander & Robert G. Picard (eds.), *In the camera's eye: News coverage of terrorist events* (pp. 75–102). New York: Brassey's (U.S.), Inc.
   See entry 720.

530. Terrorism: What is behind it and why? (1986, January 8). *AWAKE,* 68, 1: 6–10.
   See entry 284.

531. *Terrorism and the media* (1979). Report of Conference Proceedings. *Terrorism,* 2, 3: 59–60.
   See entry 722.

532. *Terrorism and the media* (1980). International Seminar held in Florence, Italy, 1978. Rome: International Press Institute with Affari Esteri.
   See entry 721.

533. Totten, Sam (1986a, Fall). A selective annotated bibliography on terrorism. *Social Science Record,* 24, 1: 40–46.
   See entry 723.

534. _____ (1986b, Fall). A selective chronology of terrorist and counter-terrorist incidents. *Social Science Record,* 24, 1: 47–50.

Author details 56 terrorist events which were covered in the world press. Includes bombing raids on Libya by the United States and Palestinian hijacking of an El Al airliner. Covers events from July 22, 1966, to April 5, 1986.

535. United States Congress. House Committee on Foreign Affairs. Subcommittee on Europe and the Middle East (1986). Hearing before the Subcommittee on Europe and the Middle East of the Committee on Foreign Affairs, House of Representative, Ninety-ninth Congress, First Session, July 30, 1985. Washington, D.C.: Supt. of Documents, U.S. GPO.
Deals with the media, diplomacy, and terrorism in the Middle East.

536. U.S. Department of State (1982). Guidelines for United States Government spokespersons during terrorist incidents. In Abraham H. Miller (ed.), *Terrorism: The media and the law* (pp. 148–152). Dobbs Ferry, NY: Transaction Publishers, Inc.
See entry 726.

537. Viera, John D. (1991). Terrorism at the BBC: The IRA on British television. In A. Odasuo Alali & Kenoye K. Eke (eds.), *Media coverage of terrorism: Methods of diffusion* (pp. 73–85). Newbury Park, CA: SAGE.
Author examines the relationship of terrorism and television within the context of the British government's responses to media coverage of Irish Republican Army's (IRA) "terrorist" activities. The author argues that one function of the British Broadcasting Corporation (BBC) is to supply information. However, given that the government's "non-exposure" position amounts to the desire to have no terrorists on television unless it is clearly "anti-terrorist" footage, the following predictions are drawn: 1) coverage of the IRA and Northern Ireland is bound to be biased towards the violent aftermath of terrorist activities, and 2) journalists risk being categorized as participants in the terrorist cause (or at least furthering it), rather than as objective reporters of it, for any coverage not explicitly anti-terrorist or failing to reveal the horrors of terrorist acts. These expectations are confirmed in the study. (Includes 23 references.)

538. Walker, Robert (1993, April 5). Most Muslims aren't terrorists but do we make that clear? *The Gazette* (Montreal), p. B3.
See entry 727.

539. Wardlaw, Grant (1982). *Political terrorism*. London: Cambridge University Press.

See entry 728.

540. Weimann, Gabriel (1987). Conceptualizing the effects of mass mediated terrorism. *Political Communication and Persuasion,* 4, 213–216.

In summer 1985, a TWA plane was hijacked by Shiite terrorists to Beirut creating what turned out to be one of the most impressive spectacles of the mass-mediated "theater of terror." After the event the American media were blamed for fanning the crisis atmosphere, giving the terrorists the publicity they craved, abetting the terrorists by reporting U.S. military movements, holding a brutal competition among themselves to get exclusive footage or interviews, harassing the hostages' families, negotiating directly with the terrorists, milking the hostages still held by the terrorists for political and ideological declarations, and propagandizing the terrorists' anti–U.S. and anti–Israeli messages. The resulting debate that followed these accusations illustrates the lingering argument regarding media and terrorism. It is also captured in the argument that the media are the terrorists' best friends. Also, the author examines the ideological loadings of definitions and arguments that are combined with confused interpretations of media effects and public opinion to yield an endless futile debate. This paper conceptualizes the basic effects of mass-mediated terrorism by relating media effects studies to the case of terrorism and public opinion. (Includes 12 notes.)

541. _____ (1987, Winter). Media events: The case of international terrorism. *Journal of Broadcasting and Electronic Media,* 31, 1: 21–39.

An analysis that highlights the uniqueness of terrorism as an electronic media drama and how its framework compares with those factors that typically are associated with other varieties of electronic media drama: those memorable programs that capture the attention of a nation or of the world, such as the Olympic games or the U.S. moon landing. The foundation of this research rests upon Katz's definition of media events and how acts of terrorism, when viewed under the camera's eye, possess some, if not many, of the same qualities Katz speaks of. The author uses the hijacking of TWA Flight 847 (to Beirut in 1985) as an example that reveals the parallel between the elements that make terrorism ideal for the electronic media (television in particular), and the attributes that define and qualify particular programs as media events. (Includes one table of data, three notes, and 41 references.)

542. _____ (1985). Terrorists or freedom fighters? Labeling terrorism in the Israeli press. *Political Communication and Persuasion,* 2, 4: 433–445.

The achievement of terrorism in gaining generous, worldwide media coverage has led to a new mode of terrorism the author refers to as the "theater of terror"; it is also known as media-oriented terrorism. Studies of public opinion and terrorism have revealed that the public is well aware of this trend, blaming vast media coverage as a major cause of terrorism. But the "theater of terror" concept should not be confined to the volume of coverage, the author argues. Rather, the author suggests that the content elements of the coverage should be considered as well. The analysis is focused on the labels used by the press in referring to terrorists. Consequently, a content analysis of press reports of 381 terrorist events yielded a variety of labels ranging from "freedom fighters" to "murderers." Measuring the evaluative meaning of these labels by their ratings on five semantic differential scales reveals the use of labels that embody a positive evaluative "load." In studying the factors that affect the choice of positive or negative labels, a log-linear analysis was used to test the various relations between the event attributes and the label's evaluative load. This analysis reveals that the most effective factor is the political distance, exceeding even that of the degree of violence employed by the terrorists. The findings of this study on the differential labeling of terrorism add a new dimension to the relationship between the three actors—the terrorists, the media, and public opinion. (Includes three tables of data and 16 notes.)

543. _____ (1983, Winter). The theater of terror: Effects of press coverage. *Journal of Communication,* 33, 1: 38–45.

Research compared attitudes before and after students read press clippings about two separate terrorist incidents. The study found that exposure to press coverage of terrorist events selectively redefines the image of the terrorists, particularly among those who do not hold strong opinions about terrorism in general. Concludes that press coverage enhances the status of the people, problems, or cause behind a terrorist event. (Includes two tables and 22 references.)

544. _____ and Brosius, Hans-Bernd (1991, June). The newsworthiness of international terrorism. *Communication Research,* 18, 3: 333–354.

See entry 732.

545. Wilber, H.B. (1977, March 19). The role of the media during a terrorist incident. *The FBI Law Enforcement Bulletin,* 54, 3: 20–23.

Terrorism is on the rise, and where there used to be difficulty in defining terrorist acts, most will agree that this violence is simply another means of war for political gain. With the technological advances in the past ten years, it is possible to see these acts as they are happening, and as a result, the world is now the terrorists' captive audience. The author argues that as the media lose interest in reporting the now mundane hijackings and kidnappings, the terrorists are searching for more spectacular methods of attracting publicity. Even though First Amendment rights are in question, the author predicts that "at some future date, assertions of national interest may ultimately take priority over the public's historic rights to be informed." The author also says that the rights to speak and publish do not include the right to gather information. Yet at the same time, terrorist activity is newsworthy as it affects our lives; anyone is a potential victim. The author argues for self-regulation of journalists when they cover such events and recommends that they should avoid creating any obvious media presence beyond that necessary to gather accurate, complete information. When covering extreme violence, the author suggests the following guidelines: 1) use of pool reporters to cover activities at incident scenes or within police lines; 2) self-imposed limitations on the use of high-intensity television lighting and camera equipment; 3) limitations on media solicitation of interviews; 4) primary reliance on officially designated spokespersons as sources of information concerning law enforcement plans; and 5) avoidance of coverage that tends to emphasize the spectacular qualities of an incident or the presence of spectators at the scene.

546. Wilkinson, Paul, and Stewart, Alasdaire M. (eds.) (1987). *Contemporary research on terrorism.* Aberdeen, MA: Aberdeen University Press, 625p.

See entry 311.

547. Winfrey, Carey (1977, March 19). Hanafi seizure fans new debate on press coverage of terrorists. *New York Times,* p. 33.

This article was prompted by the release of 135 hostages held by Hanafi Muslims in Washington, D.C. The article is a compilation of quotes from prominent federal government officials, law enforcement personnel, and media operatives. The article fairly presents both sides of the debate surrounding media coverage of terrorism. There are no new insights into the problem or solutions presented, but the article does an excellent job of relating what is already known.

548. Winkler, Carol (1989). Presidents held hostage: The rhetoric of Jimmy Carter and Ronald Reagan. *Terrorism,* 12, 1: 21–30.
See entry 736.

549. Wittebols, James H. (1989, August). The politics and coverage of terrorism: From media images to public consciousness. Paper presented at the Annual Meeting of the Association for Education in Journalism and Mass Communication (72nd, Washington, D.C., August 10-13), 23p.
See entry 737.

550. _____ (1991, Spring). Words and worlds of terror: Context and meaning of media buzzword. *ETC,* 48, 1: 336–343.
This is an analysis of the difference between U.S. and Canadian television newscasts' use of terror terms. Author suggests that they share many of the same asumptions about terrorism and the use of terror terms. (Includes four tables and ten notes and references.)

551. Wurth-Hough, Sandra (1983). Network news coverage of terrorism: The early years. *Terrorism: An International Journal,* 6, 3: 403–422.
The electronic media influence public opinion by defining which national and international issues become significant, and shape public debates by the televised images conveyed to the American audience. Based upon the Vanderbilt Television News Archive, this study examines the image projected in reporting of terrorist activities by the three major national networks (ABC, CBS, and NBC). The reality presented by the media is explored by comparing variables such as story emphasis and depiction, frequency, length of coverage, and location in the newscasts. (Includes six tables of data and 15 references.)

552. Zillman, Dolf, and Bryant, Jennings (eds.) (1985). *Selective exposure to communication.* Hillsdale, NJ: Lawrence Erlbaum, 251p.
See entry 738.

553. Zuckerman, Mortimer B. (1986, June 9). Playing the terrorists' game (Editorial). *U.S. News & World Report,* 100, 22: 86.
Discusses how media coverage of terrorism unwittingly plays into terrorists' hands. Argues that media coverage seeks to legitimize terrorists by adopting their language. Suggests that those reporting the news need to take time out to think about how they respond to terrorism.

Chapter 4

Terrorism in the Print Media

554. Alali, A. Odasuo, and Eke, Kenoye K. (eds.). (1991). *Media coverage of terrorism: Methods of diffusion.* Newbury Park, CA: SAGE, 152p.
See entry 330.

555. Alexander, Yonah (ed.) (1987). *The 1986 annual on terrorism.* Hingham, MA: Kluwer Academic Publishers.
See entry 5.

556. _____ (1979). Terrorism and the media: Some considerations. In Yonah Alexander, David Carlton, and Paul Wilkinson (eds.) (1979), *Terrorism: Theory and practice* (pp. 159–174). Boulder, CO: Westview Press.
Chapter focuses on the interaction between terrorism and the media, and how law enforcement agents (police) have handled incidents of terrorism. Author suggests 12 areas media practitioners should consider during their coverage of terrorist incidents. (Includes 39 notes.)

557. _____ (1980). Terrorism and the media: Some observations. *Terrorism: An International Journal,* 3, 179–80.
See entry 331.

558. _____ (1977). Terrorism and the media in the Middle East. In Yonah Alexander & Seymour M. Finger (eds.), *Terrorism: Interdisciplinary perspectives* (pp. 166–206). London: McGraw-Hill Book Company (UK) Limited.
See entry 333.

559. _____ (1979). Terrorism, the media, and the police. In Robert Kupperman & Darrell M. Trent (eds.), *Terrorism* (pp. 331–348). Stanford, CA: Hoover Institution Press.
See entry 334.

560. _____ (1978, Spring/Summer). Terrorism, the media and the police. *Journal of International Affairs,* 32, 1: 101–114.
See entry 335.

561. _____, Carlton, David, and Wilkinson, Paul (eds.) (1979), *Terrorism: Theory and practice.* Boulder, CO: Westview Press, 280p.
See entry 6.

562. _____, and Picard, Robert G. (eds.) (1991). *In the camera's eye: News coverage of terrorist events.* New York: Brassey's (U.S.), Inc., 156p.
See entry 338.

563. Andrews, Kate (1989, Summer). Airline disaster highlights need for ethical coverage. *Journalism Educator,* 44, 2: 50–51, 76.
Author describes a Syracuse University professor/reporter's experiences covering the airline disaster that killed 35 Syracuse students. Article discusses the problems and ethical issues involved in covering a story associated with grief.

564. Aner, Kerstin (1983, October–December). La violence et les medias [Violence and the media]. *Revue Internationale de Criminologie et de police technique,* 36, 4: 72–83.
Article reflects the recommendation adopted by the European parliament concerning methods of reducing violence and part of an associated report on violence and the media. Recommendations address many areas, including terrrorism and the role of the media. The article also deals with the European strategy to reduce the portrayal of violence in the media.

565. Association for Education in Journalism and Mass Communication (1991, August). Proceedings of the Annual Meeting of the Association for Education in Journalism and Mass Communication. (74th, Boston, MA, August 7–10), Part X: United States Coverage of International News, 459p.
See entry 346.

566. _____ (1990, August). Proceedings of the 1990 Annual Meeting of the Association for Education in Journalism and Mass Communication (73rd, Minneapolis, MN, August 1-4), Part VI: Foreign and International Media Studies, 339p.

See entry 347.

567. Austin, W. Timothy (1989, September). Living on the edge: The impact of terrorism upon Philippine villagers. *International Journal of Offender and Comparative Criminology,* 33, 2: 1-3-119.

Field observations, interviews, and content analysis of newspapers were used to determine the social and psychological consequences of terrorism on Philippine villagers. The consequences of terrorism are discussed in institutional, religious, family, educational, economic, and political terms.

568. Bandura, Albert (1990). Mechanisms of moral disengagement. In Walter Reich (ed.), *Origins of terrorism: Psychologies, ideologies, theologies, states of mind* (pp. 161-191). Woodrow Wilson Center Series. New York: Cambridge University Press.

See entry 16.

569. Bassiouni, M. Cherif (1982, Spring). Media coverage of terrorism: The law and the public. *Journal of Communication,* 32, 2: 128-143.

See entry 355.

570. _____ (1981). Terrorism, law enforcement, and the mass media: Perspectives, problems, proposals. *Journal of Criminal Law and Criminology,* 72, 1: 801-851.

Author suggests that the psychological impact of terrorism is more significant than that of most other violent acts. The study concludes that the media may be responsible for creating this effect.

571. Behm, A.J. (1991). Terrorism, violence against the public, and the media: The Australian approach. *Political Communication and Persuasion,* 8: 233-246.

This is an analysis of the Australian model for handling issues associated with terrorism and the media. The National Anti-Terrorist Plan (NATP) was developed by Australia's State Cooperation for the Prevention Against Violence (SAC-PAV) for national security interest. The plan specifies four strategies for dealing with the media on crisis management of terrorist proportion. Basically, the study suggests that all elements of society, including the media, must be encouraged to regard security as a cooperative endeavor.

572. Blaisse, Mark (1992). Reporters' perspectives. In David L. Paletz & Alex P. Schmid (ed.), *Terrorism and the media* (pp. 137–169). Newbury Park, CA: SAGE.
This chapter documents the author's personal experience in seeking out and meeting with terrorists, then publishing the results of his interviews. Author argues that reporters are free: free to be lured by different forces (i.e., political parties, lobbies, groups); free although other people may write the rules; relatively free to ignore their contacts' wishes; free to decide how they obtain their information and from whom; and free to forget the past. The result is characterized and depicted as a "tango" between the media and terrorism.

573. Bogart, Leo (1968, Summer). The overseas newsman: A 1967 profile study. *Journalism Quarterly,* 45, 293–306.
See entry 362.

574. Bremer, L. Paul, III (1987). Terrorism and the media. Washington, D.C.: U.S. Department of State, Bureau of Public Affairs, Office of Public Communication, Editorial Division.
Deals with author's view of how terrorism is recreated and represented in the media. Also describes the U.S. government's current policy on the issue.

575. _____ (1990). Terrorism and the media. In B. Schechterman & M. Slann (eds.), *Violence and Terrorism 90/91* [Annual Editions] (pp. 108–110). Guilford, CT: The Dushkin Publishing Group, Inc.
See entry 574.

576. Brown, William J. (1987, May). Mediated communication flows during a terrorism event: The TWA Flight 847 hijacking. Paper presented at the International Communication Association, Montreal.
The author proposes a theoretical approach that describes how news media mediation and control during a terrorist event can alter discourse in channels of communication. The hijacking of TWA Flight 847 is used as a case study in the analysis of terrorist discourse disseminated by the news media during events of terrorism.

577. _____ (1990, Spring). The persuasive appeal of mediated terrorism: The case of the TWA Flight 847 hijacking. *Western Journal of Speech Communication,* 54, 2: 219–236.
See entry 576.

578. Buddenbaum, Judith M. (1991). Of Christian freedom fighters and Marxist terrorists: The image of SWAPO and the Namibian independence movement in the religious and secular press. In Yonah Alexander & Robert G. Picard (eds.), *In the camera's eye: News coverage of terrorist events* (pp. 131–147). New York: Brassey's (U.S.), Inc.

This chapter examines the news coverage of the South-West Africa People's Organization (SWAPO) and the Namibian independence movement by both religious and secular press. It explores how journalists from two different persuasions select sources, facts, and justifying explanations of the situation in Namibia and the fight for independence. A study of *The New York Times* and the *Lutheran World Information* indicate that both papers rarely cover the same events or situations concerning the Namibian independence movement, and they do not rely on the same or even similar sources for their information. Correspondents for the *Times* visit the country briefly, if at all. They actually rely on highly placed political sources, who themselves have little firsthand knowledge of the situation. On the other hand, *Lutheran World Information* has limited access to political sources, yet its access to the perspectives of the natives of this land is excellent, and the publication relies on Christian sources for facts, descriptions, and interpretations and is lacking in economic and political realities. Both the *New York Times* and *Lutheran World Information* are guilty of setting policy, providing one-sided and incomplete information to their readers.

579. Burgess, Parke G. (1973). Crisis rhetoric: Coercion vs. force. *Quarterly Journal of Speech, 59, 61–73.*
See entry 28.

580. Casey, William J. (1986, November). Conquering this cancer of terrorism. *USA Today* (Magazine), 115, 2498: 10–12.
See entry 31.

581. Clark, Dennis (1978). Terrorism in Ireland: Renewal of a tradition. In Marius H. Livingston with Lee Bruce Kress & Marie G.

Wanek (eds.), *International terrorism in the contemporary world* (pp. 77–83). Westport, CT: Greenwood Press.
See entry 34.

582. Clawson, Patrick (1987, Winter). Why we need more but better coverage of terrorism. *ORBIS,* 30, 4: 701–710.
Argues that the discussion of media coverage of terrorism should focus on how media coverage can contribute to the fight against terrorism, not how much should be reported. Author sees the media as likely allies to eliminating terrorism.

583. Cooper, H.H.A. (1977). Terrorism and the media. In Yonah Alexander & Seymour M. Finger (eds.), *Terrorism: Interdisciplinary perspectives* (pp. 141–156). London: McGraw-Hill Book Company (UK) Limited.
See entry 377.

584. Cooper, Thomas (1991). Terrorism and perspectivist philosophy: Understanding adversarial news coverage. In Yonah Alexander & Robert G. Picard (eds.), *In the camera's eye: News coverage of terrorist events* (pp. 10–29). New York: Brassey's (U.S.), Inc.
See entry 379.

585. Covert, Lorrie Schmid (1984). A fantasy-theme analysis of the rhetoric of the Symbionese Liberation Army: Implications of bargaining with terrorists. Dissertation, University of Denver.
The analysis focuses on the rhetorical theme used by the Symbionese Liberation Army in execution of their actions. The analysis suggests the motivations that precipitate terrorism, at least by the SLA.

586. Cox, Robert (1981). The media as a weapon. *Political Communication and Persuasion,* 1, 297–300.
See entry 381.

587. Crelinsten, Ronald D. (1987). Power and meaning: Terrorism as a struggle over access to the communication structure. In Paul Wilkinson & Alasdaire M. Stewart (eds.), *Contemporary research on terrorism* (pp. 419–450). Aberdeen, MA: Aberdeen University Press.
See entry 46.

588. _____ (1992). Victim's perspectives. In David L. Paletz & Alex P. Schmid (eds.), *Terrorism and the media* (pp. 208–238). Newbury Park, CA: SAGE.

Author's analysis seeks to distinguish two types of terrorist victims: 1) direct victims, i.e., hostages, the disappeared, the bombed, the murdered and those who are attacked, robbed, subjected to extortion or bullied and intimidated; and 2) indirect victims, i.e., families and associates of direct victims and those who belong to related ethnic groups, political parties, governments, corporations, armies, activities, etc. Explores issues of dramatization and effects, such as fear. The nature of terrorist victimization and media coverage of terrorist victimization are also examined. (Includes 40 references.)

589. Dader, Jose Luis (1987). Periodism y pseudocomunicacion politica: Contribuciones de periodismo a las democracias symbolicas [Journalism and political pseudocommunication: Contributions of journalism to symbolic democracies]. Pamplona, Spain: Ediciones Universidad de Navarra.

This article captures various perspectives that explain how terrorists use the mass media.

590. Decker, W., and Rainey, D. (1982, November). Media and terrorism: Toward the development of an instrument to explicate their relationship. Paper presented at the Annual Meeting of the Speech Communication Association (68th, Louisville, KY, November 4–7), 23p.

This content analysis seeks to determine perceptions regarding terrorist violence and its power over mass media and to determine whether media coverage of such incidents encourages subsequent incidents. The authors chose the first three days of coverage of two terrorist incidents (the 1977 Hanafi Muslim takeover of three Washington, D.C. buildings, and the Black September killings at the 1972 Olympics in Munich, Germany) as reported by *The New York Times* and the *Washington Post*. Instrument yielded the following categories of analysis: 1) the terrorists' requests for publicity, 2) information about the hostages or victims, 3) loss of property or injuries with such activities, 4) governmental helplessness during the incident, and 5) criticism of media coverage of terrorist activity. Researchers observed that the terrorists were not always assured that their cause would be explained in any detail, or that any sympathetic education of the audience would take place; that the nature of coverage did not appear evenhanded or simply informative, but was instead neutral or negative; and that the coverage of a terrorist attack in which lives were lost did not oversensationalize the situations being reported.

591. Dowling, Ralph E. (1988, March). The contribution of speech communication scholarship to the study of terrorism: Review and preview. Paper presented at the Conference on Communication in Terrorist Events: Functions, Themes, and Consequences (Boston, MA, March 3–5), 41p.
See entry 388.

592. _____ (1989, February). The media and the terrorists: Not innocents, but both victims. (Paper presented at the Annual Meeting of the Western Speech Communication Association, Spokane, WA, February 18–21), 21p.

It is public knowledge that government officials, media critics, and the public at large believe that the media "cause" or strongly motivate acts of terrorism. Author suggests that analysis using Kenneth Burke's dramatistic method can explain political terrorism without reference to desire for coverage; terrorism would occur because of its symbolic value even with no media coverage. However, when terrorism passes into insurgency—that is, when terrorists find themselves capable of holding enemy territory and hence having traditional tactical and strategic objectives, the Burkean analysis may be less useful because communications to parties outside the inner circle of terrorists may serve instrumental objectives, while Burke's analysis best explains the consummatory functions of symbolic activity. Author suggests that Burke's analysis of society can also be applied to terrorist societies to explain their violence, and that the dramatistic approach can predict the forms in which terrorism will appear and what strategies should be pursued to control it. (Includes 83 notes.)

593. _____ (1982, February). The rhetorical genre of terrorism: Identification and policy implications. Paper presented at the Annual Meeting of the Western Speech Communication Association (Denver, CO, February 19–23), 26p.
See entry 390.

594. _____ (1986, Winter). Terrorism and the media: A rhetorical genre. _Journal of Communication,_ 36, 12–24.
See entry 391.

595. _____ (1988, September). The terrorist and the media: Partners in crime or rituals and harmless observers? Paper presented at the "Media and Modern Warfare" Conference (New Brunswick, Canada, September 30), 34p.

The author explores the idea that the media "cause" or strongly motivate acts of terrorism. The author argues that terrosim would occur because of its symbolic and communicative values even if no media coverage were provided. Four assumptions are presented that have been refuted by existing research: 1) terrorists want a propaganda platform; 2) terrorists win empathy for their causes; 3) coverage focuses on terrorists and their deeds; and 4) terrorism is contagious and the media spread it. Author also contends that terrorism "causes" media coverage, and not the reverse. Concludes that even though terrorism cannot be controlled, knowledge of the purposes it serves provides hope that it may be possible to avoid the radical estrangements that necessitate this violence, or at least find other forms for radicals' expressions of order. (Includes 67 notes.)

596. Eke, Kenoye K., and Alali, A. Odasuo (1991). Introduction: Critical issues in media coverage of terrorism. In A. Odasuo Alali & Kenoye K. Eke (eds.), *Media coverage of terrorism: Methods of diffusion* (pp. 3-11). Newbury Park, CA: SAGE.

This chapter deals with the purpose of and the rationale behind the volume edited by the authors. It begins with an examination of the definitional problems of terrorism as pointed out by the relativist conception: "One man's terrorist is another man's freedom fighter." By employing sophisticated analysis based on encyclopedic knowledge, the authors conclude that terrorism, regardless of its definitions, is an insurrectional strategy used by people of very different political convictions to achieve their objective. The essay discusses media impact on counter-terrorist strategies. Additional analyses highlight the issues articulated by various contributors to the volume. (Includes 20 references.)

597. Elliot, Deni (1988). Family ties: A case study of families and friends during the hijacking of TWA Flight 847. *Political Communication and Persuasion,* 5: 67-75.

See entry 397.

598. Farnen, Russell F. (1990, March-April). Terrorism and the mass media: A systematic analysis of a symbiotic process. *Terrorism,* 13, 2: 99-143.

See entry 400.

599. Foreign Policy Association (1986). International terrorism: In search of a response. *Great decisions '86* (pp. 35–44). New York: Foreign Policy Association.

See entry 85.

600. Friedlander, Robert A. (1982). Iran: The hostage seizure, the media, and international law. In Abraham H. Miller (ed.), *Terrorism: The media and the law* (pp. 51–66). Dobbs Ferry, NY: Transnational Publishers, Inc.

See entry 403.

601. Fuller, Linda K. (1988). Terrorism as treated by the *Christian Science Monitor,* 1977–88. *Political Communication and Persuasion,* 5, 121–137.

Standing uniquely apart from journalistic sensationalism in its reportage of terrorism, the *Christian Science Monitor* has taken a stance of trying to keep perspective on what individual events mean in terms of a wider framework. This paper discusses terrorism as treated by the *Christian Science Monitor* from 1977 through 1987 both quantitatively and qualitatively. The approach is to delineate some of the underpinning philosophy of the newspaper, to discuss its chronological treatment of terrorism, and then to draw some implications from the study. (Includes three figures, two appendices, and seven references.)

602. Gallimore, Timothy (1991). Media compliance with voluntary press guidelines for covering terrorism. In Yonah Alexander & Robert G. Picard (eds.), *In the camera's eye: News coverage of terrorist events* (pp. 103–118). New York: Brassey's (U.S.), Inc.

This is a content analysis designed to determine the extent to which media operatives comply with the voluntary guidelines that news organizations have adopted for covering terrorism. Two cases of terrorism were used as illustration: 1) media coverage of the 1982 Washington Monument seige, and 2) the hijacking of Pan Am Flight 73 in Karachi, Pakistan, in 1986. Two research questions guide this analysis of three major news magazines (*Newsweek, Time,* and *U.S. News & World Report*). Author identifies examples of violations and compliance with codes. (Includes 12 notes, and nine tables.)

603. Gallup Organization (1986). The people and the press: Part 2. An ongoing Times Mirror investigation of public attitudes towards the news media. Los Angeles, CA: Times Mirror.

This study measures public attitudes and changes in public opinion towards media coverage of specific events. Of particular interest here is how the media are perceived to have performed in various terrorist events.

604. Gerbner, George (1991). Symbolic functions of violence and terror. In Yonah Alexander & Robert G. Picard (eds.), *In the camera's eye: News coverage of terrorist events* (pp. 3–9). New York: Brassey's (U.S.), Inc.
See entry 95.

605. _____ (1988, July). Symbolic functions of violence and terror. Terrorism and the news media research project. Association of Education in Journalism and Mass Communication, 8p. (ED 312725).
See entry 95.

606. Gerrits, Robert P.J.M. (1992). Terrorists' perspectives: memoirs. In D.L. Paletz & A.P. Schmid (eds.), *Terrorism and the media* (pp. 29–61). Newbury Park, CA: SAGE.
See entry 98.

607. Gladis, Stephen D. (1979, September). The hostage/terrorist situation and the media. *The FBI Law Enforcement Bulletin,* 48, 9: 10–15.
See entry 99.

608. Goldstein, Jeffery H. (1989). Mass media and terrorism: The image of the terrorist. In Jo Groebel & Jeffrey H. Goldstein (eds.), *Terrorism: Psychological perspectives.* Series of psychobiology, (pp. 65–84). Sevilla, Spain: Publicaciones de la Universidad de Sevilla.
Chapter reports on how media convey versus construct images of terrorism. Examines selective reporting and headlines and how they shape and strengthen the public consciousness about human nature, and about violence in particular. Argues that there is no such thing as objective journalism.

609. Graber, Doris A. (1979). Evaluating crime-fighting policies: Media images and public perspective. In Ralph Baker & Fred A. Meyer, Jr. (eds.), *Evaluating alternative law-enforcement policies* (pp. 179–199). Lexington, MA: Heath Lexington Books.
This article examines the amount of coverage given to various crimes in several Midwestern U.S. newspapers and television newscasts, and

public perceptions of the frequency of these crimes. Study found that reports of political terrorism accounted for 5 percent of press reports and 8 percent of television news reports. Similar patterns were found in respondents' daily viewing diaries.

610. Graham, Katharine (1986). The media must report terrorism. In Bonnie Szumski (ed.), *Terrorism: Opposing viewpoints* (pp. 75–81). St. Paul, MN: Greenhaven Press.
See entry 413.

611. Green, L.C. (1985). Terrorism and its responses. *Terrorism,* 8, 1: 33–77.
Author discusses issues raised by the literature on terrorism and international, domestic, and individual responses to it. Among topics considered are the role of self-determination in validating terrorist actions, state-supported terrorism, the importance of the media in aiding or hindering terrorism through its effect on public reaction, and stress responses and coping mechanisms seen in hostages and other victims of terrorist acts.

612. Groebel, Jo (1989). The problems and challenges of research on terrorism. In Jo Groebel & Jeffrey H. Goldstein (eds.), *Terrorism: Psychological perspectives* (pp. 15–38). Series of psychobiology. Sevilla, Spain: Publicaciones de la Universidad de Sevilla.
Article presents results of empirical analyses that include the role of mass media and their impact on terrorism. See also entry 105.

613. _____, and Goldstein, Jeffrey H. (eds.) (1989). *Terrorism: Psychological perspectives.* Series of psychobiology. Sevilla, Spain: Publicaciones de la Universidad de Sevilla, 171p.
Presents recent research findings and perspective on terrorism. Chapters explore the role of the media and examine specific instances of national terrorism, including Basque terrorists in Spain and terrorists in Germany. See also entry 106.

614. Heisey, D. Ray (1986, Fall). Reagan and Mitterrand respond to international crisis: Creating versus transcending appearances. *Western Journal of Speech Communication,* 50, 4: 325–335.
See entry 420.

615. Hewitt, Christopher (1992). Publics' perspectives. In David L. Paletz & Alex P. Schmid (eds.), *Terrorism and the media* (pp. 170–207). Newbury Park, CA: SAGE.

Author classifies the public into three main audiences: the terrorists' constituency, the terrorists' enemy, and the uninvolved. Author's analysis of public opinion polls from several countries indicates that terrorism arouses a high degree of public concern, but rarely succeeds in getting the terrorists' cause onto the political agenda. Author also examines the role played by the media in forming public opinion about terrorists; characterizes such portrayal as problematic. Lastly, author distinguishes between the tactics of nationalist terrorists and revolutionary terrorists. (Includes 69 references, 17 notes, 13 tables, and three figures.)

616. Hocking, Jennifer J. (1992). Governments' perspectives. In David L. Paletz & Alex P. Schmid (eds.), *Terrorism and the media* (pp. 86–104). Newbury Park, CA: SAGE.

Author argues that a key element in Western nations' strategies against terrorism has been the development of a framework for media reporting of terrorist incidents. The Australian experience is based on a strategy of "voluntary restraint" or "cooperation." Author suggests a theoretical link between the Australian counter-terrorist strategy and that of the British military-based counter-insurgency approach to counter-terrorism. The concerns that result from the media/security relations are the basis for this analysis. (Includes 44 references and one note.)

617. Hoge, James W. (1982). The media and terrorism. In Abraham H. Miller (ed.), *Terrorism: The media and the law* (pp. 89–105). Dobbs Ferry, NY: Transnational Publishers.

See entry 428.

618. Holden, Robert T. (1986, January). The contagiousness of aircraft hijacking. *American Journal of Sociology,* 91, 4: 874–904.

Author develops a mathematical model of aircraft hijacking that suggests that the motivation to hijack aircraft spreads from one individual to another as a result of media coverage of hijacking events. The author applies the model to aircraft hijackings in the United States between 1968 and 1972. Analysis suggests that successful hijackings in the United States generated additional hijacking attempts of the same type. Concludes that there were no contagion effects of unsuccessful hijacking attempts in the United States or any effects on U.S. hijacking attempts of such attempts outside the United States. (Includes 52 references.)

619. Hoyt, Michael (1991a, November/December). Censorship by anti-terrorism. *Columbia Journalism Review,* 28.

Discusses the impact of an early version of an anti-terrorism bill in Greece. Suggests that the bill would have made it a crime for a newspaper to print any communication from terrorists and their organization.

620. _____ (1991b, November/December). Censorship by terrorism. *Columbia Journalism Review,* 28–29.

Discusses how violence against journalists is used to censor journalists in Guatemala. Cites numerous incidents.

621. Irvin, Cynthia L. (1992). Terrorists' perspectives: Interviews. In David L. Paletz & Alex P. Schmid (eds.), *Terrorism and the media* (pp. 62–85). Newbury Park, CA: SAGE.

Author's analysis relies on press releases and documents issued by Sinn Fein and the IRA, Herri Batasuna and ETA, and the PLO, as well as a series of interviews. Two questions shaped the analysis: 1) "Do the perpetrators of acts of insurgent 'terrorism' always perceive themselves as victors when they obtain media attention? Or, contrary to conventional wisdom, is there a recognition by the insurgents that media coverage of acts perpetrated by them can impede rather than advance their cause?" and 2) "Of the various aims attributed to insurgent 'terrorist' use of the media, which do the insurgents themselves view as most important, and do those aims change during the cause of an insurgency?" (Includes 40 references.)

622. Jaehnig, Walter B. (1978). Journalists and terrorism: Captives of the liberation tradition. *Indiana Law Journal,* 53, 4: 717–744.

Most of the controversy regarding media coverage of violent incidents, particularly terrorism, revolves around ethical issues. The author argues that traditional news values that were brought about by commercial competition compel the news industry to gravitate toward conflict-laden and tragic events. Consequently, news judgment regarding the coverage of terrorism is often made quickly without the full cooperation of police agencies.

623. _____ (1982). Terrorism in Britain: The limits of free expression. In Abraham H. Miller (ed.), *Terrorism: The media and the law* (pp. 106–129). Dobbs Ferry, New York: Transaction Publishers, Inc.

Examines the British policy of antiterrorist legislation against press coverage of terrorism. Suggests that "the British experience seems to trace the limits of free expression in a society burdened by a long campaign against political terrorism."

624. _____, Weaver, David H., and Fico, Frederick (1981, Winter). Reporting crime and fearing crime in three communities. *Journal of Communication,* 31, 1: 88–96.

See entry 133.

625. Jenkins, Brian M. (1981, February). Fighting terrorism: An enduring task. *The RAND Paper Series,* P-6585. Santa Monica, CA: The RAND Corporation, 8p.

This is an excerpt of an interview with ADN-Kronos, an Italian news service. Discusses international connections of Italian terrorism; compares international terrorism with levels of terrorism in the U.S.; discusses how to prevent the spread of terrorism; and discusses publicity as it relates to terrorist acts.

626. _____ (1981, June). The psychological implications of media-covered terrorism. *The RAND Paper Series,* P-6627. Santa Monica, CA: The RAND Corporation, 9p.

This paper expands on the author's presentation at an international seminar on "Terrorism and the Mass Media" held in Sicily, April 3–5, 1981. Author argues that media coverage of terrorism cannot be separated from acts of terrorism. Consequently, the paper focuses on the psychological effects of terrorism as reported by the news media. Specific international cases, such as the kidnapping of Aldo Moro, and domestic violence in Northern Ireland, Spain, Argentina, and Turkey are illustrative examples of this discussion. Author also examines how the public perceives the news media as encouraging acts of terrorism. Author also enumerates some of the problems terrorism poses for the news media. (Includes a bibliography of 11 references.)

627. _____ (1983). Research in terrorism: Areas of consensus, areas of ignorance. In B. Eichelman, D. Soskis & W. Reid (eds.), *Terrorism: Interdisciplinary perspectives* (p. 160), Washington, DC: American Psychiatric Association.

See entry 139.

628. _____ (1981, May). A strategy for combating terrorism. *The RAND Paper Series,* P-6624. Santa Monica, CA: The RAND Corporation, 8p.

Author discusses the trends in terrorism and the effects of terrorist actions. Suggests how the international community can combat terrorism. This paper was prepared at the request of the United States Information Agency for distribution to specific interests.

629. _____ (1982, March). Talking to terrorists. *The RAND Paper Series,* P-6750. Santa Monica, CA: The RAND Corporation, 15p.

Author argues that terrorist acts, such as political kidnappings, create many communication problems, especially when the hostage belongs to another government; often, the local governments seek to exercise control over the situation. Author suggests that while kidnapping is a good story for the mass media, there are also advantages and disadvantages of communicating through the media. The author suggests nine principles that government officials might try to adhere to in their attempt to solve communications problems during terrorism.

630. Johnpoll, Bernard (1977). Terrorism and the media in the United States. In Yonah Alexander & Seymour M. Finger (eds.), *Terrorism: Interdisciplinary Perspectives* (pp. 157–165). London: McGraw-Hill Book Company (UK) Limited.

See entry 442.

631. Jonathan Institute (1984, October). Lost in the terrorist theater. *Harper's Magazine,* 269, 1613: 43–58.

Eight prominent journalists discuss how the media can report terrorist acts without advertising terrorist causes. Two essays, by Jeane J. Kirkpatrick and Leszek Kolakowski, preface the discussion.

632. Jones, Juanita B., and Miller, Abraham H. (1979). The media and terrorist activity: Resolving the First Amendment dilemma. *The Ohio Northern University Law Review,* 6: 70–81.

See entry 444.

633. Karkashian, J.E. (1977). Problems of international terrorism: Statement. Washington, D.C.: Department of State, Bureau of Public Affairs, Office of Media Services.

This is the author's statement regarding the problems of international terrorism, and media coverage of the issue.

634. Katz, Elihu (1980). Media events: The sense of occasion. *Studies in Visual Communication,* 6, 84–89.

See entry 145.

635. Kelly, Michael J. (1989). The seizure of the Turkish Embassy in Ottawa: Managing terrorism and the media. In Uriel Rosenthal, Michael T. Charles & Paul 't-Hart (eds.), *Coping with crises: The management of disasters, riots and terrorism* (pp. 117–138). Springfield, IL: Charles C. Thomas Publishers.

Chapter discusses the case of the Quebec seige of the Turkish embassy in Canada in 1970. Author shows how the media manipulate, interfere with, and help authorities throughout a hostage incident. Author also presents a dialogue on how open societies are forced to walk a tightrope between limiting the freedom of the press, protecting operational security, and acknowledging the inevitability of intense media involvement at the risk of jeopardizing antiterrorist operations. (Policy and media guidelines are included.)

636. _____, and Mitchell, Thomas H. (1981, Summer). Transnational terrorism and the Western elite press. *Political Communication and Persuasion, 1,* 269–296.

This paper seeks to analyze transnational terrorism as a political resource or, more specifically, as a means of political communication. In order to examine how terrorists have used the media, the authors performed a content analysis of the coverage given to a selected sample of 158 incidents of transnational terrorism in two major daily newspapers of the Western world: *The New York Times* and *The Times* of London. Their findings indicate that while transnational terrorism does generate a considerable amount of press attention, the particular type of coverage it receives would appear to undermine the effectiveness of terrorism as a communications strategy. (Includes ten tables, an appendix, and 38 notes.)

637. Kent, Ian, and Nicholls, William. (1977). The psychodynamics of terrorism. *Mental Health and Society, 4,* 1–2: 1–8.

Authors propose a dynamic and social explanation for the "malignant aggression" of the terrorist. Argues that political terrorism involves the exploitation of mental illness, connived at in turn by the international public through the media. (Includes ten references.)

638. Kidder, Rushworth M. (1986, May 16). Unmasking terrorism: Manipulation of the media. *The Christian Science Monitor,* 18–20.

Argues that the cornerstone of any democracy is a free press. The following questions guide the author's analysis: 1) Are there limits to this freedom? Should there be? 2) Since terrorism seeks an audience, would the media be derelict in their duty if they didn't provide one?

and 3) How much, if at all, should the press be restricted in what they report?

639. _____ (1990). Unmasking terrorism: Manipulation of the media. In B. Schechterman & M. Slann (eds.), *Violence and terrorism 90/91* [Annual Editions] (pp. 111–115). Guilford, CT: The Dushkin Publishing Group, Inc.
See entry 638.

640. Klein, Maurice M. (1989). Terrorists and the media: A social learning approach. In Jo Groebel and Jeffrey H. Goldstein (eds.), *Psychological perspectives.* Series of psychobiology (pp. 85–117). Sevilla, Spain: Publicaciones de la Universidad de Sevilla.
Author offers a conceptual framework for the relationships between the media and terrorists. The chapter also covers the symbiotic nature of the relationships, the terrorist personality, modeling and identification processes, identification and denial processes, and the role of cognitive control.

641. Knight, Graham, and Dean, Tony (1982). Myth and the structure of news. *Journal of Communication,* 32, 2: 144–161.
This article analyzes how the Canadian press covered the British recapturing of the Iranian embassy in London. Two Toronto dailies — the *Globe and Mail* and the *Sun* — were the focus of the study.

642. Krauthammer, Charles (1985, July 15). Looking evil dead in the eye. *Time,* 126, 2: 80.
Author argues that the media have covered terrorism irresponsibly, that extensive coverage of terrorism aids terrorists by providing free publicity for their actions. Suggests that the media must impose self-enforced limits on their coverage of terrorism to help end the carnage. (Includes one illustration.)

643. Lebowitz, Michael (1983, January–March). Generalization for natural language text. *Cognitive Science,* 7, 1: 1–40.
Author describes a model of generalization that is part of a system for language understanding: the Integrated Partial Parser (IPP). IPP was applied to newspaper stories on terrorism to illustrate development and testing of generalizations. Implications of model are discussed. (Includes 25 references.)

644. Lent, John A. (1977, Winter). Foreign news in the American media. *Journal of Communication,* 27, 1: 46–50.

See entry 169.

645. Levy, Rudolfo. (1985, Oct.-Dec.). Terrorism and the mass media. *Military Intelligence,* 34–38.

See entry 459.

646. Lule, Jack (1993, Spring). Murder and myth: *New York Times* coverage of the TWA 847 hijacking victim. *Journalism Quarterly,* 70, 1: 26–39.

This dramatistic analysis explores how *The New York Times* portrayed the terrorist killing of U.S. Navy diver Robert Dean Stethem. Author suggests that news reports about the killing may have served as a mythic drama of sacrifice. "In gripping portrayals of victims sacrificed to terrorism, the language of the news reports offers readers the opportunity to participate in a great drama of hope and despair, purpose and pain." (Includes 78 footnotes.)

647. _____ (1991). The myth of my widow: A dramatistic analysis of news portrayals of a terrorist victim. In A. Odasuo Alali & Kenoye K. Eke (eds.), *Media coverage of terrorism: Methods of diffusion* (pp. 86–111). Newbury Park, CA: SAGE.

This is a dramatistic analysis of *The New York Times'* portrayal of the 1985 terrorist killing of Leon Klinghoffer, the 69-year-old American tourist on the *Achille Lauro*. The author suggests that it may contain a mythic dimension. Through an analysis of complex specifics of *New York Times* stories about Klinghoffer's widow, the author provides some consideration of possible mythic aspects of news coverage of terrorism, and the implications of mythic portrayals of terrorism for public policy. The author also suggests that, because terrorism is inherently dramatic and mythic in nature, authorities can take advantage of this and structure their policies to limit the dramatic features of a terrorist incident and manipulate such instances to their own advantage. (Includes two tables of data and 41 references.)

648. _____ (1988). The myth of my widow: A dramatistic analysis of news portrayals of a terrorist victim. *Political Communication and Persuasion,* 5.

See entry 647.

649. _____ (undated). The myth of my widow: A dramatistic analysis of news portrayals of a terrorist victim. Terrorism and the News Media Research Project, Paper No. 8. Louisiana State University.

See entry 647.

650. _____ (1991). Sacrifice and the body on the tarmac: Symbolic significance of U.S. news about a terrorist victim. In Yonah Alexander & Robert G. Picard (eds.), *In the camera's eye: News coverage of terrorist events* (pp. 30–45). New York: Brassey's (U.S.), Inc.

Author examines the myth often provided in news coverage of terrorism. Present study focuses on *The New York Times'* coverage of the TWA hijacking and the subsequent murder of Robert Dean Stethem. The news coverage is analyzed within the context of social and cultural forces. Author suggests that coverage of Stethem's killing provides insight into the relationship between terrorism, news, and social life. The mythic aspect of coverage is highlighted. (Includes 43 notes.)

651. Martin, L. John (1983). The media's role in international terrorism. Press Freedom and Responsibility Session of the International Communication Division of the Association for Education in Journalism and Mass Communication, Corvallis, Oregon.

A pilot study reviewed articles covering terrorists acts published on five alternate days in June-July 1983 in newspapers in the United States, England, West Germany, Israel, and Egypt. The study suggests that the mass media may quote someone using terms such as "terror" and "terrorism" in reference to an act performed by a group toward which the media is either neutral or opposed. However, the press never uses these terms in a headline to describe perpetrators of violence unless it disapproves or has no sympathy for them. Also discusses the symbiotic relationship between terrorism and the mass media. Concludes that 1) the press used neutral terms such as "guerrilla" and "paramilitary" in preference to more pejorative terms such as "terrorist"; 2) all newspapers, except the Egyptian paper, favored certain terrorists; and 3) the propaganda message forwarded in terrorist acts was generally not mentioned by the newspapers.

652. _____ (1985). The media's role in international terrorism. *Terrorism: An International Journal,* 8, 2: 127–146.

See entry 651.

653. Mazur, Allan (1982, June). Bomb threats and the media: Evidence for a theory of suggestion. *American Sociological Review,* 47, 3: 407–411.

Argument based on previous studies shows that publicizing suicides in the newspaper triggers additional, imitative suicides. Furthers this argument by investigating the effect of the mass media on human behavior as it relates to the incidence of bomb threats against nuclear energy facilities over 11 years. Results confirm previous findings, in that threat incidence closely followed fluctuations in mass media coverage of nuclear power issues. (Includes 11 references.)

654. Media Guideline Document (1982). National Advisory Committee on Criminal Justice Standards and Goals, Report of the Task Force on Disorders and Terrorism, 1976. In Abraham H. Miller (ed.), *Terrorism: The media and the law* (pp. 153–160). Dobbs Ferry, NY: Transaction Publishers, Inc.

Specifies responsibilities of the media when covering violence, terrorism and disorder. Specifies guidelines for covering such incidents. Examples of guidelines are drawn from a wire service and electronic and print media.

655. Media reporting of terrorism implicated as accessory to crimes. (1977, July). *Gallup Opinion Index,* No. 144, pp. 410–418.

Survey shows that 64 percent of the public believes that media coverage of terrorism encourages more acts of terrorism.

656. Meltzer, M. (1989, Summer). The social responsibility of the writer. *New Advocate,* 2, 3: 155–157.

Argues that writers, particularly those whose works are geared toward children, have a responsibility to create an early awareness of issues such as race, terrorism, poverty, and other disasters of human society. Suggests that such approach may sensitize children to develop corrective measures in their adult life.

657. Midgley, Sarah, and Rice, Virginia (eds.) (1984). *Terrorism and the media in the 1980s* (Conference proceedings). Washington, D.C.: The Media Institute and Institute for Studies in International Terror.

Discusses the relationship between news coverage and terrorist events. Experts involved in this discussion propose guidelines for responsible media coverage of terrorism. Others propose legislative policing of news organizations to insure compliance and restraint in coverage of terrorist incidents. The latter is couched on the argument that the public's right to know is secondary to the safety of the people involved.

658. Miller, Abraham H. (1980). *Terrorism and hostage negotiations.* Boulder, CO: Westview Press, 135p.
See entry 195.

659. _____ (1979). Terrorism and the media: A dilemma. *Terrorism 3,* 79–89.
See entry 470.

660. _____ (1983). Terrorism and the media: Observations from the American and British experiences. In Patrick J. Montana & George S. Roukis (eds.), *Managing terrorism: Strategies for the corporate executive* (pp. 91–107). Westport, CT: Quorum Books.
See entry 470.

661. _____ (1982). Terrorism, the media, and law enforcement: An introduction. In Abraham H. Miller (ed.), *Terrorism: The media and the law* (pp. 1–10). Dobbs Ferry, NY: Transaction Publishers, Inc.
Provides an introduction to the book and an overview of each chapter. Highlights specific issues contributors discussed in the book.

662. _____ (1982). Terrorism, the media, and the law: A discussion of the issues. In Abraham H. Miller (ed.), *Terrorism: The media and the law* (pp. 13–50). Dobbs Ferry, NY: Transnational Publishers, Inc.
See entry 473.

663. _____. (1982). *Terrorism: The media and the law.* Dobbs Ferry, NY: Transnational Publishers, Inc., 221p.
See entry 474.

664. Montgomery, Louise F. (1991). Media victims: Reactions to coverage of incidents of international terrorism involving Americans. In Yonah Alexander & Robert G. Picard (eds.), *In the camera's eye: News coverage of terrorist events* (pp. 58–64). New York: Brassey's (U.S.), Inc.
See entry 475.

665. Moreland, Richard L., and Berbaum, Michael L. (1982). Terrorism and the mass media: A researcher's bibliography. In Abraham

H. Miller (ed.), *Terrorism: The media and the law* (pp. 191–215). New York: Transnational Publishers.

Approximately 500 works, from various disciplines, relating to violence and terrorism coverage in the media are presented in this bibliography.

666. Mosse, Hilde L. (1978). The media and terrorism. In Marius H. Livingston with Lee Bruce Kress & Marie G. Wanek (eds.), *International terrorism in the contemporary world* (pp. 282–286). Westport, CT: Greenwood Press.

See entry 477.

667. Murphy, Patrick V. (1982). The police, the news media, and the coverage of terrorism. In Abraham H. Miller (ed.), *Terrorism: The media and the law* (pp. 76–86). Dobbs Ferry, NY: Transnational Publishers, Inc.

See entry 479.

668. Naco, Brigitte, Fan, David P., and Young, John T. (1989). Terrorism and the print media: The 1985 TWA hostage crisis. *Terrorism,* 12, 2: 107–115.

Authors' analysis of media coverage of the 1985 Trans World Airlines (TWA) hostage crisis by three leading U.S. newspapers showed that the press facilitated the terrorists' goals of gaining attention and airing their cause and grievances. Authors also suggest that the terrorists appeared to have had only limited success in gaining coverage that might have helped their efforts to gain acceptability and legitimacy.

669. National News Council, The (1982). Paper on terrorism. In Abraham H. Miller (ed.), *Terrorism: The media and the law* (pp. 133–147). Dobbs Ferry, NY: Transaction Publishers, Inc.

Media coverage of the Hanafi Muslim episode is examined. Argues that terrorism is a media event; that the media have increasingly become as much a part of terrorist events as the terrorists, the victims, and the authorities. Suggested guidelines for news media are included. (Includes 24 footnotes.)

670. Olson, Peter A. (1988, Summer). The terrorist and the terrorized: Some psychoanalytic consideration. *Journal of Psychohistory,* 16, 1: 47–60.

Among other issues, the media is discussed here as a powerful worldwide mirror with multi-channeled immediacy of social impact. See also entry 215.

671. O'Neill, Michael J. (1986). *Terrorist spectaculars: Should TV coverage be curbed?* New York: Priority Press Publications, 109p.
See entry 482.

672. Oots, Kent L., and Wiegele, Thomas C. (1985). Terrorist and victim: Psychiatric and physiological approaches from a social science perspective. *Terrorism,* 8, 1: 1–32.
See entry 217.

673. O'Sullivan, John (1986). Media publicity causes terrorism. In Bonnie Szumski (ed.), *Terrorism: Opposing viewpoints* (pp. 69–74). St. Paul, MN: Greenhaven Press.
See entry 483.

674. Ozyegin, Najat (1986). Construction of "Facts" of political violence: A content analysis of press coverage. Unpublished master's thesis, Annenberg School of Communications, University of Pennsylvania.
The role of the Turkish press in the creation of public image of political violence is examined. The study covers a period of five years of rising political turbulence prior to the 1980 military coup.

675. Paddock, Alfred H. (1984). Psychological operations, special operations, and U.S. strategy. In Frank R. Barnett, Tovar, B. Hugh & Schultz, Richard H. (eds.), *Special operations in U.S. strategy* (pp. 231–251). New York: National Strategy Information Center.
This study compares how Soviet media and American media cover terrorism. The former reports what should be, and the latter is passive, leaving itself vulnerable to terrorist exploitation.

676. Paletz, David L., and Boiney, John (1992). Researcher's perspectives. In David L. Paletz & Alex P. Schmid (eds.), *Terrorism in the media* (pp. 6–28). Newbury Park, CA: SAGE.
This chapter categorizes and analyzes the academic literature on media and terrorism. Central to this analysis is the question, "Does media coverage aid and encourage or obstruct and deter terrorism in general and terrorist causes in particular?" (Includes 81 references.)

677. _____, Fozzard, Peter A., and Ayanian, John Z. (1982, Spring). The I.R.A., the Red Brigades, and the F.A.L.N. in the *New York Times. Journal of Communication,* 32, 2: 162–171.

From the numerous contemporary violent groups active around the world, the authors have chosen three to study: the Irish Republican Army (I.R.A.), the Red Brigades, and the Fuerzas Armadas de Liberacion (F.A.L.N.). Coverage of the three groups relies heavily on authority sources, and hence does not serve to legitimize their causes. The authors have subjected the conventional wisdom and its suppositions to empirical test; their study of the three networks' evening news programs contradicts the standard arguments by showing that television news generally ignores the motivations, objectives, and long-term goals of violent organizations, thereby preventing their causes from gaining legitimacy with the public. In this study the authors analyze coverage of similar violence in *The New York Times.* (Includes 18 references.)

678. _____, and Schmid, Alex P. (eds.) (1992). *Terrorism and the media.* Newbury Park, CA: Sage Publications, 250p.

This book focuses on insurgent terrorism, "socio-revolutionary, separatist and single issue terrorism aimed at the top of society." This volume reflects the different perspectives on the relationship between insurgent terrorism and the media. Led by Paletz and Schmid, the contributors present the views and reactions of the terrorists themselves, of broadcast organizations, of journalists, of editors and reporters, and of the public(s) and the victims of terrorism. Interestingly, the analysis of government's perspectives takes an unusual approach here. (Includes 320 references, 30 notes, 13 tables, four figures, and an appendix.)

679. _____, and Vinson, C. Danielle (1992). Introduction. In David L. Paletz and Alex P. Schmid (eds.), *Terrorism and the media* (pp. 1–5). Newbury Park, CA: Sage Publications.

This chapter outlines the purposes and organization of the volume, discusses and connects the chapters, then analyzes the relationship of media and terrorism.

680. Pearlstein, Richard M. (1991). Tuned-in Narcissus: The gleam in the camera's eye. In Yonah Alexander & Robert G. Picard (eds.), *In the camera's eye: News coverage of terrorist events* (pp. 49–57). New York: Brassey's (U.S.), Inc.

Author examines the psychodynamic interrelationship between the news media and the terrorist. Emphasis is placed on the psychological types of individuals who commit terrorist acts; and the psychodynamic rewards that attract individuals to perpetrate terrorist acts. (Includes 18 notes.)

681. Peretz, D. (1982). *Reporting Lebanon the Christian way: The media in the United States on Lebanon: Part I, A media source guide, Issues for the '80s.* New York: Council on International and Public Affairs, 14p.
See entry 495.

682. Pfaff, William (1986, September 19). Terrorists call the shots — On front page. *Miami Herald.*
Author argues that publicity both motivates and encourages terrorists. Further, author suggests that terrorists, rather than journalists, control what is seen on television. Observes that the media are caught between this possibility and the equally offensive alternative — censorship.

683. _____ (1990). Terrorists call the shots — On front page. In B. Schechterman & M. Slann (eds.), *Violence and terrorism* (p. 121). Guilford, CT: The Duskin Publishing Group, Inc.
See entry 682.

684. Picard, Robert G. (undated). The conundrum of news coverage of terrorism. Terrorism and the news media research project, Paper No. 1, Louisiana State University.
Paper examines media coverage of terrorism and argues that the media support the existing social, political, and economic orders.

685. _____ (1991c). Journalists as targets and victims of terrorism. In Yonah Alexander & Robert G. Picard (eds.), *In the camera's eye: News coverage of terrorist events* (pp. 65–71). New York: Brassey's (U.S.), Inc.
Author's analysis focuses on the journalist as target of terrorism. Explains the problems and dangers journalists face in trying to cover political violence, including language and cultural barriers. Analysis suggests that the dangers and problems journalists face are often ignored in research literature. Determines implications for journalists. (Includes 17 notes.)

686. _____ (1991a). The journalist's role in coverage of terrorist events. In A. Odasuo Alali & Kenoye K. Eke (eds.), *Media coverage*

of terrorism: Methods of diffusion (pp. 40–48). Newbury Park, CA: Sage Publications, Inc.
 See entry 500.

687. _____ (1993). *Media portrayals of terrorism: Functions and meaning of news coverage.* Amex, IA: Iowa State University Press, 147pp.
 This book should make a reader aware of the common confusions about terrorism's definition, goals, and practice. More interesting is that it examines the role of mass communication in terrorism. It poses and answers questions such as: Is media coverage essential to terrorism? Does media coverage generally produce sympathy for terrorists? Are there types of terrorism that are almost never covered by the media? Overall, "the book explores problems and benefits of media coverage of terrorist acts; analyzes research that provides an understanding of the role of media in terrorism; examines terrorism as persuasion; and studies specific criticisms concerning media's coverage of terrorism." (Includes seven chapters, six figures, and an extensive bibliography.)

688. _____ (1991b). News coverage as the contagion of terrorism: Dangerous charges backed by dubious science. In A. Odasuo Alali & Kenoye K. Eke (eds.), *Media coverage of terrorism: Methods of diffusion* (pp. 49–62). Newbury Park, CA: Sage Publications, Inc.
 Author uses this chapter to answer serious charges and questions about the role of journalism in the spread of terrorism. Ignoring the questionable evidence about media effects that government officials offer, the author suggests that rather than being a contagion of terrorism, the media may possibly aid the campaign against terrorist violence. Study also explores diffusion theory possibilities, and explores whether the media are useful in preventing or reducing the scale of violence in terrorist attacks. (Includes 17 references.)

689. _____ (1989, Winter). Press relations of terrorist organizations. *Public Relations Review,* 15, 4: 12–23.
 Examines the different types of press relations commonly undertaken by terrorist organizations. Argues that commonality exists in publicity tactics used by large and small terrorist groups; patterns of press relations activities differ.

690. _____, and Adams, Paul D. (1991). Characterizations of acts and perpetrators of political violence in three elite U.S. daily newspapers. In A. Odasuo Alali & Kenoye K. Eke (eds.), *Media coverage of terrorism: methods of diffusion* (pp. 12–22). Newbury Park, CA: SAGE.

> This chapter considers the characterizations of acts of political violence in three elite U.S. daily newspapers, the *Los Angeles Times, The New York Times,* and the *Washington Post,* for the years 1980–1985. The study suggests that significant differences exist in the ways media practitioners, government officials, and witnesses characterize acts of political violence and those who perpetrate the acts. Typical is the example that media personnel and witnesses to violence tend to use nominal characterizations, while government officials employ the use of descriptives in their characterizations. (Includes ten tables and an appendix.)

691. _____, and _____ (1987). Characterizations of acts and perpetrators of political violence in three elite U.S. daily newspapers. *Political Communication and Persuasion,* 4: 1–9.

> See entry 690.

692. _____, and Sheets, Rhonda (1986). *Terrorism and the news media research bibliography.* Boston, MA: Terrorism and the News Media Research Project, Emerson College.

> See entry 693.

693. _____, and _____ (1986). *Terrorism and the news media research bibliography.* Columbia, S.C.: Association for the Education in Journalism and Mass Communication.

> This is an extensive research bibliography on terrorism and the mass media. provides researchers with resources, including scholarly analysis, on how media have covered terrorism.

694. Purnell, Susanna W., and Wainstein, Eleanor (1981, November). *The problems of U.S. businesses operating abroad in terrorist environments.* RAND Report R-2842-DOC.

> The escalation of terrorist assaults on United States interests abroad prompted this report. The authors conclude that because terrorists are dissatisfied with U.S. policies toward governments they are trying to overthrow, terrorist acts are aimed at U.S. interests. Through these actions, terrorists are able to receive the publicity on which they thrive.

695. Quester, George H. (1986). Cruise ship terrorism and the media. *Political Communication and Persuasion,* 4: 355–370.

> See entry 505.

696. Rabbie, J.M. (1989). Terrorism and the media: A social psychological approach. In Jo Groebel & Jeffrey H. Goldstein (eds.), *Psychological perspectives*. Series of psychobiology (pp. 119–133). Sevilla, Spain: Publicaciones de la Universidad de Sevilla.

Shows how author's experimental and theoretical work on intergroup conflict and aggression may have some relevance in understanding the intricate relationships between terrorist groups, the mass media, the public and the authorities involved.

697. Rabe, Robert L. (1982). The journalist and the hostage: How their rights can be balanced. In Abraham H. Miller (ed.), *Terrorism: The media and the law* (pp. 69–75). Dobbs Ferry, NY: Transnational Publishers, Inc.

See entry 507.

698. Rada, S.E. (1985, Fall). Trans-national terrorism as public relations. *Public Relations Review,* 11, 3: 26–33.

See entry 508.

699. Revzin, Philip (1977, March 14). A reporter looks at media role in terror threats. *The Wall Street Journal,* p. 16.

Author suggests that media coverage of terrorism is partly to blame because it glorifies lawbreakers and makes heroes out of nonheroes. He argues that the media are losing control over their news departments. Concludes that media are being used by terrorists.

700. Rosenfeld, S.S. (1975, November 21). How should the media handle deeds of terrorism? *Washington Post,* p. A19.

See entry 513.

701. Rubin, Jeffrey Z., and Friedland, Nehemia (1986, March). Theater of terror. *Psychology Today,* 20, 3: 18–28.

Authors discuss the motivation of terrorists and the effect their actions have on the public. It suggests that terrorists attempt to amplify their impact on society by grasping public attention, giving terrorist actions clear symbolic significance, and involving innocent figures in terrorist acts that are sure to evoke strong emotions for the public at large. Recommends that negotiations be conducted out of view of the public and news media to reduce the chance of either party appearing weak in front of the public and to deprive terrorists of their audience. A description of the 1985 *Achille Lauro* ship hijacking is presented.

702. Salwen, Michael B., and Lee, Jung-Sook (1988). News of terrorism: A comparison of the U.S. and South Korean Press. *Terrorism,* 11: 323–328.

   See entry 703.

703. _____, and _____ (1988, March). Terrorism and the crash of KAL Flight 858: A comparison of U.S. and South Korean newspaper coverage. Paper presented at the Spring Conference of the Mass Communication Division of the Association for Education in Journalism and Mass Communication (Boston, MA, March 3–5), 14p.

   This is a case study comparing United States and South Korean press coverage of the November 29, 1987, crash of Korean Air Lines (KAL) flight 858 in order to examine how the press reported the terrorist angle before evidence supporting the charges of terrorism was uncovered. Stories dealing with the crash reported in four prestigious U.S. newspapers and two leading South Korean newspapers from November 30 to December 3, 1987, were analyzed. Analysis focused on whether references were made to the terrorism angle. Results 1) did not suggest evidence that the press plays up or sensationalizes terrorist events; 2) showed that neither the South Korean nor United States press gave much coverage to the terrorist angle until a major event was uncovered suggesting North Korean involvement; 3) suggested that public officials exercised at least a degree of "agenda control"; and 4) suggested that mere allegations or rumors of terrorism alone will not lead the press to report about terrorism in great detail and that some evidence is needed before the press focuses on the possibility of terrorism.

704. Savarese, Rossella and Perna, Antonio (1981). Strategic arms and guerrilla weapons: A content analysis of articles from Italian newspapers of the 70s. Paper presented to the International Peace Research Institute Association, Orillia, Canada.

   A critical analysis of how the Italian press covers terrorists' weapons of choice. The analysis of about 2,700 headlines of one of the most important Italian newspapers, *Corriere della Sera,* suggests that because the daily press lacks an appropriate communication strategy about these issues, their coverage is designed to make news and attract, rather than inform, the reader.

705. Scanlon, Joseph (1984). Domestic terrorism and the media: Live coverage of crime. *Canadian Police College Journal,* 8, 2: 154–178.

   Author presents two case studies of the role of media at hostage-taking in Calgary and Edmonton, Canada. Incidents suggest that the police must pay attention to the media in hostage-takings and similar incidents and that the media create some particular problems. The author warns that the police contingency must include plans for dealing with the media, and the trained personnel must include not just negotiators, hostage commanders, and a task force, but also public relations officers. Suggests that the force handling such incidents must have an established and positive track record of media relations. (Includes one reference.)

706. Schaffert, Richard W. (1992). *Media coverage and political terrorists: A quantitative analysis.* Westport, CT: Greenwood Publishing Group, 271p.

An analysis of three leading newspapers in the United States *(The New York Times),* Britain (London *Times*), and Germany *(Die Welt)* indicates that the coverage of political terrorism may be socially irresponsible. Does not explore television news. Author argues that the nature of terrorism incidents requires self-restraint on reporting about goals, aspirations, and demands of terrorists.

707. Schlesinger, Philip (1981). Terrorism, the media, and the liberal-democratic state: A critique of the orthodoxy. *Social Research,* 48: 74–99.

See entry 518.

708. Schmid, Alex P. (1992). Editor's perspective. In David L. Paletz & Alex P. Schmid (eds.), *Terrorism and the media* (pp. 111–136). Newbury Park, CA: Sage Publications, Inc.

Author argues that the revolution in communication technology since the 1870s has favored the emergence of terroristic "propaganda by the deed"; they create violent pseudo-events to gain access to the news media. With the coverage of the hijacking of TWA Flight #847 in June 1985 as an example, the author compares media principles and news practices and the agenda-setting power of the media. Examines the dilemmas associated with news as a commercial product as well as a social product. Suggests that existing codes of ethics are insufficient and that new journalistic codes and rules of enforcement need to be formulated to prevent a rise in violent pseudo-events. (Includes 19 references, 12 notes, and an appendix.)

709. _____, and de Graaf, Janny (1982). *Violence as communication: Insurgent terrorism and the Western news media.* Beverly Hills, CA: SAGE Publications, Inc., 283p.

See entry 521.

710. Shaw, David (1976, September 15). Editors face terrorist demand dilemma. *Los Angeles Times,* Part 1, p. 14–15.

This article resulted from the 1976 hijack of a jetliner, from New York to Chicago, by Croatian nationalists. The hijackers demanded that their manifesto be printed on page one in five major newspapers. The manifesto was left in a locker in a New York subway station along with a bomb. The bomb exploded, killing one policeman. According to the hijackers, another bomb would explode in a busy location unless the manifesto was published. The newspapers complied with their request. The main point of this article was to present opinions of editors of major newspapers regarding what was done and what should be done in such situations in the future. Robert McCord, president of the National Journalist Society, said the policy should be not to print items on demand. He cited such a policy being followed successfully by Israel. A.M. Rosenthal, editor of *The New York Times,* stated, "The last thing I want is guidelines. . . . The strength of the press is its diversity." Benjamin Bradley, editor of the *Washington Post,* consulted with other editors before printing the manifesto, but he opposed editors acting in concert in such a case. He emphasized that the terrorists had already killed once, and therefore his paper had no alternative but to print the item in hopes of saving lives. William F. Thomas of the *Los Angeles Times* felt that the incident was an isolated case that would not lead to a rash of similar cases. Thomas emphasized that this was a genuine news story. The Croatians wanted independence from Yugoslavia, and no one had ever heard of them or their goals. He added that there is "nothing so sacrosanct about our columns . . . when human lives are in danger." All editors agreed that they were glad they did not have to make the decision. Also, most did not want to speculate about hypothetical cases in the future. Larry Jinke of the *Miami Herald* said that if such demands continued, a public policy might be needed.

711. Signorielli, Nancy, and Gerbner, George (1988). *Violence and terror in the mass media: An annotated bibliography.* Westport, CT: Greenwood Press, 233p.

This annotated bibliography represents scientific research on violence and terror in the mass media. The "Terrorism and the Media" section (pp. 201–219), which has 73 entries, should be of particular interest to researchers in the area.

712. Silj, Alessandro (1978). *Brigate Rosse-Stato: Lo scontro spettacolo nella regia diella stampa quotidiana* [Red Brigade-State: Confrontation spectacle directed by the daily press]. Firenze, Vallecchi.

Analysis of five Italian newspapers' coverage of the kidnapping of Aldo Moro indicates that the press was used by various political forces for ideological ends. Political ideology often hinders recognition of danger faced in terrorist incidents.

713. _____ (1982). *Stampa, radio e TV di fronte al processo Moro di terrorismo* [Press, radio and television before the Moro trial, the cases of La Torre, Delcogliano, Cirillo, and other stories of terrorism]. Rome: RAI Radiotelevisione Italiana, Verifica dei Programmi Trasmessi.

A comparison of the RAI information on the problem of Italian terrorism with those published in nationally distributed newspapers suggests that information on terrorism in the media is neither a response to a concern for an exhaustive review of terrorism nor a response to orientations and choices that are continual and coherent. Consequently, the author concludes that "this type of information has not yet found its own code of behaviors and that the performance of broadcast groups and newspapers is often the result of conflict."

714. Simmons, Brian K. (1991). U.S. magazines' labeling of terrorists. In A. Odasuo Alali & Kenoye K. Eke (eds.), *Media coverage of terrorism: Methods of diffusion* (pp. 23–39). Newbury Park, CA: SAGE.

This chapter is a content analysis of three U.S. weekly magazines' labeling of terrorists. Author determines which labels were often used by the newsmagazines and under what circumstances. Three hypotheses guided the study: 1) U.S. newsmagazines will label terrorists with a more negatively perceived term when their acts affect U.S. citizens; 2) U.S. newsmagazines will label terrorists with a more negatively perceived term when their acts oppose U.S. foreign policy; and 3) there will be a significant positive correlation between the degree of carnage resulting from a terrorist act and the use of a negative label by U.S. news magazines. The study found that 13 different labels were used often to describe the perpetrators of terrorism. Data supported the first hypothesis; no support was offered for the other two hypothesis. (Includes 20 references.)

715. Sloan, Stephen (1978). International terrorism: Academic quest, operational art and policy implications. *Journal of International Affairs,* 32, 1: 1–6.

See entry 264.

716. Sommer, Michael, and Sommer, Heidi (1982). The project of media coverage of terrorism: A summary of national surveys and other investigations, 1977–79. In Abraham H. Miller (ed.), *Terrorism: The media and the law* (pp. 161–187). Dobbs Ferry, NY: Transaction Publishers, Inc.

Authors summarize the findings of three studies on media coverage of terrorism: one on police chiefs, and two each on police chiefs and the media. Includes implications and recommendations.

717. Spates, C.R., Little, P., Stock, H.V., and Goncalces, J.S. (1990). Intervention in events of terrorism. In L.J. Hertzberg, G.F. Ostrum, J.R. Fields (eds.), *Violent behavior, Vol. 1: Assessment & intervention* (pp. 185–199). Costa Mesa, CA: PMA Publishing Group.

See entry 270.

718. Stephens, Lowndes F. (1983). Press and public reaction to "special bulletin." Paper presented to the Association for Education in Journalism, International Communication Division.

This paper analyzes a made-for-television movie, "Special Bulletin," about a group of anti-terrorists who take hostages. Author evaluates episodes in the movie and the script to determine their reflections on "real world" events.

719. Steuter, Erin (1990). Understanding the media/terrorism relationship: An analysis of ideology and the news in *Time* magazine. *Political Communication and Persuasion,* 7: 257–278.

The article provides quantitative and qualitative data from an analysis of *Time* magazine in 1986; it suggests that the media are not a propaganda tool for terrorists, and neither are they sympathetic in their portrayals of terrorist activities. The author argues that because news production is a social process that informs and obscures, it is not a neutral process that provides objective facts. Consequently, terrorism news is presented at seven ideological levels: semantics, language, headlines, social and historical context, treatment of objectives, trivialization, and amplification of violence. The paper elaborates on how this kind of presentation supports the view that the media are a propaganda tool for terrorists.

720. Terrell, Robert, and Ross, Kristina (1991). The voluntary guidelines' threat to U.S. press freedom. In Yonah Alexander & Robert G. Picard (eds.), *In the camera's eye: News coverage of terrorist events* (pp. 75–102). New York: Brassey's (U.S.), Inc.

A thorough analysis of the "guideline" controversy in media coverage of terrorism is provided. Examines the attention focused on news media coverage of terrorism under specific U.S. presidents; the view of terrorism; and those who are key participants in the voluntary guidelines debate. Author vehemently opposes a system of censorship, yet argues that media should adopt guidelines that promote accuracy and informative, unbiased reporting. Proposes eight guidelines for U.S. news media. (Includes 60 notes and one table.)

721. *Terrorism and the media* (1980). International seminar held in Florence, Italy, 1978. Rome: International Press Institute with Affari Esteri.

This work captures one of the troubling aspects of covering terrorist acts. The assumption is that media coverage is sometimes irresponsible, and that a low-profile police investigation of incidents of terrorism is needed, but that the public has a right to information about terrorist acts. It is a conflict that concerns many.

722. Terrorism and the media (1979). (Report of Conference Proceedings), *Terrorism,* 2; 3: 59–60.

This is a case presentation and analysis of specific terrorist events (TWA hijacking by Croatian nationalists, the Hanafi raid on Washington, D.C., and the South Moluccan cases) and the role of the media in handling these situations. The report concludes with what the media have learned from these experiences and their responsibility for the future.

723. Totten, Sam (1986a, Fall). A selective annotated bibliography on terrorism. *Social Science Record,* 24, 1: 40–46.

Author's annotated bibliography covers four areas of discourse: 1) 28 items for teacher background; 2) a seven-item listing of films and filmstrips; 3) 27 print items for classroom use; and 4) a list of 43 novels dealing with terrorist themes.

724. _____ (1986b, Fall). A selective chronology of terrorist and counter-terrorist incidents. *Social Science Record,* 24, 1: 47–50.

See entry 534.

725. United States Congress. House Committee on Foreign Affairs. Subcommittee on Europe and the Middle East (1986). Hearing before the Subcommittee on Europe and the Middle East of the Committee on Foreign Affairs, House of Representatives, Ninety-ninth Congress, first session, July 30, 1985. Washington, D.C.: Supt. of Documents.

See entry 535.

726. U.S. Department of State (1982). Guidelines for United States Government spokespersons during terrorist incidents. In Abraham H. Miller (ed.), *Terrorism: The media and the law* (pp. 148–152). Dobbs Ferry, NY: Transaction Publishers, Inc.

Articulates guidelines for U.S. spokespersons both at home and abroad during a terrorist crisis. The guidelines provide U.S. spokesperson with general instructions of what to do before, during, and after a terrorist incident.

727. Walker, Robert (1993, April 5). Most Muslims aren't terrorists but do we make that clear? *The Gazette* (Montreal), p. B3.

Writer argues that Western journalists' lack of familiarity with Islam creates mythologies which associate Muslims with terrorism. Suggests that media personalities educate themselves about Islam as much as they have been educated about Christianity and Judaism.

728. Wardlaw, Grant (1982). *Political terrorism.* London: Cambridge University Press.

The author argues that there is a symbiotic relationship between terrorists and the media. Clearly, each side gains from such incidents because terrorists get their publicity as media sensationalism leads to commercial success.

729. Weimann, Gabriel (1987). Conceptualizing the effects of mass mediated terrorism. *Political Communication and Persuasion, 4,* 213–216.

See entry 540.

730. _____ (1985). Terrorists or freedom fighters? Labeling terrorism in the Israeli press. *Political Communication and Persuasion,* 2, 4: 433–445.

See entry 542.

731. _____ (1983, Winter). The theater of terror: Effects of press coverage. *Journal of Communication,* 33, 1: 38–45.

See entry 543.

732. _____, and Brosius, Hans-Bernd (1991, June). The newsworthiness of international terrorism. *Communication Research,* 18, 3: 333–354.

The study investigates the newsworthiness of international terrorism.

The authors conclude that specific attributes such as "the level of victimization, the type of action, the identity of the perpetrators, and an attributable responsibility" were the best predictors of media selection and coverage of international terrorism. Also important is the authors' suggestion that a two-step process of selection is used to determine cases of international terrorism in the news.

733. Wilber, H.B. (1977, March 19). The role of the media during a terrorist incident. *The FBI Law Enforcement Bulletin,* 54, 3: 20–23.
See entry 545.

734. Wilkinson, Paul, and Stewart, Alasdaire M. (eds.) (1987). *Contemporary research on terrorism.* Aberdeen, MA: Aberdeen University Press, 625p.
See entry 311.

735. Winfrey, Carey (1977, March 19). Hanafi seizure fans new debate on press coverage of terrorists. *New York Times,* p. 33.
See entry 547.

736. Winkler, Carol (1989). Presidents held hostage: The rhetoric of Jimmy Carter and Ronald Reagan. *Terrorism,* 12, 1: 21–30.
Author argues that rhetoric is a key variable in understanding the public's disparate response to two United States presidents who dealt with hostage crises. Analysis suggests that Jimmy Carter's early rhetorical choices during the Iranian hostage crisis placed him in an untenable posture with the public. However, Ronald Reagan's early rhetorical choices allowed him sufficient flexibility to retain a successful image for resolving hostage crisis. Argues that rhetoric should be considered along with other factors, such as media coverage, that contribute to the public's evaluation of presidents.

737. Wittebols, James H. (1989, August). The politics and coverage of terrorism: From media images to public consciousness. Paper presented at the Annual Meeting of the Association for Education in Journalism and Mass Communication (72nd, Washington, D.C., August 10–13), 23p.
Author presents a typology of terrorism which is grounded in how media differentially cover each type. The typology challenges some of the basic assumptions, such as that the media "allow" themselves to be exploited by terrorists and "encourage" terrorism, and the conventional

wisdom about the net effects of the media's portrayal of each type of terrorism. The model emphasizes the amount of coverage each form of terrorism receives, the flavor or tone of the coverage, and the political effects of such coverage in influencing public opinion and consciousness. Two types of terror are discussed: grievance terror, identified as terror which challenges power, and institutional terror, which seeks to maintain the status quo and power. Concludes that in assessing the net effects of the way terrorism is covered there are several dimensions to consider: a de-emphasis and reframing of United States/state sponsored terror, the portrayal of anti–United States grievance terror as irrational and without just cause, and a siege mentality among the larger population resulting from the way news skews the coverage toward grievance terror committed against U.S./Western interests and away from terror resulting from United States government policies. (Includes 56 references.)

738. Zillman, Dolf, and Bryant, Jennings (eds.) (1985). *Selective exposure to communication.* Hillsdale, NJ: Lawrence Erlbaum, 251p.
This is an edited collection of how media influence people and affect their behavior. Emphasizes selective exposure behavior; specifies aspects of fear and crime.

Author Index

References are to entry numbers, not page numbers.

Author Index

Author Index

Title Index

References are to entry numbers, not page numbers.

Title Index

Title Index

Title Index

206

Subject Index

References are to entry numbers, not page numbers.

Subject Index

Egypt: in the media 333
Electronic media: broadcast gatekeepers and terrorism 463; communicative function of television programs on terrorism 351; perspectives on how television mediates terrorism 399; reporting hostage crises 445; televised image of terrorism 516, 519; television 96; television and diplomacy 418; television and political accountability 433; television and U. S. foreign policy 457; television coverage of hostage-takers 446; television coverage of international affairs 327; television news coverage of terrorism incidents 340–341; television news format and terrorism 340–341; television newscasts' use of terror terms 550; terrorism in 326–553; terrorism on television 395–396, 417, 425–426, 482, 489
El Salvador 11
Entebbe: military response in 264
ERP 381
ETA 227, 233, 621
Ethno-political terrorism 64
European Award for Non-Violence 44
Euzkadi Ta Azkatasuma see ETA

FALN 489, 677
Fatah: as portrayed in the media 333
FBI: terrorism and 83, 303
Fear arousal 110
Federal Bureau of Investigation see FBI

First Amendment: media self-regulation and 335, 372; news guidelines and 529, 602; terrorism and 632
Foreign policy rhetoric 420
France: counterterrorism unit 172; government attitude towards terrorism 202; response to terrorism 420; terrorism in 109, 202
Freedom fighters: terrorism and 542
Fuerza Armadas de Liberacion see FALN
Fugitive political offenders 301

Gabon: and terrorism 279
Global terrorist coalition 317
Government: responses to terrorist activity 174; support of terrorism 211; terrorism and 616
Government sponsored terrorism: on Guatemalan children 190; on Mayan children 190
Government/terrorist response options 43
Great Britain: terrorism in 623, 435; terrorism on television in 509
Greece 619
Guatemala 11, 620

Hanafi Muslims 722, 735; hostages and 547, 590, 669; press coverage of 547
Hezbullah 56
Holy war see Jihad
Honduras 11
Hostages: at the U.S.

Embassy in Tehran 403; behavior 113; coverage of 370; international law and 403; media and 99, 469; negotiations 195; political 13; survival of 182; taking 113
Human aggression: terrorism and 276

Institutional terrorism 203
Insurgent terrorism 107, 272; in Europe 98; media and 678; the Western news media and 521, 709
International terror: victims of 197
International terrorism 4, 43, 58, 76, 78, 85, 87, 128, 136–138, 171, 174, 205, 309; causes of 259; media coverage of 475, 651–652; nature and extent of 200; network coverage of 349–350; newsworthiness of 732, 544; policy implications 525; problems of 447, 633; public perceptions of 61; purposes 254; reactions to coverage of 664; response to 401, 599; secret war of 271; spread of 194; state support of 205; studying 715; tackling 31
IRA: on British television 537; terrorism and 1, 77, 184, 219, 263, 489, 621, 677
Iran: network coverage of hostages 343, 457, 467; hostage seizure in 600; hostages and Reagan inaugural address 363; media response to crisis in 491; television news coverage of hostage release 342, 363;

208

Subject Index

U.S. television news and the 328
Mogadishu: military response in 264
Moro, Aldo 626, 712–713; news reports about the kidnap of 461; trial coverage on television 524
Mount St. Helens 210
Mujaheddin 305
Muslims: Asian 53; Middle East 53; terrorism and 538, 727

Namibia: news coverage of 578
Narcissus 494
Narco-terrorism 69, 132, 431
The National Liberation Front: terrorism and 187
NBC: interview with Abul Abbas 450; terrorism and 99
The Netherlands: terrorism and 64, 258
News coverage of terrorism 562: contagion of 688; conundrum of 498, 684; defining boundaries of 384; functions and meaning of 501
News media: contagion of terrorism and 502; public attitudes towards the 404; psychodynamic relationship between the terrorist and 680; terrorism in the 5, 338
News value: terrorism and traditional 622
Nidal, Abu 189
NORAID 1
Northern Ireland: domestic violence in 626; political violence in 199; terror in 292; terrorism and 29, 34, 77, 79, 104, 157, 167, 373

Nuclear terrorism 170, 212, 290

Overseas newsmen 362, 573

Pakistan 602
Palestine Liberation Organization see PLO
Palestinian: acts of violence 216; terrorist organizations 189
Pan Am Flight 103 72
Paramilitary activity 104
People's Revolutionary Army see ERP
People's Temple 210
Persian Gulf: war and television coverage 449
Perspectivist philosophy: terrorism and 584
Persuasive appeal: mediated terrorism and 577
Peru: terrorism and 245
Philippines: terrorism and villagers 567
Pirates of the Barbary Coast of North Africa 163
PLO: in the media 333; terrorism and 27, 70, 621
Police: response to terrorism 255
Political: economy of terrorism 224; reality of terrorism 239
Political terrorism 42, 107–108, 150, 266, 274, 539; analysis of 262; causes of 13; controlling 315; coverage of 706; impact on corporate activities 8; threat of 8; types of 130
Politics: coverage of terrorism and 549
Press release: by terrorists 621
Printed media: political violence in U.S. news-

papers 690–691; *Rocky Mountain News* 83; terrorism in 554–738; terrorism in the *Christian Science Monitor* 601; *The New York Times* and terrorist killings 646–650; U.S. magazines' labeling of terrorists 714
Propaganda: terrorism and 295, 595, 708
Psychological: impact of terrorism 570; implications of media-covered terrorism 626; mechanisms 16; operations and terrorism 484; perspective and terrorism 416; roots of 18
Psychology of terrorism: research on the 238
Public opinion 54, 112, 120; media coverage of events and 603
Public perceptions: media coverage of terrorism and 655
Public relations: terrorism and 508; terrorist organizations and 689

Qur'an: semantics of the 186

RAID 172
RAND Corporation 123
Reagan, Ronald: rhetoric of 548
Red Army 109, 299
Red Brigade 109, 400, 489, 677, 712
Religious: fanaticism and terrorism 252; violence 186
Research bibliography: on terrorism 503–504, 523, 533, 665, 723–724, 692–693; on violence

Subject Index

218; liberal-democratic state and 707; liberation theology and 282; logic of 237; managing 81, 700; mass destruction and 203; modern 6; in the modern world 244; motivation of 10, 284; natural disasters and 302; nature of 49, 161; new forms 109; perspectives on 300, 311; persuasive appeal of mediated 367; political chaos and 294; political significance of 88, 176; as a political strategy 245; politics and coverage of 737; portraying 191; power and 512; preventing 228; price of 116; problems of 88; psychodynamics of 452, 637; public's perspectives on 615; purposes of 88; questions about 256; rape and 114; recommendations about 166; reporters' perspectives on 361; response to 8, 28; revolutionary 281; rhetoric of 27; roots of 204; scope of 116; social structure of 274; spread of 12; studying, 47, 49, 105, 118, 141, 153, 275; teaching the semantics of 460; teaching students about 154; theological concepts and 234; theory and practice of 6; threat of 37, 232; trends in 144, 162; understanding 1–325, 696; understanding the semantics of 460; viewpoints about, 22; young people and 2
Terrorist: attacks and media events 53, 145; behavior 237; counter-

terrorist incidents and 534; demands 710; female 93; hijacking 514; manipulation of the media 453–454, 459; manipulations of the democratic process 320; media and 99; mindset 40; motivations 40, 289, 323, 682–683; operatives and controls 316; political 222; strategies 74, 138; theater 443, 631
Terrorist groups: Armenian 75; Croatian 75; Cuban 75; Jewish 75; Libyan 75; methods of operation and 9; political economic power of 10; private 108; social psychology of 180–181; in Western Europe 9
Terrorist incidents 193: characteristics of 43; corporate executives and 198; covering 721; role of the media during 733; spectaculars 671; television coverage of 348
Terrorists: categories 229; characteristics 124; death penalty for 243; goals of 152; image of 608; live-action spectaculars and 358; motivations of 246; as murderers 261; reasoning processes 230; silent treatment of 359–360; symbiotic relationship between the media and 728; talking to 441, 629; target of civilians 183
Theater of terror 731, 542–543, 701
Third World: conflicts in 160
Three Mile Island 210

Transnational: as public relations 698; flow of information 236; terrorism 107, 193, 636; terrorism and slave trade 197
Turkey: domestic violence in 626
Turkish Embassy seizure 451, 635
TWA Flight 847 366–367, 397–398, 668, 708; network evening news coverage 349–350; television coverage of 422
Tylenol poisonings 210

United Kingdom 54, 104
United Nations 78
Urban guerrillas: terrorist organizations and 41; warfare 213
Urban terrorism 164
Urban terrorist: groups 318; operations 321
Urban terrorists 103
U.S.: terrorism in 66, 74, 123, 159
U.S. government: attacks against terrorism 168; bombing of Libya 188, 385; definition of terrorism 188; foreign policy on terrorism 23; guidelines for spokespersons during terrorist acts 536, 726; policy on international terrorism 156; response to terrorism 92, 131, 420; strike on suspected terrorists 173; support of terrorists 67, 146
U.S. Information Agency 628
U.S. media: coverage of international news 346–347; international coverage of terrorism in 169; the Iranian crisis

212